PETER AITKEN

DAVID H. FRIEDEL, JR.

ANTHONY POTTS

CORIOLIS GROUP BOOKS

PUBLISHER	**KEITH WEISKAMP**
PROJECT EDITOR	**RON PRONK AND PAULA KMETZ**
COVER ARTIST	**GARY SMITH**
COVER DESIGN	**ANTHONY POTTS**
INTERIOR DESIGN	**MICHELLE STROUP**
LAYOUT PRODUCTION	**PROIMAGE**
PROOFREADER	**MARY MILLHOLLON**
INDEXER	**LAURA LAWRIE**

The Coriolis Group, Inc.
7339 E. Acoma Drive, Suite 7
Scottsdale, AZ 85260
Phone: (602) 483-0192
Fax: (602) 483-0193
Web address: http://www.coriolis.com

1-57610-064-2 : $34.99

Printed in the United States of America

10 9 8 7 6 5 4 3 2 1

The first guy in the door has to turn on the lights.

That's true whether you're the first member of a team to adopt a new technology, or whether you're doing it all by yourself. Being "first" means that you have no one to ask for help—and that you must find the light switch on your own.

There are undeniable benefits to being a technology frontrunner: Those first in the door can set the standards, test new approaches, and be first to market with major products. There could be millions of dollars lying on the table, waiting for the first hand that learns how to grab them.

We at Coriolis Group Books created the FrontRunner Series so that you'd have help on Day One: the day you bring that new technology product home and crank it up. This will be true even if Day One for you is Day One for the product, too. We've built working relationships with the technology leaders in our industry so that our teams of analysts and writers can be working as soon as new technology is out of the labs. When it comes to a new technology product, you're not all alone anymore. The Front Runner is here to help.

Our goal is to provide you with the best possible information on new technology products the day they're released to the public. Not "soft stuff" or hot air, either—just real, useful, practical information that you can put to work right away. We hope that this book gives you whatever additional power you need to make that final sprint over the line—and on to outstanding success in your study or business.

Jeff Duntemann

Contents

Chapter 5 Java Language Fundamentals 103

Chapter 6 Operators, Expressions, And Control Structures 139

Chapter 7 Java Classes And Methods 161

Chapter 9 Java Exceptions 225

Chapter 10 Threads 249

Chapter 14   Dances With Databases   367

Chapter 15   Networking With Java   431

Hello, Visual J++

Peter Aitken

In this chapter, you will be introduced to Java and Visual J++ and will see what they can do for you. You'll also create and run your first Java applet.

We don't know about you, but we were certainly excited when we heard that Microsoft was releasing an integrated Java development environment called Visual J++. We were not alone, either. Lots of programmers who wanted to start working with Java were waiting for just such a product, and we suspect you may be one of them.

Why all the excitement? The way we look at it, Visual J++ is a beautifully complementary combination of the new and the old. The "new part" is, of course, the Java programming language, newly created to provide the platform independence, object-oriented capabilities, security, and other features needed for today's interactive Web development. We'll learn more concerning what's special about Java later in this chapter. While some cynics think the fuss about Java is overblown, we are not among them. We believe that Java is a truly significant advance that is here to stay. If you are a professional developer, you avoid Java at your own peril!

The "old" part of the Visual J++ equation is Microsoft's visual development technology. We use "old" not to mean outdated or obsolete, but rather in the sense of being thoroughly tested and finely honed. Microsoft originated

1

the concept of visual program design with the first release of Visual Basic many years ago and has been improving it over the years. Known as the Developer Studio, it is used in Microsoft's C++ and Fortran development environments and now, as Visual J++, with Java. The Developer Studio combines visual interface design, debugging, code editing, online reference information, and time-saving Wizards in an easy to use integrated development environment. One of our major goals in this book is to teach you how to effectively use Microsoft Developer Studio to maximize your productivity as a Java programmer. If you're new to Java programming, you've made a wise choice starting out with Visual J++. If you have previously written Java programs the old way, Visual J++ will make you think you have traded in your roller skates for a Ferrari!

Applications And Applets

Java can be used to create both full applications and applets. You need to understand the difference between these two terms before we move on.

◆   An *application* is a complete, self-contained program. For example, the Microsoft Word word processing program is an application, as is the Quicken financial management program. An application does not necessarily have anything to do with the Internet or the World Wide Web. From the end user's standpoint, an application created with Java is not any different from an application created with Delphi, Visual Basic, or any other programming language.

◆   An *applet* is a small program designed specifically for use on the Web. It is dynamically downloaded over the network connection and is executed by the browser program that the end-user is using (e.g., Navigator or Internet Explorer). The output of an applet appears as part of the Web page being viewed in the browser.

Internally, an applet is somewhat simpler than an application because some of the work that an application must do for itself—for example, creating an on-screen window to display its output—is done for an applet by the browser. Fortunately, Visual J++ lets you specify at the beginning whether your program will run as an applet only or as an applet and as an application. The details are all taken care of automatically.

Visual What?

In the "old" days (a couple of months ago!), your only option for developing Java applets and applications was the Java Development Kit, or JDK, from Sun Microsystems (the creators of the Java language). The JDK was positively primitive by today's Windows development standards. You had to type in your Java source code using a text editor, then compile it using a command-line compiler named *javac*. If you needed any visual elements, such as a window or a dialog box, you had to write the code by hand—none of this newfangled drag-and-drop visual design stuff! Debugging was primitive at best.

To be honest, using the JDK had one advantage—you were forced to develop a thorough knowledge of the language and the JDK object libraries. Today's sharpest Java programmers are the people who learned the hard way, using the JDK—sort of like a master woodworker who learned to make furniture using only hand tools before learning about power tools. Still, learning all of the inner workings of a programming language is a luxury that most developers do not have the time for. Your boss or your client is not interested in a theoretical discussion of Java classes—they want results, and they want them yesterday!

Visual J++ cannot do yesterday, but it can certainly help you get that Java applet up and running as quickly and easily as possible. Among its powerful features are:

◆ A powerful text editor that supplies a wide variety of productivity tools and lets you work on multiple files at once.

◆ The Applet Wizard that performs all the grunt-work of creating the basic code framework of your project.

◆ A menu editor that makes it a cinch to create regular and pop-up menus, and to assign accelerator keys and status bar prompts to your menu commands.

◆ A visual dialog editor for designing dialog boxes.

◆ A graphics editor for creating and modifying GIF and JPEG graphics (these are the two graphics formats that Java can work with).

◆ A debugger that greatly simplifies the task of finding bugs (errors) in your Java programs and applets.

We'll be showing you how to use Visual J++'s arsenal of tools throughout the book.

Java Language Overview

You can learn a lot about a language by looking at its original design specifications—in other words, what was the language originally designed for? For example, Basic was originally designed as a simple, easily understood language for beginning programmers (Beginner's All-purpose Symbolic Instruction Code). In contrast, C was designed to write operating systems and hence needed access to all of the hardware internals. Despite many evolutionary changes, Basic remains a relatively simple and easy to understand language, while C (and its descendant C++) remain complex, difficult to use, and potentially dangerous.

What, then, was Java designed for? Hard as it may be for you to believe, Java began life as a language to control household appliances. That's right! Some people at Sun Microsystems envisioned a time when the various electronic appliances in a house—TV, thermostat, video cassette recorder, stereo, etc.—would all be connected to a network and run by a single controller. The demands of such an application defined many of Java's most important attributes:

1. It is *architecture neutral*. The language operation does not depend on any of the details of the hardware it is running on. A Java program must be able to run equally well not only on PCs and Macs, but also on controller chips in VCRs, cellular phones, and toasters.

2. It is *robust*. Java programs must be highly resistant to crashes and other runtime problems.

3. It is *object oriented*. By packaging instructions and information in self-contained packages called objects, Java greatly reduces the chance of unforeseen errors. In addition, once you are used to the object-oriented model, writing programs is a lot easier.

4. It is *powerful* yet *simple*. Java lets you implement just about any programming idea you may have, placing almost no limitations on your creativity. It remains relatively simple by hiding the inner workings of the hardware from the programmer and by offering only a small number of ways to accomplish most tasks.

5. It is *safe*. The sort of distributed computing for which Java was designed opens the possibility of viruses and Trojan Horses. Rather than simply protecting against such problems, Java prevents them from the outset by not permitting those programming actions that hackers typically use to cause mischief. Java simply does not permit the type of actions, such as free access to system resources, that are required to hack a system.

None of the individual features in Java are new. What's new is putting them all together in one language and designing the features in from the beginning rather than adding them on later as an afterthought. If you have some programming experience, whether C/C++, Basic, Pascal, or some other language, you'll probably find Java programming a bit strange at first. It won't be long, however, before you find yourself wishing that Java had been invented a long time ago.

Your First Applet

We are strong believers in hands-on learning. We know from experience that you'll learn more by creating and running a real Java applet than by reading another 100 pages of text. Therefore, the remainder of this chapter walks you through the steps of using Visual J++ to create an applet. We have designed this applet to be relatively simple while providing a demonstration of many of Java's more important components. Best of all, it is a real-world applet and not just some silly demo program. This means that it is a useful applet that you'll be able to use on your own Web pages.

The remainder of this chapter shows you how to create and run the sample applet. Later, in Chapter 2, we'll examine the applet code in detail and explain exactly how it works.

The Tickertape Applet

Our applet is called *tickertape*, and its name pretty well describes its function: to scroll a message from right to left across the screen. You've probably seen tickertape-like effects in your Web wanderings, displaying stock quotes or sports scores. We won't get quite so involved. This tickertape applet is limited to displaying a custom message, and you also have the ability to control the scrolling speed. When the tickertape is running, the user can stop and then restart the scrolling by clicking with the mouse.

To create and run the tickertape applet you need to have Visual J++ installed on your system. You also need a Java-capable browser. While there are several such browsers available, we will assume that you are using the version of Microsoft Internet Explorer that is provided with the Visual J++ package.

Step 1: Running The Applet Wizard

1. Select New from the File menu.

2. In the dialog box that is displayed, select Project Workspace then click OK.

3. Visual J++ displays the New Project Workspace dialog box. Under Type select Java Applet Wizard. In the Name box, type "tickertape" (without the quotes). Then click the Create button.

4. The Applet Wizard will now take you though five steps, displaying a series of dialog boxes to gather the information it needs to create the basic structure of your applet. The first dialog box is shown in Figure 1.1. At the top, select the As an applet only option. All of the other dialog box items can be left at their default values. Click the Next button when you are done.

5. The Step 2 dialog box does not need any changes, so you can click Next to go on to the third step. This dialog box is shown in Figure 1.2. Click the mouseDown(), mouseUp() option, then click Next. This selection tells the Wizard to add the code required for your applet to detect the corresponding mouse actions.

6. The fourth Applet Wizard step lets you specify your applet's parameters. A *parameter* is a piece of information passed from the browser to the

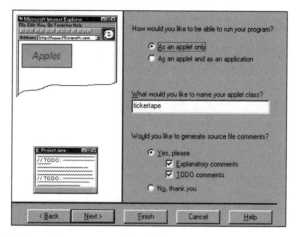

Figure 1.1 Step 1 of starting a new applet with the Java Applet Wizard.

applet when the applet is executed. The tickertape applet needs two parameters named SPEED and TEXT. These will specify the tickertape scrolling speed and its text, respectively. Enter SPEED in the first line under the Name column, then enter TEXT on the second line in the same column. The other columns (Member, Type, etc.) will be filled in automatically. When you're done, this dialog box will look as shown in Figure 1.3. Click Next when you are finished.

7. The fifth dialog box does not require any input, so you can click the Finish button.

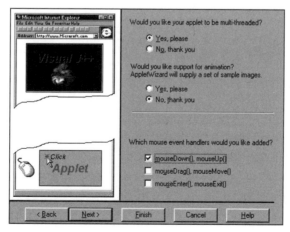

Figure 1.2 In Step 3, you specify which mouse actions your applet will respond to.

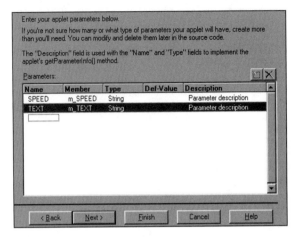

Figure 1.3   Specifying the applet's parameters.

8. The final dialog box, titled New Project Information, presents the details of the project specifications you have entered. You cannot make changes here, but if you discover an error, you can select Cancel and start over. Otherwise, select OK.

Once you've completed the final Applet Wizard step, Visual J++ will create the project folder and files. You're now ready to add your own code to change the applet from a generic "do nothing" program to an applet that performs the specific tasks you want—in this case, displaying a tickertape message. That's our next task.

Step 2: Customizing The Tickertape Applet

Once the Applet Wizard has completed its job, you'll have the complete skeleton of a Java applet. It contains all of the basic code that every applet requires, as modified by the selections you made in the Applet Wizard dialogue boxes. However, this applet will not do anything—it is like a blank canvas waiting for you to add your personal touches. In this case, the personal touches consist of Java code to give the applet the functionality you desire. The program's code is located in a file named tickertape.java, and when the Applet Wizard is finished, this file should be displayed in the Visual J++ editor. If it is not, open the Window menu and select the file from the list.

The Visual J++ editor works just like most other Windows text editors, so you shouldn't have any trouble modifying the code in tickertape.java. We will explain details of editor operation in a later chapter.

First, look for a line in tickertape.java that reads:

```
private final String PARAM_TEXT = "TEXT";
```

Immediately after this line, add the following code:

```
Color color = new Color(255,255,255);
int xpos, fontLength, fontHeight, animSpeed;
Font font;
Image im;
Graphics osGraphics;
boolean suspended = false;
```

Next, look for the following line and delete it; while added by the Wizard, it's something we don't need.

```
resize(320, 240);
```

Then, immediately following the location where you delete this line, add the following code:

```
m_TEXT = getParameter(PARAM_TEXT);
m_SPEED = getParameter(PARAM_SPEED);
animSpeed = Integer.parseInt(m_SPEED);
im = createImage(size().width, size().height);
osGraphics = im.getGraphics();
xpos = size().width;
fontHeight = 4 * size().height / 5;
font = new Font("Ariel", 1, fontHeight);
```

In this and all other code editing, you need to be careful. Java is not only very picky when it comes to spelling, but is also case-sensitive. This means you must enter upper and lowercase letters exactly as shown.

The next step is to look for the following line of code:

```
public void paint(Graphics g)
```

Delete this line and everything following it up to and including the first right curly brace }. You will delete a total of about five lines of code. We will be replacing this deleted code with code of our own later.

Now, look for a line of code that reads:

```
public void run()
```

Delete everything following this line up to, but not including, the line that mentions MOUSE SUPPORT. Then, add the following code in the same location:

```
{
  while (m_tickertape != null)
  {
  try {Thread.sleep(50);}
  catch (InterruptedException e){}
  setcoord();
  repaint();
  }
}
```

Next, look for the following line of code:

```
public boolean mouseDown(Event evt, int x, int y)
```

You need to add code within the curly braces following this line as shown here:

```
{
  if (suspended)
  {
  m_tickertape.resume();
  }
  else
  {
  m_tickertape.suspend();
  }
  suspended = !suspended;
  return true;
}
```

Finally, move to the very end of the file and add the following code. Be sure to add this code before the final right curly brace } in the file.

```
//Override Applet class paint method.
  public void paint(Graphics g)
{
  paintText(osGraphics);
```

```
            g.drawImage(im, 0, 0, null);
}

  public void paintText(Graphics g)
{
  g.setColor(Color.black);
  g.fillRect(0, 0, size().width, size().height);
  g.clipRect(0, 0, size().width, size().height);
  g.setFont(font);
  g.setColor(color);
  FontMetrics fMetrics = g.getFontMetrics();
  fontLength = fMetrics.stringWidth(m_TEXT);
  fontHeight = fMetrics.getHeight();
  g.drawString(m_TEXT, xpos, size().height - fontHeight / 4);
}

  public void setcoord()
{
  xpos = xpos - animSpeed;
  if (xpos < -fontLength)
  {
  xpos = size().width;
  }
}

  public void update(Graphics g)
{
  paint(g);
}
```

That's all the code modifications that are required (the complete listing of the final version of tickertape.java is presented at the end of the chapter, in Listing 1.2). At this time, you need to save the source code file to disk so your changes will be preserved. This is done by selecting Save from the Visual J++ File menu, by pressing Ctrl+S, or by clicking the Save icon on the toolbar. Once the file has been saved, you are ready for the next step.

Step 3: Building The Tickertape Applet

The term *build* refers to the process of compiling your Java source code, converting it to a binary form that the computer can recognize. To build the tickertape applet, simply select Build tickertape from the Build menu, or press F7. For a small program like this, the build process will occur almost instantaneously. Visual J++ will display a message in the lower part of the screen indicating the results of the build. You should see the following message:

```
tickertape - 0 error(s), 0 warning(s)
```

If any errors or warnings are reported, it most likely means that you have made an error typing in the code. Each error or warning will be identified by its line number. Here's an example:

```
C:\Msdev\projects\tickertape\tickertape.java(101,3) : error J0049:
 Undefined name 'n_TEXT'
Error executing jvc.exe.
tickertape - 1 error(s), 0 warning(s)
```

This message tells you that an "undefined name" error has occurred on line 101. In this case, the error was the result of misspelling the variable name m_TEXT as n_TEXT. You must locate your errors in the source code, repeating the build process as needed until Visual J++ reports no errors or warnings. Once this is accomplished, you are ready to run your applet. Well, almost ready—you first need to make some minor modifications to the HTML file that runs the applet.

Step 4: Editing The HTML File

Remember that an applet is run in a browser program, and that browsers read HTML files. Remember also that we asked the Visual J++ Applet Wizard to create an HTML file for us. We must edit this file before we can load it into our browser to execute the applet that we just created. To open the file, select Open from the Visual J++ File menu. In the Open dialog box, pull down the Files of Type list and select HTML files. Then, select tickertape from the file list and click the OK button. A new editing window will open with the contents of tickertape.html displayed for editing. Make the changes shown in the following listing, then save the file.

LISTING 1.1   TICKERTAPE.HTML AFTER EDITING.

```
<html>
<head>
<title>tickertape</title>
</head>
<body>
```

```
<hr>
<applet
    code=tickertape.class
    width=500
    height=50
    PARAM NAME=TEXT VALUE="Visual J++ Hangs Ten..."
    PARAM NAME=SPEED VALUE="4">
</applet>
<hr>
<a href="tickertape.java">The source.</a>
</body>
</html>
```

Step 5: Running The Applet

OK, folks—we are finally ready to try our first applet. You have several options for running it. The easiest is to select Execute from the Visual J++ Build menu, or press Ctrl+F5. Visual J++ will start the Microsoft Internet Explorer browser, assuming it has been installed, and load the tickertape.html file. The <APPLET> tag in the HTML file instructs the browser to load and execute the applet. You can also start your browser in the usual fashion and use its File Open command (or equivalent) to load tickertape.html. Finally, if you have created an association between HTML files and your browser, you can open the Windows Explorer, locate tickertape.html, and double-click the file name.

Whatever method you use, the result should be that your browser loads the HTML file and executes the tickertape applet. Figure 1.4 shows the applet executing in the Microsoft Internet Explorer browser. If you click on the tickertape display, the scrolling will stop. Click again and it restarts.

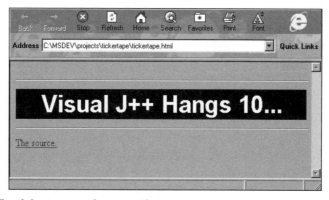

Figure 1.4 The tickertape applet executing.

Summing Up

We hope that you are suitably impressed! With relatively little work, we have created a real, useful Java applet. When you compare the code that you had to type with the full source code of tickertape.java in Listing 1.2, you will realize just how much work Visual J++ has done for you. Typing in the entire source code listing yourself is certainly possible, and many terrific Java applets have indeed been created just this way. Still, the computer's job is to save you work, and compared to other Java development tools, Visual J++ does just that.

In the next chapter, we will take a closer look at the Java language and object oriented programming. We will also take a closer look at the code in tickertape.java, explaining what each part does. Armed with this hands-on introduction, you'll be ready to tackle the detailed Java language information to come in later chapters.

LISTING 1.2 TICKERTAPE.JAVA, SOURCE CODE FOR THE TICKERTAPE DEMONSTRATION PROGRAM.

```
//
   ************************************************************************
// tickertape.java: Applet
//
//
   ************************************************************************
import java.applet.*;
import java.awt.*;

//
_____

// Main Class for applet tickertape
//
//
_____

public class tickertape extends Applet implements Runnable
{
  // THREAD SUPPORT:
  //      m_tickertape is the Thread object for the applet
  //-----------------------------------------------------------------
  Thread m_tickertape = null;

  // PARAMETER SUPPORT:
  // Parameters allow an HTML author to pass information to the applet;
```

```
// the HTML author specifies them using the <PARAM> tag within the
// <APPLET> tag.
// The following variables are used to store the // values
// of the parameters.
//-----------------------------------------------------------------

// Members for applet parameters
// <type>         <MemberVar>    = <Default Value>
//-----------------------------------------------------------------
private String m_SPEED = "";
private String m_TEXT = "";

// Parameter names. To change a name of a parameter, you need only
// make a single change. Simply modify the value of the parameter
// string below.
//---------------------------------------------------------------
private final String PARAM_SPEED = "SPEED";
private final String PARAM_TEXT = "TEXT";

Color color = new Color(255,255,255);
int xpos, fontLength, fontHeight, animSpeed;
Font font;
Image im;
Graphics osGraphics;
boolean suspended = false;

// tickertape Class Constructor
//-----------------------------------------------------------------
public tickertape()
{
     // TODO: Add constructor code here
}

// APPLET INFO SUPPORT: The getAppletInfo() method returns a string
// describing the applet's author, copyright date, or miscellaneous
// information.
//-----------------------------------------------------------------
public String getAppletInfo()
{
     return "Name: tickertape\r\n" +
          "Author: Peter G. Aitken\r\n" +
          "Created with Microsoft Visual J++ Version 1.0";
}

// PARAMETER SUPPORT
// The getParameterInfo() method returns an array of strings
// describing
// the parameters understood by this applet.
```

```
//
// ttape Parameter Information:
//   { "Name", "Type", "Description" },
//-------------------------------------------------------------------
public String[][] getParameterInfo()
{
      String[][] info =
      {
        { PARAM_SPEED, "String", "Parameter description" },
        { PARAM_TEXT, "String", "Parameter description" },
      };
      return info;
}


// The init() method is called by the AWT when an applet is first
// loaded or reloaded. Override this method to perform whatever
// initialization your applet needs, such as initializing data
// structures, loading images or fonts, creating frame windows,
// setting the layout manager, or adding UI components.
//-------------------------------------------------------------------
public void init()
{
    // If you use a ResourceWizard-generated "control creator"
    // class to arrange controls in your applet, you may want to
    // call its CreateControls() method from within this method.
    // Remove the following call to resize() before adding the call
    // to CreateControls();
    // CreateControls() does its own resizing.
//-------------------------------------------------------------------
      //resize(320, 240);

      // TODO: Place additional initialization code here

      m_TEXT = getParameter(PARAM_TEXT);
      m_SPEED = getParameter(PARAM_SPEED);
      animSpeed = Integer.parseInt(m_SPEED);
      im = createImage(size().width, size().height);
      osGraphics = im.getGraphics();
      xpos = size().width;
      fontHeight = 4 * size().height / 5;
      font = new Font("Ariel", 1, fontHeight);
}


// Place additional applet clean up code here. destroy() is called
// when your applet is terminating and being unloaded.
//-------------------------------------------------------------------
public void destroy()
{
```

```
            // TODO: Place applet cleanup code here
}


//----------------------------------------------------------------
public void start()
{
      if (m_tickertape == null)
      {
        m_tickertape = new Thread(this);
        m_tickertape.start();
      }
      // TODO: Place additional applet start code here
}

//      The stop() method is called when the page containing the
applet is
// no longer on the screen. The AppletWizard's initial
// implementation of this method stops execution of the applet's
// thread.
//----------------------------------------------------------------
public void stop()
{
      if (m_tickertape != null)
      {
        m_tickertape.stop();
        m_tickertape = null;
      }

      // TODO: Place additional applet stop code here
}


// THREAD SUPPORT
//      The run() method is called when the applet's thread is
// started. If your applet performs any ongoing activities without
// waiting for user input, the code for implementing that behavior
// typically goes here. For
// example, for an applet that performs animation, the run() method
// controls the display of images.
//----------------------------------------------------------------
public void run()
{
      while (m_tickertape != null)
      {
        try {Thread.sleep(50);}
        catch (InterruptedException e){}
        setcoord();
        repaint();
      }
}
```

```
// MOUSE SUPPORT:
// The mouseDown() method is called if the mouse button is pressed
// while the mouse cursor is over the applet's portion of the
// screen.
//-------------------------------------------------------------
public boolean mouseDown(Event evt, int x, int y)
{
      // TODO: Place applet mouseDown code here
      if (suspended)
      {
        m_tickertape.resume();
      }
      else
      {
        m_tickertape.suspend();
      }
      suspended = !suspended;
      return true;
}


// MOUSE SUPPORT:
// The mouseUp() method is called if the mouse button is released
// while the mouse cursor is over the applet's portion of the
// screen.
//-------------------------------------------------------------
public boolean mouseUp(Event evt, int x, int y)
{
      // TODO: Place applet mouseUp code here
      return true;
}


// TODO: Place additional applet code here

// Override Applet class paint method.
// public void paint(Graphics g)
{
      paintText(osGraphics);
      g.drawImage(im, 0, 0, null);
}

public void paintText(Graphics g)
{
      g.setColor(Color.black);
      g.fillRect(0, 0, size().width, size().height);
      g.clipRect(0, 0, size().width, size().height);
      g.setFont(font);
      g.setColor(color);
```

```
        FontMetrics fMetrics = g.getFontMetrics();
        fontLength = fMetrics.stringWidth(m_TEXT);
        fontHeight = fMetrics.getHeight();
        g.drawString(m_TEXT, xpos, size().height - fontHeight / 4);
}

public void setcoord()
{
        xpos = xpos - animSpeed;
        if (xpos < -fontLength)
        {
          xpos = size().width;
        }
}

public void update(Graphics g)
{
        paint(g);
}
}
```

Do You Speak Java?

Peter Aitken

2

We start this chapter with a detailed overview of Java and object-oriented programming. We also take a closer look at Chapter 1's Tickertape applet, and see how Java handles the classic "Hello, World!" program.

Java is an *object-oriented* language and as a result is quite different from all other popular programming languages. If you're totally new to programming and have no experience with C, Basic, Pascal, and so on, programming with Java will seem perfectly natural to you. Otherwise, it may take you a little time to adapt. At least that was our experience—it took a bit of practice to switch our mode of thinking from the old paradigm to the new. This transition would have been a lot easier if we had access to a clear explanation of the overall structure and concepts of Java. Such explanations were not to be had in the early days, but now we can distill our experience to make things easier for you.

This chapter is by no means intended only for those readers with prior programming experience. Even if you're a total programming novice with no preconceptions or outmoded ideas to discard, the material in this chapter is essential. The details of Java will fall into place and make sense much more readily if you have a clear understanding of the "big picture."

Java not the first?

To be strictly accurate, Java is not the first object-oriented programming language. Several languages, most notably C++ but also some others including Borland's Delphi and Microsoft's Visual Basic, have a greater or lesser degree of "object-orientedness." The difference is that these other languages permit you to use OOP techniques, but do not demand that you do. For example, you can write a purely procedural C++ program. In contrast, Java is a pure OOP language that forces you to use OO techniques. True, there have been a few other pure OO languages such as Smalltalk, but Java is the first one to catch on and move beyond a small group of dedicated users.

The Old Way

Every computer program is comprised of two types of elements: data (or information) and instructions for manipulating that data. For example, if you have a program to alphabetize a list of names, the list is the data, and the code to perform the ordering is the instructions. Similarly, in a multimedia program, the pictures, sounds, and so on are the data; and the code to display the pictures and play the sounds are the instructions.

From the genesis of computing until very recently, the instructions were given primary importance. The design of programs, and indeed of entire programming languages, was such that specifying a program's instructions came first. Data representations were necessarily designed (and sometimes were jury-rigged) to fit the available instructions. It was soon discovered that it was very helpful to divide the instructions into relatively small, partially independent sections called functions or procedures. Hence, this programming paradigm became known as *procedural programming*.

There can be no doubt of the power and efficacy of procedural programming. Until very recently, just about every program in existence was written this way. This includes not only ground-breaking productivity applications for the PC, such as Lotus 1-2-3 and WordPerfect, but also everything else, from the original DOOM to the programs controlling the space shuttle. Without question, procedural programming is a powerful tool that is capable of producing some very impressive results in the hands of expert practitioners. All of the popular programming languages—C, Pascal, Basic, Fortran, and COBOL—were procedural languages, at least in their original incarnations.

As programs increased in size and complexity, problems began to surface. These problems resulted from the fact that the procedural paradigm made it almost impossible to create programs where the various parts of the program are truly independent of each other, interacting only in those ways specified by the programmer. Unintentional interactions between parts of a large, complex program would result in errors that were impossible to test for and difficult to fix. Such interactions also made program development and maintenance more difficult, as programmers creating or modifying one part of the program could not work without constantly dealing with these interactions with other parts of the program. Something entirely different was needed, a whole new programming paradigm.

Object-Oriented Programming To The Rescue

Object-oriented programming (OOP) is more data-centric. The program is designed around the data it needs to manipulate, rather than the data being shoehorned into a form that the program can handle. An *object* is a programming construct designed to hold data in a form that corresponds to the way the data exists in the real world. Crucially, an object also contains the code required to manipulate the data. Thus, an object is an independent entity containing both data and code—in a sense, an object is "smart data" that knows what to do with itself.

As an example of OOP concepts, we'll use a simple but common programming task: maintaining a list of numbers. We'll also suppose that there are a limited number of things we need to be able to do with this list:

◆ Print the list.

◆ Get the total number of items in the list.

◆ Get the largest and smallest values in the list.

◆ Sort the list into numerical order.

A real program would most likely need to do a larger number of things with such a list, but these four will serve well enough for this example. With traditional procedural programming, you would keep the list in an array and write procedures (functions) to perform the various needed tasks. You would pass the array as an argument to each procedure, and the code in the procedure would perform the task. If necessary, it would also pass the result back to the program as its return value. The general structure of this procedural program is shown in Figure 2.1. Note that the list data and the functions that work with the list are all separate and independent from each other.

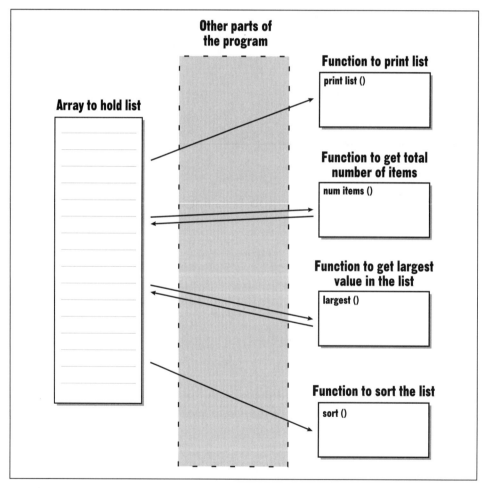

Figure 2.1 The structure of a procedural program to maintain a list of numbers. The data storage and functions for data manipulation are separate.

An object-oriented programming language would approach this same task quite differently. You would define a *class* that defines both the data storage for the list and the actions (such as printing and sorting) that you need to perform with the list. The list data would still most likely be stored in an array, and the code to perform the various actions would not be much different from the code you would use in a procedural program. The primary difference here is that the list's data and the code necessary to manipulate it are not separate and independent parts. They are all integral parts of the same object—the list class. Data variables in a class are called *instance variables* and the procedures in a class are called *methods*. The structure of an object-oriented list maintenance program is shown in Figure 2.2.

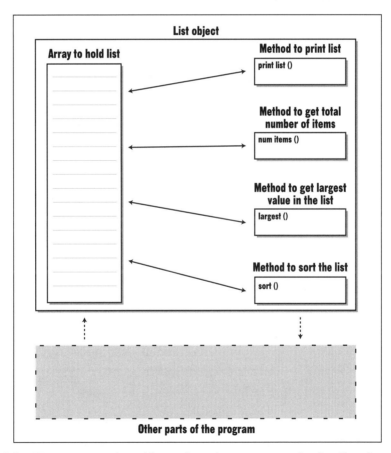

Figure 2.2   The structure of an object-oriented program to maintain a list of numbers. The data and functions (methods) are part of the same object.

Classes, objects, and instances.

These three terms can be confusing—while they are related, they do not mean the same thing. A CLASS is the plan or design for an object, similar in concept to the blueprints for a car. When you actually create something from those plans, you have an OBJECT, analogous to the car built from those blueprints. An object is sometimes referred to as an INSTANCE of its class, just like a car is an instance of its blueprints. When you create an object, you INSTANTIATE a class.

An important benefit of OOP is that you can (and in fact should) design your classes to model the real-world items or concepts that your program is handling. For example, a checkbook maintenance program would probably include a "check" class containing instance variables and methods corresponding to the information and actions associated with a real-world check. Likewise, a mailing list program would define a "person" class.

Now that you have had a brief overview of how OOP works, we need to take a closer look at the important characteristics of OOP.

Encapsulation

You've seen that OOP combines data and the code needed to manipulate that data together in something called a *class*. This is referred to as *encapsulation*, and it is this concept that forms the heart of OO programming techniques. The code and data within an object (remember, an object is an instance of a class) are hidden from the rest of the program and protected from unwanted interactions and arbitrary accesses. The only exceptions are those class methods and instance variables that you, the programmer, have declared to be *public*, rendering them accessible from the rest of the program. These public methods and variables form the class's *interface*, and it is by means of the interface that the remainder of the program can make use of the object's functionality.

Because a class's interface is the only part that the rest of the program is aware of, other parts of the class can be changed without worrying about unintended effects on the program as a whole. As long as the interface remains the same, you can modify the inner workings of a class as much as you like, and then plug it into the program without concern about your changes having unintentional effects.

Built-in classes.

Java not only lets you create your own classes, it also comes with an extensive library of predefined classes for a wide variety of programming needs. Whether it be screen display, file access, mathematical calculations, or whatever—you should always look in the Java class library first before trying to do it yourself.

Inheritance

In the world of object-oriented programming, the term *inheritance* refers to the ability to create a new class based on an existing class. The new class automatically has all the elements—methods and instance variables—of the parent class. You then add new methods and/or variables to customize the new class to meet your specific needs.

Inheritance is an incredibly powerful tool. Used properly, inheritance means you never have to write code twice. Once you have coded a particular functionality in a class, you can reuse it over and over again in derived classes. You can derive classes not only from other classes you have created, but also from classes in the Java class library. If you cannot find an existing class that does everything you need, look for one that does at least some of what you need and derive a new class from it.

There is some inheritance-related terminology you need to know. A *base class* is a class that is not derived from any other class. The immediate parent of a derived class is called its *superclass*. A class derived from a particular class is called a *subclass*. Thus, if class A was derived from class B, we say that class B is class A's superclass, and class A is a subclass of class B.

A subclass is not forced to use all of its superclass's methods unchanged. A subclass can *override* any of the methods that it inherits from its superclass. This feature further enhances your ability to customize a subclass. Of course, there's no point in doing too much overriding—you might as well create a new class from scratch!

In any collection of related classes such as the Java class library, there will exist a complex hierarchy of classes. At the "top" of the hierarchy is a relatively small number of base classes. A given class may have multiple levels of inheritance between it and the base class from which it is ultimately derived. Remember that a class inherits all of the methods and instance variables from not only its superclass, but from every class in the hierarchy between it and the ultimate base class.

Java does not support multiple inheritance, where a new class is based on two or more superclasses. The complexities and potential pitfalls of multiple inheritance outweighed its benefits. Even so, Java uses interfaces (to be covered soon) to achieve many of the advantages of multiple inheritance.

Polymorphism

The literal meaning of the term *polymorphism* is "many forms." In object-oriented programming, it refers to the ability to call different methods with the same name. Which of the methods is invoked depends on the type of object passed to it. You could have two methods called **print**(), one containing code to display text on the screen, the other with code to display a bitmapped graphic. When you call the **print**() method, the appropriate method is called depending on whether you pass a string object or a bitmap object as the method's parameter.

Polymorphism is sometimes referred to as *method overloading*. The same method name—**print**() in our example—is overloaded by having two or more "meanings" depending on the context. Note, however, that operator overloading (a similar capability found in some other object-oriented languages) is not supported by Java. It was decided that the disadvantages of operator overloading outweighed the advantages.

Java Language Overview

Most of this book is devoted to teaching you the details of Java, but we think that it's very helpful to start out with a general overview of the language first. In other words, start with the big picture, then zoom in on the details. We'll start with a comparison between Java and C++. If you don't know C++, this won't be helpful; but for the many programmers who do know C++, it's an excellent place to start.

Java And C++

If you are familiar with C++, then Java code will look very familiar to you. In fact, Java is based on C++, but not in the usual sense. In other words, not in the same way that C++ is based on C. Rather than thinking of Java as C++ with some more features added (as C++ is C plus some new features), it's more accurate to think of it as C++ with some features removed (C++ minus, as we have heard it dubbed!).

Say what? Isn't removing features from an established language a step backward? Not necessarily, if the removals are carefully selected. C++ is an immensely powerful language; but all that power, plus the fact that C++ was designed as a superset of C, has resulted in a language that is also complicated and dangerous. Think of C++ as a Swiss Army Knife with every possible attachment. Sure, it looks appealing in the store. After using it for a while, however, you may find that you impale yourself on the corkscrew while trying to use the screwdriver. Perhaps a smaller, carefully selected set of attachments would actually allow you get things done faster. Thus, Java is lacking C++ features that would:

◆ Introduce non-essential complexity for the developer.

◆ Prevent implementation of true cross-platform support.

◆ Compromise the robustness of final applications.

◆ Jeopardize security measures.

As a result, you won't find #defines, header files, typedefs, pointers, multiple inheritance, operator overloading, or general functions in Java (functions are replaced by methods). You will, however, find the familiar C/C++ syntax for most program statements, operators, and so on.

Bytecode And The Java Virtual Machine

This section needs to begin with a brief review of a few computer basics. Our apologies to those readers who already know this stuff.

When you write a computer program, be it in Java, C++, or whatever; you write in *source code*, English-like expressions that detail the actions the program is to take. Of course, your computer can't understand these statements! Before the program can be executed, the source code must be translated into machine language instructions, the binary codes that the system's CPU can understand. There are two basic approaches to performing this translation.

The most common is called *compilation*. The source code is translated into machine code during the process of program development, and the program file that is distributed to end-users contains the program's machine code instructions. When the program is executed, all that is necessary is to load the file into memory. Compiled programs have the advantage of speed, since the machine code requires no addition processing during program execution. Compilation is used by C, C++, Pascal, and most other languages.

The second method is called *interpretation*. The program distribution files contain the actual source code, or a partially processed version of it. When the program is executed, another program, called the *interpreter*, loads the source code and translates it into machine code on the fly as the program is executing. A speed penalty results from the extra processing required by the interpreter. Interpreted languages do have their advantages, however. Some of these advantages involve error handling and resource management, because the interpreter can be aware of the state of the host system in ways that are not possible for a compiler. Cross-platform support is another advantage, because you can distribute the same source code to multiple platforms as long as each one has its own interpreter.

The designers of Java wanted the best of both worlds: the advantages of an interpreted language without the speed tradeoff. They achieved it by fine-tuning the interpretation process. Here's how it works.

When you compile a Java program, the output is called *bytecode*. Bytecode is a representation of the source code in a form that can be translated directly and quickly into machine code. One can look at bytecode as sort of an intermediate between source code and machine code. It retains the significant advantages of an interpreted language with very little performance hit. The identical Java bytecode can run on any platform with a Java interpreter.

The Java interpreter is called the *Java Virtual Machine*. This rather fancy name reflects the way it works. Rather than simply translating the bytecode into platform-specific machine code, the virtual machine simulates a central processing unit (CPU) in software. The bytecode can be thought of as machine code for this virtual, or simulated, CPU. The platform-specific parts of the virtual machine provide the links between the virtual CPU and the physical CPU.

What about applets? They work the same way, except that the Java interpreter is part of the browser rather than a separate program.

Packages

One of the major advantages of Java programming, and indeed of object-oriented programming in general, is the ease with which code can be reused. Inheritance, of course, is the main mechanism of code reuse. In addition, Java uses *packages* to simplify and streamline the reuse of code. Packages also assist in the management of *name spaces*.

What the devil is a name space? When you define a class, you must give it a unique name to distinguish it from other classes. Since we all want to assign our classes names that are meaningful, it's pretty easy to run out of good names. Remember, because of the distributed nature of Java, you're not just competing for names against other classes you write—you're competing with the entire Internet community. Your applet that contains a class named **FooBar** may be running alongside an applet written by Joe Shmoe from Kokomo who also has created a class named **FooBar**. Possibilities for confusion clearly exist.

Java solves this problem with the concept of name spaces. A class name need be unique only within its name space. Putting a class in a package also specifies its name space, and potential conflicts are avoided. Thus, a specific class is identified by both its package and its name.

Interfaces

The term *interface* is used not in the sense of a visual graphical interface, but rather the ways in which an object interacts with the rest of the program. In other words, an object's interface consists of all its public methods—

those methods that can be accessed from outside the class. Sometimes you need to be sure that a class has one or more specific methods, usually because the internal workings of Java require it. For example, a class that uses threads must have a **run**() method, because the browser or Java Virtual Machine calls **run**() repeatedly to activate thread processing.

Note that the requirement here is that the class have one or more certain methods, and note that those methods contain certain code. The exact code in **run**(), for example, will depend on the number of threads in the applet.

Java implements interfaces using the **implements** keyword. When a class implements an interface, as tickertape implements the **Runnable** interface, it is required to define those methods that are in the interface. In effect, the interface contains one or more empty methods. If you do not implement these methods properly in your class, the compiler reports an error. By "properly" we mean that your implementation of the method must have the same type signature as the empty method template in the interface—the same parameters and return value. For example, if your class implements the **Runnable** interface, it must include a **run**() method that takes no parameters and has a type **void** return value.

Java includes several predefined interfaces, and you can also create your own. Note that a class can implement more than one interface. Through the use of interfaces, Java achieves most of the advantages of multiple inheritance without its disadvantages.

Garbage Collection

One of the things we like best about Java is its built-in garbage collection. No, Java won't pick up all the Jolt Cola cans on the floor; but it will automatically take care of system memory, allocating and releasing it as needed.

In all but the simplest programs, the amount of memory needed changes throughout program execution. Temporary data storage, new objects, and so on all require allocation of memory from the system's RAM. When a program no longer needs memory, perhaps because an object went out of scope, that memory needs to be freed up so it can be used for something else.

In other languages, most notably C and C++, dealing with memory is left to the programmer to a great degree. Your source code would have to include a statement to allocate memory for a specific purpose—a linked list, for example—and then another statement to free that memory when the list is no longer needed. Much of this allocation involves pointers, and the use of pointers opens the door to the possibility of serious bugs.

The designers of Java decided that all allocating and freeing of memory should be done automatically—which is exactly what the term *garbage collection* means. From the programmer's perspective, garbage collection means a lot fewer programming headaches. From the system's point of view, garbage collection means that improper memory management never hogs unneeded system resources. Automatic garbage collection does slow things down a little bit, but on today's fast systems, it will hardly be noticed.

Threads

When someone says "Nice threads, man" to a Java programmer, it is not a complement about his or her clothing! Rather, the term *thread* refers to the way Java can divide up a program's various tasks to enhance responsiveness and maximize efficient use of the CPU. Each thread is a partially independent process, and to a certain degree, it has complete use of the system's resources while it is running. Typically, you would program an individual thread to perform a task or, at most, a few specific tasks, such as performing animation, getting user input, downloading data, or accessing disk files.

The concept of threads is similar to that of multitasking, a capability found in most modern operating systems, including Windows 95. For example, if you are printing a document from your word processor while performing calculations in a spreadsheet, multitasking is at work. Multitasking is performed at the operating system level to permit more than one program to run concurrently. In contrast, threads work within a single program to permit more than one process to operate at the same time.

What's the point of threads? First of all, modern programs often need to do more than one thing at a time. A Java program could be animating a couple of icons, downloading data from the net, and accepting keyboard input all at the same time. Of course, strictly speaking, the system CPU can only do one thing at a time. However, almost every task that a program requires actually takes up very little of the CPU's processing power. The overall speed with which a process operates is almost always limited by something external to the CPU such as the network connection, user response speed, and so on. By splitting the CPU time among the various tasks—5 milliseconds downloading data, 10 milliseconds performing animation, 2 milliseconds getting keyboard input—the CPU can perform multiple tasks at the "same" time without actually slowing down any individual task.

The beauty of Java threads is that Java takes care of almost all the work for you. The methods you use to start, pause, and stop threads are all quite simple, and you need not be concerned with all the complicated stuff that's going on behind the scenes.

A Java program or applet does not have to use threads, and in fact, sometimes threads are not even advised. An applet that performs simple actions and requires little user interaction is a good example, such as an applet that plays a sound when clicked on. When this applet is not playing a sound, it is not doing anything and does not require system resources; so there is no advantage to using a thread.

You may be wondering why we used a thread in the tickertape demo, since it has only a single process. Remember that a given applet may not be the only one running. We could have implemented tickertape without using threads, but this approach would have required writing a loop to control the animation. This loop would hog system resources, and the performance of other running applets would suffer.

Another reason for using threads is the **run**() method, part of the **Runnable** interface. The **run**() method is called by the browser once each cycle. It's important to remember that this means *every* **run**() method, in every class, in every running applet, is called. By letting the browser/Java Virtual Machine take care of running processes, you are using Java the way it was designed.

Synchronizing Threads

Normally, multiple Java threads are *asynchronous*, meaning that each thread goes about its business without any regard for what other threads are doing.

This is desirable in most situations. If one thread becomes blocked—waiting for something to happen, for example—all other threads continue executing and do not have to wait for the blocked thread to continue.

At times, however, two or more threads need to be synchronized in some way. A common example is when two threads access the same data file on disk—you want to be sure one thread is finished writing new data to the file before the other thread accesses it. You need to synchronize the threads to prevent simultaneous access.

Java accomplishes this with the **synchronize** keyword. You use this keyword when declaring a shared object's methods. When a thread enters a synchronized method, no other thread is permitted to call any synchronized method of the same object instance until the first thread has exited the method. Thus, the object—representing, say, a disk file—can be accessed by only a single thread at a time.

Applications Vs. Applets

As we have mentioned, Java is designed to write two types of programs: full-fledged applications and applets for distribution over the Internet. Applets are a bit simpler to write because the browser in which an applet runs performs some of the tasks that an application must do for itself.

One important difference between applets and applications is that only the latter have a **main**() method. The Java interpreter needs to know where to start program execution, and by convention, this is done in **main**(). Applets are controlled by the browser, so a **main**() method is not needed. If a Java program is designed to be both an applet and an application, the **main**() method is present but is ignored by the browser.

Java's Object Environment

Java consists of a lot more than just a programming language. It also includes a rich collection of classes that are already written and ready to use. In many ways, Java's class packages are similar in concept to libraries in

C/C++ and to Basic's built-in functions. The language designers considered the various tasks that programmers would most often use the language for and created classes to simplify these tasks. Some of Java's classes are intended to be used as-is, others are designed to be used as base classes from which you can derive your own classes. In any case, you'll find that Java's predefined classes make many otherwise complex programming tasks a lot easier. Let's take a brief look at what's in the Java class packages.

Core Classes

The core classes provide the fundamental capabilities that most programs need. They can be divided into several categories.

LANGUAGE

These are the most basic classes, required for any program to function. String manipulation is handled by the **String** class, and it's a rare program that doesn't use strings in some fashion. Multithreading is handled by the **Thread** class, and errors by the **Exception** and **Error** classes. Mathematical operations are encapsulated in the **Math** class. These core language classes are automatically available in every Java program, not requiring the use of an **import** statement.

UTILITIES

The Utilities classes consist mainly of commonly used data structures and their associated methods, such as growable arrays, hash tables, and stacks. Date and time functions are included, too.

INPUT/OUTPUT

The Input/Output classes use a uniform stream model based on C/C++ streams for all forms of I/O: keyboard, console, etc.

LOW-LEVEL NETWORKING

The low-level networking classes are an abstraction of network "sockets" that encapsulate the idea of Internet addresses and input/output streams to the sockets on other computers. Note that these classes are part of Java's core classes and not part of the Internet classes (to be discussed). This is an indication of the extent to which Java is Internet-aware in its basic design and not as an afterthought.

GRAPHICAL USER INTERFACE

Java implements a program's graphical user interface by means of the Abstract Window Toolkit, or AWT. The AWT includes classes that abstract common GUI elements, such as windows, menus, and scroll bars. This may be the most complex and difficult set of Java classes, and we'll be spending a lot of time on it in a later chapter.

Internet Classes

Java's Internet classes provide abstractions of all the common Internet protocols. The basic Internet connectivity is part of the core classes, as described above.

TCP/IP

Transfer Control Protocol/Internet Protocol is the basis of most Internet communication. TCP/IP actually embraces several individual protocols, including FTP (File Transfer Protocol), HTTP (Hypertext Transfer Protocol), and SMTP (Simple Mail Transfer Protocol). By using these classes you can write Internet-aware programs without having to deal with the bloody details of the various protocols.

WORLD WIDE WEB

Since one of Java's main goals is the delivery of interactive Web page content via applets, it makes perfect sense that it would include a comprehensive set of classes in this area.

DISTRIBUTED PROGRAMS

Java was designed to easily implement distributed programs, in which the various components of a Java program may not reside on the same system. The fact that Java's file system and network implementation have the same interface makes it simple to load a Java class over the Internet (this is, of course, how Java applets work).

Dissecting The Tickertape Demo

Now that you know a bit about Java, it will be instructive to look back at the code for the tickertape demo that we developed in Chapter 1, explaining what the various source code statements do. We won't be explaining every line of code from the listing in Chapter 1. First of all, any line that begins with a double slash (//) is a *comment*, ignored by the Java compiler and placed there as documentation and explanation by the programmer. We'll omit comments from this discussion. Also, there's a bit of code placed there by the Applet Wizard that the program does not end up using; we'll ignore this, too. The explanations below will not strictly follow the order of statements in the program, but will be modified to more closely follow the order of things as they happen when the applet is executed. In the sections that follow, the explanatory text follows each piece of code.

```
import java.applet.*;
import java.awt.*;
```

It's a rare Java program that does not make use of the Java Class Library, a collection of predefined classes for a wide variety of tasks. The library is divided among several *packages*, with each package containing related classes (e.g., graphics, file access). The **import** statements tell the Java compiler which packages the applet will need—in this case, the applet package and the graphics package (AWT stands for Abstract Window Toolkit, Java's collection of graphical classes).

```
public class tickertape extends Applet implements Runnable
```

This single line begins the definition of the tickertape class. This is a confusing line, so let's take it apart in Table 2.1.

The remainder of the source code file consists of the code that defines this class, the single class used in this demonstration applet.

```
Thread m_tickertape = null;
```

Table 2.1 The tickertape class definition.

Keyword(s)	Meaning
public	The tickertape class will be accessible from other packages. If the public keyword is omitted, the class will be accessible only from within its own package.
class tickertape	We are defining a class named tickertape. Technically, tickertape is the class name space.
extends Applet	We are specifying that tickertape's superclass is the Applet class. This is one of Java's predefined classes and is part of the Applet package. As a result, tickertape will inherit all of Applet's instance variables and methods.
implements	Runnable is a Java interface; as you may remember
Runnable	from earlier in the chapter, it is a collection of method declarations. The Runnable interface contains only the single method run().

This line creates a type **Thread** variable that will be used to refer to the applet during program execution. Because the applet is not yet running, this variable is set to the special value **null**.

```
private String m_SPEED = "";
private String m_TEXT = "";
```

These lines create, or *declare*, two type **String** variables and initialize each to a blank string. The **private** keyword specifies that these variables will not be accessible to other classes. Since there's only the one class tickertape in this Java application, using **private** is not really necessary; but in a more complex multiple class Java application, the use of **private** is an essential part of encapsulation—one of the cornerstones of object-oriented programming.

```
private final String PARAM_SPEED = "SPEED";
private final String PARAM_TEXT = "TEXT";
```

Here we create and initialize two more type **String** variables. The **final** keyword specifies that the value of these variables cannot change. They are, in effect, constants and are used in the same manner as #define in C++ and const in Basic.

```
Color color = new Color(255,255,255);
int xpos, fontLength, fontHeight, animSpeed;
Font font;
Image im;
Graphics osGraphics;
boolean suspended = false;
```

These lines of code declare additional variables that the applet needs. In some cases, such as **color,** the variable is initialized to a specific value. In other cases, such as **font,** the variable value is left undefined and will be set later.

```
public void init()
```

The **init()** method is called when an applet is first loaded or reloaded. You use this method to perform whatever initialization your applet needs. In this example, we have the following code in **init()**:

```
m_TEXT = getParameter(PARAM_TEXT);
m_SPEED = getParameter(PARAM_SPEED);
animSpeed = Integer.parseInt(m_SPEED);
```

These lines obtain the parameters passed in the HTML file when the applet is loaded and assign the values to the appropriate variables. We also have the following in **init()**:

```
im = createImage(size().width, size().height);
osGraphics = im.getGraphics();
xpos = size().width;
fontHeight = 4 * size().height / 5;
font = new Font("Ariel", 1, fontHeight);
```

This code initializes the Java graphics system, creating an image that is as wide as the applet and 80% of its height. Also, the display font is selected and initialized.

```
public void destroy()
```

The **destroy**() method is called when a Java object terminates. If there are any required "clean-up" operations, the code would be placed here. However, the tickertape applet does not require any such clean-up code.

```
public void start()
{
    if (m_tickertape == null)
    {
        m_tickertape = new Thread(this);
        m_tickertape.start();
    }
}
```

The **start**() method is executed after the **init**() method—when the applet is first loaded and each time its page is referenced again from a browser. It checks to see if the applet thread has already been started. If not, as indicated by the value **null** in the **m_tickertape** variable, a new thread is created and started. It is important to note the difference between the applet's **start**() method and a thread's **start**() method, as they are two completely different things. An applet can have only one **start**() method, and it is called automatically by the Java interpreter as needed. An applet can contain one or more threads, each representing a separate process. Each of these threads has its own **start**() method, and whether a particular thread has been started has nothing to do with whether its applet has been started.

```
public void run()
{
    while (m_tickertape != null)
    {
        try {Thread.sleep(50);}
        catch (InterruptedException e){}
        setcoord();
        repaint();
    }
}
```

The **run**() method is called when the applet's thread starts executing (which is done in the **start**() method, above). In this applet, the **run**() method contains a **while** loop that will execute repeatedly. The statements in the **while** loop do three things: 1) Pause for 50 milliseconds, 2) Call the **setcoord**() method to update the text's display position, and 3) Call the **repaint**() method.

But wait! You say there's no **repaint()** method in this applet? Yes and no—
repaint() is an internal method, part of Java's Applet class. You don't have
to write it; it's already there, hidden from view but part of the material
included in the project with the import statements earlier. And one of the
things that **repaint()** does is to call the **update()** method.

```
public void update(Graphics g)
{
    paint(g);
}

public void paint(Graphics g)
{
    paintText(osGraphics);
    g.drawImage(im, 0, 0, null);
}

public void paintText(Graphics g)
{
    g.setColor(Color.black);
    g.fillRect(0, 0, size().width, size().height);
    g.clipRect(0, 0, size().width, size().height);
    g.setFont(font);
    g.setColor(color);
    FontMetrics fMetrics = g.getFontMetrics();
    fontLength = fMetrics.stringWidth(m_TEXT);
    fontHeight = fMetrics.getHeight();
    g.drawString(m_TEXT, xpos, size().height - fontHeight / 4);
}
```

The **update()** method is called by the internal Java method **repaint()**, as
described above. In this demonstration, **update()** does nothing but call the
paint() method. The job of **paint()** is to update and display the text on-
screen by calling **paintText()** and **drawImage()**. Most of the actual display
work is done by the code in the **paintText()** method, but we won't get into
details here.

Around and around we go.

You may think this code is convoluted and wasteful: the program calls REPAINT(),
which calls UPDATE(), which calls PAINT(). Why not just call PAINT() directly? The
reason is that REPAINT() does a lot more than call UPDATE(). If we called PAINT()
directly without calling REPAINT(), things would not work properly.

```
public boolean mouseDown(Event evt, int x, int y)
{
    if (suspended)
    {
        m_tickertape.resume();
    }
    else
    {
        m_tickertape.suspend();
    }
    suspended = !suspended;
    return true;
}
```

The **mouseDown()** method is executed when the user clicks the mouse over the applet's screen area. If the applet is running, it is suspended; if the applet is currently suspended, it is restarted.

```
public void setcoord()
{
    xpos = xpos - animSpeed;
    if (xpos < -fontLength)
    {
        xpos = size().width;
    }
}
```

The method **setcoord()** is called once each "cycle" of the program by the code in the **run()** method. Its job is to scroll the text by moving it a little bit to the left each time. Once the text has scrolled completely off the screen, the text position is moved to the right edge of the window so it can scroll into view again.

```
public void stop()
{
    if (m_tickertape != null)
    {
        m_tickertape.stop();
        m_tickertape = null;
    }
}
```

The **stop()** method is called when the page containing the applet is no longer on the screen. As implemented here by the Applet Wizard, this method stops execution of the applet's thread.

Hello, World!

Traditionally, the first program that C and C++ programmers learn is the simple program to display the text "Hello, world!" on the screen. It's too late for Hello, World! to be your first Java program, but it's still worth a glance. In fact, we'll look at two ways of doing it.

The Console Version Of Hello, World!

A *console* program is one that does not make use of any graphical interface, being limited to displaying text on the screen and accepting keyboard input. If you've been around since the pre-Windows days of DOS, you know what I'm talking about. To be honest, console programs are not too common these days, and you may never have call to write one. Even so, it's worth reviewing to see how simple a Java program can be.

To create this program, start Visual J++ and select New from the File menu. Select Project Workspace, then click OK. In the next dialog box, select Java Workspace under Type, and enter "helloworld1" in the Name box. Finally, click Create.

Visual J++ will create the workspace, and the ClassView box in the upper left portion of the screen will contain the entry "helloworld1 classes." The project does not yet contain any classes, and the next step is to add the one class it needs.

Select New Class from the Insert menu. In the dialog box that is displayed, type "helloworld" in the Name box, and turn the Public option on. Then select OK. Visual J++ will open an editor window with the skeleton of the class definition displayed:

```
/*
 *
 * helloworld
 *
 */
public class helloworld
{

}
```

The next step is to add code for the class's **main**() method. Here's the code; place it between the braces in the helloworld class listing:

```
public static void main(String args[])
{
    System.out.println("Hello, world!");
}
```

That's it—the program is complete. To run it, select Execute from the Build menu, or press Ctrl+F5. When Visual J++ asks if you want to build the files, select Yes. In the next dialog, specify "helloworld" as the class to use. Visual J++ will compile helloworld1, then open a DOS box and start the Java interpreter to run the program's bytecode. You'll see "Hello, world!" displayed briefly before the box closes. This is shown in Figure 2.3.

Don't knock console programs!

While they may seem quaint and old fashioned, there are places where a console program is perfectly appropriate and in fact, may be preferable to a graphical interface program. For example, a program to convert graphics files from one format to another is a good candidate for a console program. It doesn't need to display anything to the user except perhaps a "file not found" or "disk full" message, and the only input it requires is the name of the files to convert. And believe me, I can open a DOS box and type

```
PCX2GIF *.PCX
```

a lot faster than you can click an icon, select a menu command, and select files in a dialog box! In addition, the console program is easier to write.

```
 jview.exe                                                                _ □ ×
Microsoft (R) Visual J++ Command-line Interpreter Version 1.00.6173
Copyright (C) Microsoft Corp 1996. All rights reserved.
Hello, world!
_
```

Figure 2.3   The output of the console version of Hello, World!

The Windows Version Of Hello, World!

Now that you've seen the console version of Hello, World!, let's take a look at the Windows version. Here are the steps to follow:

1. Select File, New, then choose Project Workspace and click OK.

2. In the next dialog box, select Java Applet Wizard under Type, enter "helloworld2" in the Name box, then select Create.

3. In the next dialog box (Step 1), be sure the As an Applet and as an Application option is selected, then choose Next.

4. In the Step 2 dialog box, accept the default settings, then select Next.

5. In the Step 3 dialog box, select No under Multithreading, then click Next.

6. In the Step 4 and 5 dialogs boxes, no entries are required, so select Next then Finish.

Once the project has been created, the ClassView window will display the name of the project. Click the + sign next to the project name to see a list of the project's classes. There are two: helloworld2 and helloworld2Frame. Click the + sign next to the helloworld2 class name to see a list of the class methods. This list is shown in Figure 2.4.

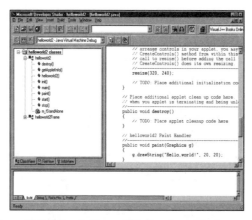

Figure 2.4   Displaying a list of the helloworld2 class's methods.

Two classes?

Why does the helloworld2 project have two classes? We mentioned earlier that one of the main differences between a Java applet and an application is that an application must take care of creating its screen window. That's the function of the second class, helloworld2Frame. If this program is run as an applet, this frame class is not used since the browser takes care of allocating a screen window.

The source code for all of these methods is located in the same file, helloworld2.java (a class is required to be in a file with the class name). Double-clicking a method name takes you to the appropriate section of code—a real time saver when you are working with a large, complex class! We need to modify the **paint**() method, so double-click paint and the editing window will display the code, as shown in Figure 2.5. At present, the **paint**() method is empty.

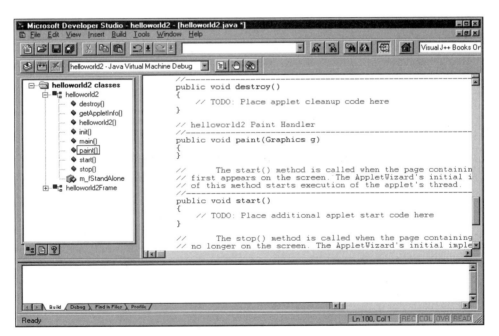

Figure 2.5   Editing the paint() method.

We need to add only a single line of code; when we're finished, the method will look like this:

```
public void paint(Graphics g)
{
  g.drawString("Hello, world!", 20, 20);
}
```

We are now ready to run the program. Press Ctrl+F5, or select Run from the Build menu. A window will open and display the "Hello, world!" message, as shown in Figure 2.6. This time, the message is displayed in a "Windows" window, complete with title bar, maximize button, and so on. Click the close button (the X at the right end of the title bar) to close the program.

If you examine the full source code for this second version of Hello, World!, you'll see it's a lot more complex than the original console version. Even so, the amount of work that you had to do was not any greater.

What's Next?

If we have been successful as authors, you should have a pretty good idea of the overall picture as regards Java and Visual J++. Now, it's time to start getting into the details. The next two chapters teach you how to use the Visual J++ programming environment to create Java applications and applets and their visual interfaces. With Chapter 5, we start covering the Java language in depth. Have fun!

Figure 2.6   Running the Windows version of Hello, World!

Using Visual J++

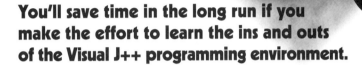

3

Peter Aitken

You'll save time in the long run if you make the effort to learn the ins and outs of the Visual J++ programming environment.

Writing Java programs with Visual J++ requires that you know two things. The most important, of course, is the Java language and object library. Most of this book is devoted to teaching you Java, and we will get started on the details in Chapter 5. The second thing you need to know is how to use Visual J++. Since programming is a complex business, Visual J++ is unavoidably somewhat complex, and if you are going to use Visual J++ efficiently, you need to know its ins and outs. That's the job of this chapter and the next.

Workspaces And Projects

Before we get started with the details of using Visual J++, you need to understand the concepts of *workspaces* and *projects*. These terms refer to the way Visual J++ manages and organizes the components of your Java programs. Because most Java programs are comprised of multiple files, it would not be trivial if you had to keep track of everything yourself. Fortunately, Visual J++ provides a variety of tools for these tasks.

A *workspace* contains all of the files and configuration information that are required to create a Java applet or application. You can have only one workspace open in Visual J++ at a time. The files that comprise a workspace are kept in their own folder, although you can add files from other folders to a workspace, if necessary.

A *project* is a set of source code files and the association configuration. In most cases, a workspace contains only a single project, and the terms *workspace* and *project* are synonymous. For some more complex programming tasks, the workspace can contain multiple projects—one master project and one or more sub-projects. In a multiple-project workspace, the output is still a single Java applet or application. The use of sub-projects is rarely necessary and will not be covered further. In the remainder of this book, we will often use the term *project* to mean workspace.

A *configuration* is the collection of settings that will be used when the project is built (*building* is the process of compiling the project's files into bytecode). By default, every project has two configurations: *debug* and *release*. The debug configuration results in bytecode that contains various information required to debug the program, while the release configuration does not. Typically, you work with the debug configuration while developing your project, then switch to the release configuration when the program is thoroughly debugged and ready for distribution.

The Visual J++ Screen

When you first start using Visual J++, the screen will probably seem a bit intimidating. Once you learn how to use it, however, we think you'll agree that it has been very well designed to provide you with access to the wide range of information you need while working on a Java project.

The main part of the Visual J++ screen is divided into three sections. These are identified in Figure 3.1. Each of these sections presents certain types of information to you, as described here.

◆ The Project Workspace window provides a hierarchical view of the elements of your project and the contents of the Help system (also called the Infoviewer).

◆ The Editing/Infoviewer area is used to display one or more independent windows containing project source code and Infoviewer information.

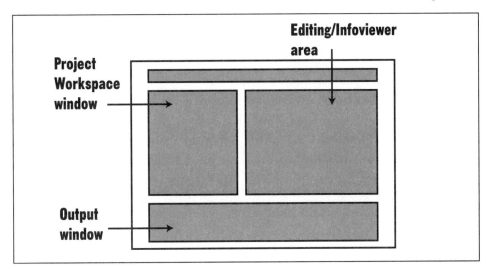

Figure 3.1   The main parts of the Visual J++ screen.

◆ The Output window is used to display error messages, debugging results, and other information generated by Visual J++ as you work on your project.

You can control the relative sizes of these screen areas. With the mouse, point at the border between two areas and drag until things are sized as you like. To activate the Workspace, Infoviewer, or Output window, click on it with the mouse or pull down the View menu and select the desired window.

Note that both the Workspace and Output windows have a row of file folder-like tabs along the bottom. This permits the same window to display different information depending on which tab you click. We will learn more about the specialized uses of these screen areas, as needed, throughout the book.

Using The Workspace Window

Understanding how to use the Workspace window is essential if you are to utilize Visual J++ efficiently. There are three tabs in this window. Let's look at how they are used.

The Infoviewer tab provides access to the online help information that is installed with Visual J++. A book icon represents a collection of related material. Click the plus sign next to the icon, or double-click the icon itself or its title, to open the book and display its contents. Double-click again, or click the minus sign, to close the book. A book can contain other books, also identified by the book icon, or articles, identified by a page icon. To display the contents of an article, double-click its icon or title. We will cover Infoviewer use in more detail later in the chapter.

The Class View tab provides a view of the contents of the current project, organized by classes. Under each class, its methods and instance variables are listed, each identified according to type by its icon. You expand and contract the class listing by clicking plus and minus signs, just as you did with the Infoviewer tab. Double-clicking a class name takes you directly to the source code where the class definition begins. Double-clicking a method or variable name takes you to the source code location where that item is defined.

The FileView tab presents your project organized by file name. This view is primarily useful when working on a complex project that uses many files. Double-click a file name to open it in the editor.

Right button magic.

If you right-click on almost any item in the Workspace window, Visual J++ displays the context menu for that item. This menu contains commands related to the item. All context menu commands can be carried out by other means, but the menu is often more convenient, particularly if you like to use the mouse. Context menus are widely used in Visual J++, so we suggest that you try right-clicking on various screen items to see what pops up.

Working With Projects

At the heart of creating any Java program are two related processes: using the Java Class Library and writing Java source code. Most of the remainder of this book is devoted to teaching you about these things. At another level, however, there are many other things that you need to learn in order to use the Visual J++ programming environment efficiently. For example, it's all very well to say that writing Java code is important, but if you don't know how to use your text editor, you won't get very far!

Visual J++ offers a collection of well-designed tools to help make these other tasks as easy as possible. We will approach these tools by looking at the steps required to create a Java program, which are as follows:

1. Creating a new project, or opening an existing one.

2. Adding new elements to the project—for example, creating a new class or adding a new method to an existing class.

3. Inserting existing elements into the project. For example, you will often include a class that you created as part of an earlier project, or one that you obtained from a colleague.

4. Editing the source code.

5. Working with resources. The term *resources* refers to visual elements, such as menus and dialog boxes. We'll cover resources in the next chapter.

6. Compiling and building your project—converting the Java source code into bytecode that can be executed by the Java Virtual Machine.

7. Testing the program and debugging, if necessary.

Creating A New Project

You have already seen the process of creating a new project in both of its flavors. The two "flavors" refer to whether or not you use the Applet Wizard. We haven't looked at all the options yet, however, and that's what we will do here.

You start a new project by selecting File|New, then selecting Project Workspace from the dialog box. You then must name the project and choose between creating a Java Workspace or running the Applet Wizard. What's the difference between these two choices?

◆ The Applet Wizard asks you a series of questions about the program you will be creating—for example, Will it be multithreaded? Will it use parameters?—and then generates the source code to create the skeleton of the program. The end result is a Java Workspace, but with a lot of the coding work already done for you.

◆ When you simply create a Java Workspace, nothing is generated for you. You are responsible for writing every single bit of code.

We find the Applet Wizard to be a terrific time saver and use it almost all the time. The only situation where it is not useful is when you are creating a console application, with text-only output and keyboard-only input. As you have seen previously, the Applet Wizard presents a series of dialog boxes that gather information from you about the program. Let's take a look at all the options.

First, however, we want to emphasize that the choices you make in the Applet Wizard do not lock you into anything. If you do not ask for a feature—say, animation support—you can always add it to the project later. Of course, you'll have to add the code manually, and it's always easier to let the Wizard do it, which is a good reason to plan thoroughly before firing up the Applet Wizard.

Applet Wizard Step 1

The first Applet Wizard dialog box is shown in Figure 3.2. You are asked for several pieces of information:

◆ Will the program be used as an applet only or as both an applet and application? Your choice depends on your needs, of course. Note that there is not an "application only" option, as there is nothing "extra" in an applet that is not also required in an application.

◆ The name of the applet class is, by default, the name that you assigned to the project. You can enter a different name if you wish.

◆ Visual J++'s default is to add explanatory comments and "to do" notes to the generated source code. The "to do" notes are particularly useful for beginners as they identify locations in the program where you will probably need to add more code. You can turn these options off if, once you become more experienced, you find that they just get in the way.

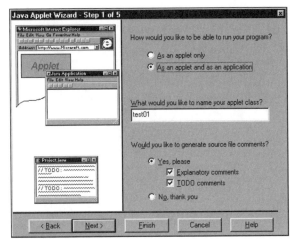

Figure 3.2   Applet Wizard Step 1.

Applet Wizard Step 2

The second step lets you choose whether to have a sample HTML file created. This will be a brief file containing nothing but an <APPLET> tag to call the applet and a link to the applet's source code. You can also specify the applet's initial screen size during this step.

Applet Wizard Step 3

The third Applet Wizard dialog box is shown in Figure 3.3. Here you choose whether your program will be multithreaded, as described in Chapter 2. A multithreaded program also has the option of animation support. If you select animation support, the Wizard adds code and member variables for animation support, as well as some sample images. This Wizard-generated animation support is so complete that, if you build and run the applet without adding any code, you'll see an animated spinning globe!

In this step, you also select the mouse support your applet needs. The mouse actions that a program can detect are as follows. Note that these apply only when the cursor is over the program's screen area.

◆ **mouseDown, mouseUp.** Pressing or releasing the mouse button.

◆ **mouseDrag.** Moving the mouse when the left button is depressed.

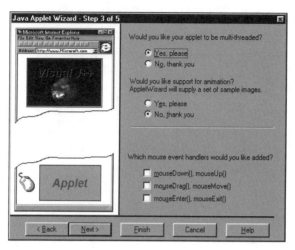

Figure 3.3   **The third Applet Wizard step.**

◆ **mouseMove.** Moving the mouse when the left button is not depressed.

◆ **mouseEnter.** The mouse cursor moves into the program's area.

◆ **mouseExit.** The mouse cursor moves out of the program's area.

Applet Wizard Step 4

The fourth step lets you specify parameters used to pass information from the calling HTML file to the applet. The dialog box is shown in Figure 3.4. The only piece of information you must fill in for each parameter is the name; the Wizard will automatically generate default values for the other items. You can, however, specify your own values for these items. They are described here:

◆ **Name.** The parameter name.

◆ **Member.** The name of the class member variable that will be created to receive the parameter variable.

◆ **Type.** The data type of the member variable.

◆ **Def-value.** The parameter's default value, used if an HTML file calls the applet without passing a value for the parameter.

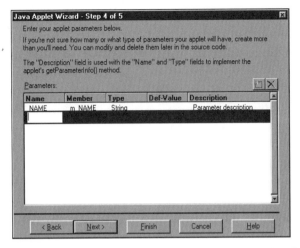

Figure 3.4   Specifying applet parameters in Step 4 of the Applet Wizard.

◆ **Description.** The parameter description used in the Wizard-generated comments.

If you specify parameters in this dialog box, the Wizard will generate code in the class source file that provides member variables to hold the parameter values, as well as code to assist you in retrieving the values from the HTML file with the **getParameter**() method. If you requested a sample HTML file, its <APPLET> tag will include tags for passing the parameters.

Applet Wizard Step 5

The fifth step lets you enter information about the applet that will be returned by the applet's **getAppInfo**() method. You can accept the default information that is supplied or edit it as desired.

Applet Wizard Step 6

The final "step" is not really a step at all, as there is no information for you to enter. Visual J++ displays the New Applet Information dialog box, listing all of the details of the new program that you specified in the Applet Wizard steps. If you notice a mistake here, there's nothing you can do except click on Cancel and start all over again. If you click on OK, Visual J++ will go to work for a few seconds, generating the project files. You are now ready to start adding your own elements.

Adding New And Existing Elements To A Project

All of the Java code that you write will be "in" something—a class, to be precise. And within a class, most code will be inside methods. Clearly, you need a way to add classes to your project and to add methods to classes.

Creating A New Class

To add a new class to your project, select New Class from the Insert menu. The Create New Class dialog box is displayed, as shown in Figure 3.5. Make entries as follows:

◆ **Name.** Type the class name, remembering the advantages of using descriptive names for your classes. The class name can be any length and should begin with a letter or number. Recall that Java is case-sensitive.

◆ **Extends.** Enter the name of the class, if any, that the new class is derived from. Pull down the list to see the names of the project's existing classes.

◆ **Package.** Enter the name of the package that the new class will be part of, or select from the drop-down list. If you type a new name, a new package will be created.

Figure 3.5   The Create New Class dialog box.

◆ **Modifiers.** Select the class modifiers. A *Public* class is accessible from outside its package. An *Abstract* class is one that cannot be instantiated, but rather is intended for use as a base class for other classes. A *Final* class can have no subclasses—in other words, no new classes can extend it.

Microsoft goofed?

Given Visual J++'s generally excellent approach to making the programmer's life easier, we were surprised to see that the New Class dialog box does not provide a list of Java's built-in base classes to select from. Likewise, there is no way to select an interface to implement. You must type these elements into the class definition yourself. Perhaps this shortcoming will be remedied in the commercial version of Visual J++ (we are using a pre-release beta).

After you have entered the necessary information, click on OK. Visual J++ will create the skeleton code for the new class and a file to hold it. Recall that each class is in a separate file with the .JAVA extension and the same name as the class. You can now edit the class source code to add methods, member variables, and so on.

Adding An Existing Class

By *existing class,* we mean a Java class that has already been defined but whose file is not yet part of your project. An existing class may be one that you wrote as part of another project or one that you obtained from a friend or online service. To add a class file to your project:

1. Select Files Into Project from the Insert menu.

2. Use the dialog box to locate the desired .JAVA file. It does not need to reside in the same folder as the other project files.

3. Click on OK.

After inserting a file, its class will automatically be listed in the Class View window and you can work with it like any other class. Generally, you will add a class file from another project only if you are going to instantiate it unchanged. If you plan to modify it, you are better off putting the class in a package to access it, then creating a subclass with the desired modifications.

Adding A Method To A Class

To add a method to a class, right-click on the class name in the Workspace window. Visual J++ will display the Add Method dialog box, as shown in Figure 3.6. The information to enter in this dialog box is described here:

◆ **Return type.** Enter the Java data type of the method's return value. Enter **Void** if the method does not return a value.

◆ **Method declaration.** Enter the method's declaration, including its name and its parameters. You'll learn the details of method declarations in Chapter 7.

◆ **Access.** Select the desired access level from the pull-down list. *Package* (the default) permits the method to be called by any class within the same package. *Public* access permits the method to be called by any class regardless of its package. *Private* access permits the method to be accessed only from within its own class. *Protected* is similar to *Package* but also allows access from subclasses of the method's class.

The other access modifiers—Static, Final, etc.—will be explained in Chapter 7.

Add Method

Return type:

Method declaration:

Modifiers

Access: Default (Package)

☐ Static ☐ Final ☐ Synchronized
☐ Abstract ☐ Native

Full Declaration:

OK
Cancel
Help

Figure 3.6   Adding a new method to a class.

When you click OK, the skeleton of the method will be added to the class source code, and the method name will be displayed under the class name in the Class View window. Note that you do not have to use this technique to add a method to a class—you can simply type the method definition into the source code. If you use this technique, however, the method name will not be displayed in the Class View window until the class is compiled.

Adding A Member Variable

Adding a member variable to a class is similar to adding a method. Right-click the class name in the Class View window, and select Add Variable. Fill in the variable type and name, and select other options as desired. You'll find more information on declaring member variables in Chapter 5.

Using The Text Editor

Visual J++ includes a powerful text editor for editing your Java source code files. You can actually use this editor to edit any text file, but it differs from a basic text editor, such as the Windows Notepad, in that it has a number of specializations for working with code. It also permits you to use commands from several popular third-party programmers' editors, including Brief and Epsilon. We'll be explaining the default Developer Studio commands, however.

Entering And Manipulating Text

Text that you type appears in the editing window at the location of the cursor. Of course, the editing window must be active to receive input. The editing cursor does not display unless the window is active. Press Enter to start a new line; use the arrow and other navigation keys, or the mouse, to move the editing cursor. Hold down the Ctrl key while pressing left and right arrows to move a word at a time.

Many editing operations require that you select the text to operate on. Selected text is displayed in reverse video—white letters on a black background. To select text, hold down the Shift key while using the navigation keys to move the cursor, or drag over the text with the mouse. To deselect text, press Escape or click anywhere with the mouse. You can also select one or more entire lines of text by dragging in the left margin with the mouse. This area is called the *selection margin,* and you can identify it because the mouse cursor displays as an arrow when over this area. The selection margin is an editor option that you can turn on or off, as explained later in this chapter in the section on options.

Once you have selected text, you can delete it by pressing the Del key. To move or copy the text to a different location, in the same or another file, select either Cut or Copy from the edit menu, then move the editing cursor to the destination location and select Edit Paste.

Quick line copy.

If you issue the Edit|Copy command with no text selected, the entire current line is copied to the clipboard. This is very handy, because working with entire lines of code is a common task. If line copy is not working, you need to set editor options, as explained later in the chapter.

Certain mistakes are easily corrected using the editor's Undo and Redo commands. As is probably obvious, Undo reverses your most recent editing action, while Redo reverses the most recent Undo command, in effect restoring the action that was undone. Both Undo and Redo "remember" quite a few actions, so you are not limited to undoing only your most recent action. To use these commands, pull down the Undo or Redo list from the toolbar, and select the desired action. Or, press Ctrl+Z or Ctrl+Y to Undo or Redo the most recent action.

Indentation

It is customary to write source code using indentation to set off sections of code based on their logical organization. Proper use of indentation makes it much easier to read and understand the source code. To indent a line of code, press the Tab key one or more times at the start of the line. Even better, use the editor's *smart indentation* capability. When activated, smart indentation analyzes the code you have typed and automatically indents the next line, if needed, according to standard indentation rules.

In our opinion, automatic indentation is a terrific help, and we use it all the time. To turn this feature on or off, and to set other indentation options, select Options from the Tools menu. In the dialog box, click the Tabs tab and make the desired entries. You'll see a File Type entry in this dialog box. This is because the indentation rules are different for different types of files. For example, Java source code is indented differently from an HTML file. The Default entry specifies indentation for all file types not specifically identified.

Multiple Files

The Visual J++ editor can edit multiple text files at the same time. Each file is displayed in its own window, and only one window can be active at a given time. Information from the Help system is also displayed in a window in this part of the screen. Managing multiple editing windows can sometimes require a bit of juggling unless you are lucky enough to have a huge monitor that can display everything at the same time. Table 3.1 shows some window commands you can use.

Each file that you open with the File|Open command is displayed in its own window. To start a new, blank file, click the New button on the toolbar or select New from the File menu, then select Text File. To close the active

Table 3.1   Windowing commands.

To	Do This
Switch to a specific window	Select the desired window from the Window menu, or click its title bar if visible
Cycle from one window to the next	Press Ctrl+F6
Display all windows overlapping with title bars visible	Select Cascade from the Window menu
Display all windows non-overlapping	Select Tile Vertically or Tile Horizontally from the Window menu
Display a window at its maximum size	Click the window's Maximize button

Continued

Table 3.1   Windowing commands (Continued).

To	Do This
Return a maximized window to its original size	Click the window's Restore button
Move a window	Point at the window's title bar and drag to the new location
Change the window size	Point at the window border and drag to the desired size

window, select Close from the File menu or click the window's Close button. Visual J++ will prompt you to save the file, if necessary.

The big picture.

If you find the editing window a bit cramped, you can expand it to full-screen size by selecting Full Screen from the View menu. Click the button to return to normal view. You can still access the menus in full screen view by pressing Alt plus the first letter of the menu title. Shortcut keys, such as Ctrl+O for File|Open, work too.

Splitting Windows

A useful technique, particularly when editing large files, is to split your editing window. You can then view two different sections of the same file at once. You can split a window into as many as four separate views, or *panes*. To split a window, select Split from the Window menu. Visual J++ displays one vertical and one horizontal line in the window with the mouse cursor centered on the intersection of the lines. Move the mouse until these lines are positioned where you want the split(s) to be located, then click. To split the window horizontally into two panes, one above the other, drag the vertical split line to one edge of the window before clicking.

Once the window has been split, you can scroll independently in each pane to bring different parts of the file into view. To move the editing cursor from one pane to another, click. To rearrange or remove the split, point at the dividing line and drag it to the new position.

Find In Files

The Find in Files command lets you search through files on your disk for specified text. It can be a lifesaver when you forget where a certain section of code is. To use this command:

1. Select Find in Files from the Files menu.

2. Enter the text to find, in the Find What box. Click the down arrow to retrieve recent search strings. Click the right arrow to select certain options, such as looking for characters only at the beginning of a line.

3. Specify the type of files to search for, in the In Files of Type box. Use the pull-down list to select frequently needed settings. Use standard wildcard specifications. For example, *.JAVA looks only in files with the .JAVA extension.

4. In the In Folder box, specify the disk folder (directory) to be searched. Click the button with the "..." on it to use a dialog box to locate the search directory. Click the Look In Subfolders option to extend the search to subfolders of the selected folder.

5. Click the Find button. If any matches are found, they are listed on the Find in Files tab in the Output window. Each entry lists the path and name of the file, the number of the line the text was found on, and the actual line of text.

After the search has been completed, double-click on any entry in the Find in Files list to open that file, if necessary, and go to the specified line.

Bookmarks And Go To

When you are editing Java source code, particularly in a large, multiple file project, you'll often find yourself hopping back and forth from one section of code to another. Visual J++'s bookmarks and Go To command can be very useful. A bookmark is a name that you assign to a particular location in a file. Once you've set a bookmark, you can go to that location by referring to the bookmark name. The Go To command also lets you move directly to specific lines, object references, and so on.

To set a bookmark, position the editing cursor at the desired location, then:

1. Select Edit Bookmark, or press Alt+F2. Visual J++ displays the Bookmark dialog box.

2. Type the name for the bookmark in the Name box.

3. Select Add.

This dialog box also lists existing bookmarks. If you select a bookmark name, you can delete it or go to it by clicking the appropriate button.

To use the Go To command, select Go To from the File menu, or press Ctrl+G. This dialog box is shown in Figure 3.7. In the Go To What list, select the type of target, then enter the target identifier in the box and click Go To.

Note that not all Go To target types will be available at all times. Some are used for debugging and are not relevant for source code files.

Quick Go To.
Press F2 to move to the next bookmark following the current location. Press Shift+F2 to go to the immediately previous bookmark.

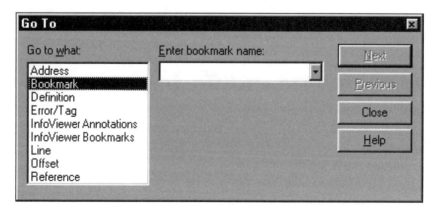

Figure 3.7   Using the Go To command to move to a specified file location.

You can also set a temporary bookmark, one that is not assigned a name. You can have multiple temporary bookmarks, with each one marked in the left margin by a blue rectangle. Press Ctrl+F2 to add or remove a temporary bookmark from the current line. Because you cannot refer to a temporary bookmark by name, you must use the Next and Previous commands (F2 and Shift+F2 respectively) to move to them.

Compiling And Building A Project

The process of compiling and building a project converts the Java source code into bytecode that can be executed by the Java Virtual Machine or a browser. There is some confusion between the terms *compile* and *build* because they have slightly different meanings.

When you compile, you are converting a single source code file (with the .JAVA extension) to a bytecode file (with the .CLASS extension). If your project contains only a single class, then compiling it is the same as building it. The process of building has a different meaning only for projects that contain more than one source code file. With multiple file projects, you are dealing with *dependencies*.

The term *dependency* refers to the fact that certain classes depend on other classes. If class A is a subclass of class B, then class A depends on class B—changes to class B may affect class A. However, class B does not depend on class A. Likewise, if class C calls methods in class D, then class C is dependent on class D.

Visual J++ can keep track of dependencies and determine when updating is required. Let's say you modify DRAW.JAVA, but do not recompile it. Then, the file DRAW.JAVA will have a newer time/date stamp then DRAW.CLASS, so Visual J++ knows it requires updating (that is, it needs to be recompiled). If, however, the file DRAW.CLASS is newer than DRAW.JAVA, Visual J++ knows that updating is not required.

With this background, you will now be able to understand the various commands on Visual J++'s Build menu. The ones you need to know about at present are:

◆ **Compile.** Compiles the current source code file. In a single file project, this is equivalent to the Build command.

◆ **Build.** Compiles only those files in the project whose dependencies are out of date.

◆ **Rebuild All.** Compiles all of the files in the project regardless of whether their dependencies are out of date.

◆ **Execute.** Builds the project, if necessary, and then executes the program.

If your project is being developed as an applet only, then of course the program will execute within your browser. If it is both an application and an applet, you select how the Execute command will work, as follows:

1. Select Settings from the Build menu.

2. In the dialog box that is displayed, click the Debug tab. Be sure that General is selected in the Category box. This dialog box is shown in Figure 3.8.

3. Select either the Browser option or the Stand-alone Interpreter option.

4. Click OK.

Just because the Browser/Interpreter option is available does not mean that both options will work. An applet-only project has no **main**() method, so

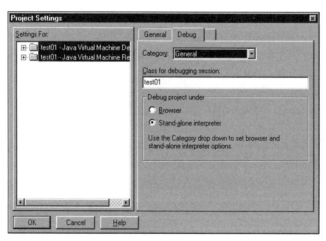

Figure 3.8 Setting the project's Execute options.

the interpreter cannot execute it. An applet/application project will have **main**(), but remember the differences between running a Java program in a browser versus running it in an application. The Java Virtual Machine (interpreter) starts off in the **main**() method, so the code that starts things off—creating and starting threads, for example—must be located there. A browser, in contrast, starts off in the **run**() method. Special coding is required for a Java program to run either as an applet or as an application.

How does Visual J++ know which browser to use when running an applet? Display the Project Settings dialog box as above, then select Browser in the Category box. You'll then be able to specify the path to your browser in the dialog box, as well as whether the applet should get its parameters (if any) from the associated HTML file or from values you enter in the dialog box.

Using two browsers?

Many developers like to test their applets in more than one browser to be sure the applet is compatible. The easiest way we have found to do this, without having to constantly change the Browser setting in Visual J++, is as follows: Set the Visual J++ Browser setting to one browser (say, Microsoft Internet Explorer), then use the Windows command to associate another browser (say, Netscape Navigator) with .HTML files. Then, run the applet in one browser with Visual J++'s Execute command and run it in the other by double-clicking the HTML file name in the Explorer.

To associate a file type with a program, open My Computer and select Options from the View menu, then select the File Types tab. Scroll through the list to "Internet Document (HTML)," click the Edit button, and in the next dialog box select Open in the Actions list. Click Edit again, and enter the name of your browser in the Application box (or click Browse to locate it on disk).

Dealing With Errors And Bugs

It's a rare Java project that moves straight from conception to completion without problems along the way. Finding these problems is an essential part of program development, because if you don't find the problems, your customers most certainly will! These problems fall into two general categories.

Program Errors

An *error* is a problem that prevents the project from compiling or building correctly. For example, you might have spelled a class name incorrectly, forgotten the semicolon at the end of a line of code, or mismatched parentheses. Errors are relatively easy to fix because they are caught by Visual J++ during the build process. Even better, Visual J++ will display a message identifying both the error and its location. For example, using the HELLO WORLD1 project, suppose you had made a typing error in this line:

```
System.out.println("Hello, world!");
```

Instead of "out" you typed "ot":

```
System.ot.println("Hello, world!");
```

When you try to compile this file, Visual J++ will display the following message in the Output window (on the Build tab):

```
C:\Msdev\projects\helloworld1\helloworld.java(11,9) : error J0072:
 'ot' is not a  member of class 'System'
Error executing jvc.exe.
helloworld.class - 1 error(s), 0 warning(s)
```

The first line of this message identifies the path and name of the source code file in which the error occurred. The numbers in parentheses identify the line and column numbers where the error was found. In my experience, the line number is almost always correct, while the column number is not always accurate but will at least get you close. This is followed by the error number and a brief description of the error.

Line numbers?

Note that the Visual J++ editor displays the current line and column number in the status bar—a real help in locating errors.

There are several methods for moving the editing cursor to the location of the error, so that you can fix it:

◆ Double-click the error message in the Output window.

◆ Press F4 to go to the next error in the list.

◆ Press Shift+F4 to go to the previous error in the list.

◆ Right-click the error message and select Goto Error|Tag from the popup menu.

You can get a more detailed description of an error by clicking the error number (so the vertical cursor displays in it), then pressing F1. The more detailed error descriptions can be useful if the brief message that the compiler displays is not sufficient for you to identify the error.

Bugs

A *bug* is a problem that prevents your program from performing as intended. It does not interfere in any way with building the project, nor does it generate any error messages in Visual J++. Rather, it causes the program to crash or to operate incorrectly. For example, a graphics program that displays things in the wrong colors, a financial calculator that gives incorrect answers, and a database that performs inaccurate searches are all examples of bugs. Likewise, when a program that "hangs" and requires the old three-finger salute (Ctrl+Alt+Del) to get out, that's a bug, too. It is essential that your Java programs be thoroughly debugged before you release them to your users.

Fortunately, Visual J++ provides a variety of debugging tools that make the job a lot easier. We will cover these tools in detail in a later chapter.

Warnings

The compiler will sometimes display warnings. A *warning* is displayed when the compiler detects something in your source code that is not an error—it will not prevent the program from compiling—but that may cause problems during program execution. Examples of conditions that will generate warnings are the use of methods with no declared return type, failure to put **return** statements in methods that aren't **void,** and data conversions that would cause loss of data or precision. You can move to the locations of warnings, as you would do for errors.

Visual J++ provides five levels of warning messages, ranging from ignoring all warnings to displaying all warnings—even the least severe. You set this option by selecting Settings from the Build menu, clicking the Java tab in the dialog box, and selecting the desired level in the Warning Level box. Higher-valued warning levels are stricter.

We suggest that you use the default level, which is 2, unless you have a good reason to do otherwise. As a learning exercise, try setting Level 4 to see the warnings that are generated. While this type of warning rarely causes problems in a real-world program, experimenting with them can provide you with additional insight into the workings and fine points of Java.

Customizing Visual J++

Visual J++ provides you with lots of options for customizing the environment to the way you like to use it. The following sections provide some good examples of what you can do to adapt Visual J++ to the way you like to work.

Toolbars

If you like using the mouse, you'll love Visual J++. Its extensive use of toolbars makes maximum use of the graphical environment. Tooltips, displayed when you rest the mouse cursor over a toolbar button, make things even easier. Better yet, you can customize the toolbars to your heart's content—controlling which toolbars are displayed, where they are located, and which buttons are on them.

Visual J++ has a variety of different toolbars, each containing buttons for related tasks. You can, for example, display the Edit toolbar while editing your source code, then hide it and display the debug toolbar during debugging. To control which toolbars display, select Toolbars from the View menu and turn individual toolbar displays on or off. By default, toolbars all display together in the same area at the top of the screen. You can make a toolbar "float" by pointing at it with the mouse (between buttons, of course) and dragging it to the desired screen location. If you drag it to the left, right, or bottom edge of the screen, it will automatically dock along that edge. The size and shape of a floating toolbar can be adjusted by pointing at its border and dragging. To return a toolbar to the default position at the top of the screen, simply drag it there.

You can customize any toolbar by adding, removing, and rearranging buttons. This way, you can set up the toolbars so the commands that you use most often are arranged in a convenient manner. You can also create totally new toolbars. Any command button can be placed on more than one toolbar, which gives you added flexibility.

To modify a toolbar, first make sure that the toolbar is displayed as described above. Then, select View Toolbars and click the Customize button in the dialogue box, or select Customize from the Tools menu and click the Toolbars tab. Either way, the dialogue box shown in Figure 3.9 will be displayed.

Select a button category in the Categories list, and the available buttons will be displayed in the right section of the dialogue box. Click a button to see a description of its function. Drag a button to any toolbar to add it to that toolbar. To delete a button, drag it off the toolbar. To rearrange buttons, drag a button to a new location on the toolbar. When you are finished, click the Close button.

To create a new toolbar, select View Toolbars then click the New button in the dialogue box and enter a name for the toolbar. Visual J++ creates a new, empty toolbar and displays it (it's small because it doesn't yet have any buttons, so you may have to look carefully to find it!). Then, follow the procedures in the preceding paragraph to add buttons to the new toolbar.

The Keyboard

A *shortcut key* is a key or key combination that has been assigned to a Visual J++ command. Pressing a shortcut key has the same effect as selecting the corresponding command from the menus or a toolbar. Many shortcut keys are part of Visual J++'s default configuration, following the Windows

Figure 3.9   You customize toolbars in this dialog box.

standard or one of the alternate editor emulations that are available. You can change these key assignments and create your own, as follows:

1. Select Customize from the Tools menu, then click the Keyboard tab in the dialog box that is displayed. This dialog box is shown in Figure 3.10.

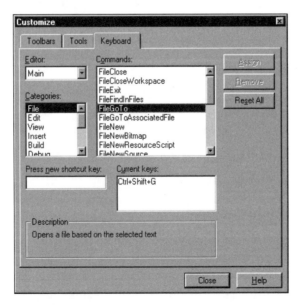

Figure 3.10   Customizing the keyboard.

2. In the Editor list, select the editor that you wish to customize. You have not seen all of these editors yet; briefly, they are:

   ◆ **Text.** The source code editor.

   ◆ **Image.** Used for editing bitmap images.

   ◆ **Dialog.** Used for creating and editing dialog boxes.

   ◆ **InfoViewer.** Used for accessing and manipulating Help information.

   ◆ **Main.** General commands.

3. In the Category list, select the desired category of commands.

4. The Command list will display all of the commands for the selected category/editor combination. Select the desired command by clicking on it. The Description box displays a brief description of the selected command.

5. If the command already has a shortcut key assigned to it, the key is displayed in the Current Key box. To "unassign" a shortcut key, select it and click on Remove.

6. To assign a shortcut key to a selected command, tab or click to the Press New Shortcut key box and press the desired key or key combination. You can use essentially any keys alone or in combination with the Ctrl, Alt, and/or Shift keys. If the key combination you press is currently assigned to a command, its assignment will be displayed above the Description box. Press Backspace to erase the key so that you can enter a new combination.

7. Select Assign to assign the entered key combination to the command.

If you click the Reset button in the Customize Keyboard dialog box, all of the key assignments for the selected editor will be returned to their default values. To get a list of all key assignments, select Keyboard from the Help menu.

The Help System

One of the best things about Visual J++, particularly for less experienced programmers, is its extensive online help system (also referred to as the

Infoviewer). You can obtain detailed and easy-to-use information on just about every aspect of Visual J++, not only on how to use the program but also on the Java language and API. The help system is rather involved, and we can cover only the basics of using it. We encourage you to explore it on your own.

Using extension help.

For Help to operate as we describe next, you must enable Extension Help. To toggle this setting on and off, select Use Extension Help from the Help menu. A checkmark is displayed next to the command when it is active.

The Help Menu

Your main access to the help information is via Visual J++'s Help menu. The commands you'll need most often are explained here.

◆ **Contents.** Displays the table of contents for the available online documentation.

◆ **Search.** Lets you search for terms of interest. You can use the index, which is an alphabetical listing of terms, or the Find tab, which lets you search for a specific term.

◆ **Define Subset.** Lets you define a subset of the available topics to which searches can be confined. For example, you might define a subset that contains information only relating to the Java API. If you restrict searches to this subset while you are working on API-related tasks, your searches will run faster and will turn up fewer irrelevant matches.

◆ **Set Default Subset.** Lets you specify which subsets are used by the Help system.

◆ **Open Information Title.** Lets you specify which set of help files is accessed. This command is relevant only if you have another Help title installed on your system, such as the Microsoft Developers Network.

- **Tips of the Day.** Lets you browse the tips and set whether a tip is automatically displayed when Visual J++ starts.

- **Web Favorites.** Provides a list of Java and Visual J++ related Web sites. You can edit the list and add new sites. When you select Go To, the default browser is opened to connect to the Web site.

Context-Sensitive Help

Context-sensitive help provides information about the task you are performing. The help system is "smart" and knows, within certain limitations, what task you are performing. There are two main methods for activating context-sensitive help. While editing code, place the cursor on a keyword and press F1 for information about that term. While a dialog box is open, click the Help button or press F1 for information about using that dialog box.

The Infoviewer toolbar.

The Infoviewer toolbar provides quick access to certain Help function, such as selecting an information title and performing searches. Select Toolbars from the View menu to turn the Infoviewer toolbar display on and off.

Your Visual Interface

Peter Aitken

Visual J++ provides tools that simplify the task of creating your program's visual interface.

Just about any Java program you write is going to have a visual interface or screen display of some sort. Because the Web is such a visually oriented medium, a program's visual interface is often critical in determining its success. Two programs may offer essentially the same functionality, but the one with the more convenient and appealing visual interface is able to attract more customers and users. It follows that successful Java programmers must be skilled in designing and creating visual interfaces.

Fortunately, the Java language provides a rich set of visual elements for use in your programs. These elements are part of the *Abstract Window Toolkit*, or AWT, a library of predefined classes for commonly needed visual elements such as windows, menus, images, and dialog boxes. The hard work has already been done—all you need to do is utilize the AWT classes in your code to create the visual interface that you need.

You still have one little obstacle to hurdle, however. Despite all the power of the AWT, you are still required to write the code to create your visual interface. Anyone who has used the type of visual design tools introduced by Visual Basic many years ago will find this hand-coding method to be unbearably tedious. It's faster, easier, and more intuitive to "draw" the interface using visual design tools.

Well, "visual" is Visual J++'s first name! The development environment provides an assortment of visual design tools that permit you to create your program's interface using convenient drag-and-drop techniques. You can then use the *Resource Wizard* to translate your interface into the Java AWT statements necessary to generate it.

Java And Windows Resources

If you've dabbled with any Windows programming, you are probably familiar with the term *resources*. A Windows resource is a visual program element such as menus, images, dialog boxes, and their contents. Windows is organized such that a program's resources are defined in a resource definition file, which in turn is compiled by a resource compiler into a resource file. When the project is built, the compiled resources are combined with the compiled code to create the final program.

Java works differently. Because it is designed to be platform-independent, Java cannot make use of any elements or techniques that are specific to Windows or any other platform, such as Macintosh. Therefore, a Java program cannot use Windows resources—at least not directly. A Java program can utilize only elements of the Java AWT to create visual elements.

Visual J++ bypasses this apparent dilemma in the following way. The resource editors in Visual J++ work in the same manner as any other Windows resource tools, creating dialog boxes and menus in the Windows format. But instead of using a Windows resource compiler, you translate the resources into Java AWT code using the Visual J++ *Resource Wizard*.

Resource Template Files

The resources that you create using Visual J++'s Dialog Editor and Menu Editor are stored in a *resource template file*, the input to the Resource Wizard. This resource template file is not part of your project, strictly speaking. Rather, the Java source code files produced by the Resource Wizard are part of the project. The Wizard will create one Java file for each resource (dialog box or menu) in the template file, plus one additional Java file that contains information used in dialog box layout.

You can edit the Java source code files created by the Resource Wizard, but we do not advise it. Unless you really know what you are doing, you can easily create some real havoc. Furthermore, these Java files are regenerated each time you run the Resource Wizard, and any changes you make will be overwritten.

How you arrange your resources within one or more template files is completely up to you. Most often, particularly while you are just getting started with Visual J++, you'll keep each project's resources together in a single template file located in the project folder. If you start to share resources—for example, using one dialog box in multiple projects—you may want to arrange things differently.

The basic steps you'll follow are as follows:

1. Create a new resource template file or open an existing one.

2. Add one or more new dialog or menu resources to the file using the Visual J++ Dialog Editor and Menu Editor.

3. Use the Resource Wizard to convert the resource template file into Java source code files.

4. Add the Java files to your project.

5. Add code to your project to display and respond to the resource elements.

When you create or open a resource template file, it will not be listed in the FileView window because it is not part of your project. Rather, it gets its own window in the Editing area of the screen. You can have more than one resource template file open at a time, and each will have its own window. Use the Window menu command to display the desired resource template window (note the example in Figure 4.1). Click the + sign next to the file name to open the resource list. In Figure 4.1, you can see that the file name is TEMPL1.RCT. It contains two dialog box resources (named IDD_DIALOG1 and NewDialog) and one menu resource (named IDR_MENU1). Double-click a resource name to open it for editing.

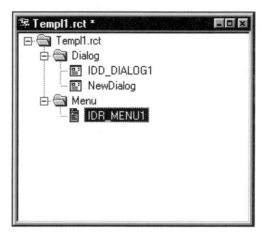

Figure 4.1   The Resource Template window lists the resources contained in a particular resource template file.

If you want to add a new resource to an existing resource template, be sure that the template file is open and displayed in its window. Otherwise, Visual J++ tends to create a new resource template for a new resource.

Dialog Box Resources

A dialog box is a small window that a program displays to present information and/or accept input from the user. In creating a dialog box, you select from a set of available elements and arrange them in the window to suit the needs of the program. The Visual J++ Dialog Editor lets you perform this task visually, sizing and arranging elements with the mouse. You will encounter a limitation, however. As we mentioned earlier, a Java program can display only those visual elements that are part of the Java Abstract Window Toolkit, including all of the commonly needed dialog box elements. However, some dialog box elements are available in Windows but are not part of the AWT. The Visual J++ Dialog Editor lets you add these unsupported elements to a dialog box, but they will not appear in the final Java program. It's unclear to us why Microsoft left these unsupported elements in the Visual J++ Dialog Editor, but that's the way it is. You just have to learn which elements are supported, as listed in Table 4.1.

Table 4.1   Dialog box elements supported in Visual J++.

Visual J++ Control	Function	Java Class
Static Text	Display text that cannot be edited by the user	Label
Edit Box	Entry/editing of text	TextField (or TextArea for multi-line edit controls)
Button	Triggering of actions	Button
Check Box	Selecting on/off options	CheckBox
Radio Button	Similar to a Check Box except that only one Radio Button in a group may be "on" at a time	CheckBox (Resource Wizard generates and adds the control to a CheckboxGroup member)
List Box	Presenting a list of items from which the user can choose	List
Combo Box	Similar to List Box except the list is hidden until the user selects the control	Choice
Horizontal Scrollbar	Left-right scrolling	Scrollbar
Vertical Scrollbar	Up-down scrolling	Scrollbar

Not just for dialogs.

The Visual J++ Dialog Editor can do more than design dialog boxes. The code that results from a dialog box that you have designed specifies the arrangement of certain visual elements—buttons, text boxes, etc.—within a container. A dialog box is just one type of container available in Java, the others being window, panel, and applet.

Adding A New Dialog Box

To add a new dialog box, select Resource from the Insert menu or press Ctrl+R. Select Dialog, then click OK. Visual J++ opens the Dialog Editor with a basic dialog box displayed and ready for editing, as shown in Figure 4.2. This dialog box contains only OK and Cancel buttons, which are components of most dialog boxes. If you don't need them, they can be deleted.

Next to the dialog box is the *control palette*. Each button on the palette represents a control, or object, that you can place on your dialog box (within the restrictions mentioned previously). The top left button with the arrowhead symbol is not a control, but rather the *selector* that is used to work with existing controls. If you let the mouse cursor rest over a control button for a few seconds, Visual J++ will display a brief description of the corresponding control. To add a control to your dialog box, click the control's button in the control palette and then:

◆ Click in the dialog box at the desired location to place a default-size control.

◆ Drag in the dialog box to place a custom-size control.

You'll note that the newly added control is surrounded by small black boxes, called *handles*, indicating that the control is currently selected. The Edit Box in Figure 4.3 is selected. You can select any control or the dialog box

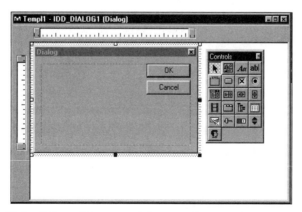

Figure 4.2   The Dialog Editor with a new dialog box displayed for editing.

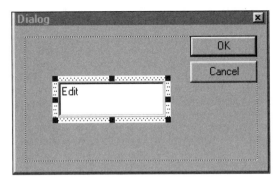

Figure 4.3   The black handles around the Edit Box indicate that it is currently selected.

itself by clicking or by pressing Tab or Shift+Tab to move the selection from one object to another. You can take the following actions with the selected object:

◆ Move. Point at the center of the object; the mouse pointer changes to a 4-headed arrow. Then, drag the object to the new position. You cannot move the dialog box itself, only controls on the dialog box.

◆ Resize. Point at one of the handles; the mouse pointer will change to a 2-headed arrow. Then, drag the object to the desired size.

◆ Delete. Press Del or Backspace; you can also select Delete from the Edit menu.

Using The Alignment Tools

A visually appealing dialog box will not have its controls scattered haphazardly here and there. Careful attention to the sizes and locations of the controls can result in dialog boxes that are more attractive and easier to use. The Dialog Editor's Dialog toolbar makes this task a lot easier. This toolbar is normally displayed at the bottom of the screen but can be moved around like any other toolbar. If it is not displayed, right-click any toolbar and select Dialog.

To use some of the tools on the Dialog toolbar, you need to select more than one control. Select the first, or dominant, control by clicking it in the usual manner. Next, hold down the Shift key while clicking one or more additional controls. Note that if only one control is selected, the buttons on the Dialog toolbar that work only with multiple controls are not available. The Dialog toolbar buttons perform the following alignment/sizing tasks:

◆ Align Left. Aligns the left edges of the selected controls with the left edge of the dominant control.

◆ Align Right. Aligns the right edges of the selected controls with the right edge of the dominant control.

◆ Align Top. Aligns the top edges of the selected controls with the top edge of the dominant control.

◆ Align Bottom. Aligns the bottom edges of the selected controls with the bottom edge of the dominant control.

◆ Center Vertically. Centers the selected controls vertically within the dialog box.

◆ Center Horizontally. Centers the selected controls horizontally within the dialog box.

◆ Space Across. Spaces the controls equally left-to-right.

◆ Space Down. Spaces the controls equally top-to-bottom.

◆ Same Width. Makes the width of all controls the same as the dominant control.

◆ Same Height. Makes the height of all controls the same as the dominant control.

◆ Same Size. Makes the height and width of all controls the same as the dominant control.

In addition, there are three more buttons on the Dialog toolbar.

◆ Grid. Toggles the display of a grid of dots in the dialog box. When the grid is displayed, control position and size changes are restricted so that control boundaries fall on the grid.

◆ Guide. Toggles the display of ruler guides above and to the left of the dialog. You can use these guides to change the dialog box's margin, the area indicated by a thin blue line where controls cannot be placed.

◆ Test. "Runs" the dialog box so you can see its final appearance. You can also run the dialog box by pressing Ctrl+T. After viewing the "running" dialog, click the X button in its title bar to close it.

Working With Object Properties

The dialog box itself, as well as the controls you place on it, are all objects. Each object has a set of properties that control its appearance and behavior. Much of the work involved in designing a dialog box consists of working with object properties. You need to know the properties for each type of object and the effects of the various settings in order to make maximum use of the Dialog Editor.

To display an object's property sheet, either double-click it or right-click it and select Properties from the pop-up menu. Property sheets will typically have two or more tabs that permit you to access different subsets of the object's properties. Note the Keep Visible button and the Help button in the upper right. The former keeps the property sheet displayed even when you switch away from it, and the latter displays Help information.

A couple of properties are common to all or most objects, while others are unique to just one object. In the following sections, we'll explain the various object properties and how to use them, although we won't cover every single property. Some of the ones available are simply not supported by Java. Others are very specialized, and you'll rarely, if ever, need them. We'll confine our explanation to those properties that you'll use most often. Many of the other properties are self-explanatory, and you can always obtain information from the Help system. In addition, not all of the properties available in the Dialog Editor will translate into Java code. Details on which properties do and which do not translate was unavailable in the beta version of Visual J++ that we are using, but you should be able to find this information in the online Help of the released version.

COMMON PROPERTIES

Properties that are common to all or many dialog box-related objects. See Table 4.2.

Table 4.2 Common object properties in dialog boxes.

Property	Function
ID	The object's name. You'll use this name to refer to the object in code, so choose something meaningful. The default ID names assigned by Visual J++ are fine for objects that you won't need to access in code.
Caption	The text displayed on the object—or in the case of the dialog box itself, in the title bar.
Visible	A boolean value that determines whether the object is visible.
Tab Stop	A boolean value specifying whether the user can move the focus to the object by pressing Tab.
Disabled	A boolean value. A disabled control is visible but cannot be accessed by the user.

DIALOG OBJECT PROPERTIES

The dialog box itself has a variety of properties that control various aspects of its appearance and behavior. The important ones follow:

◆ Font. Sets the typeface and size of the font used in the dialog box. Changing the font size also changes the overall size of controls and the dialog box itself.

◆ System Modal. A modal dialog box prevents the user from switching to another window or program while the dialog is displayed. The default is False.

EDIT BOX OBJECT PROPERTIES

The Edit Box object is used for the entry and editing of text. Its important properties are explained here:

◆ Multi-line. Permits the Edit Box to contain more than one line of text. Behavior of a Multi-line Edit Box is controlled by the Auto HScroll and Want Return properties.

◆ Auto HScroll. If True, text scrolls to the left when it reaches the right edge of the box. If False, text is automatically wrapped to a new line (if Multi-line is True). The default is True.

◆ Want Return. If True, pressing Enter starts a new line of text in a Multi-line Edit Box. If False (the default), pressing Enter selects the dialog box's default Button object.

◆ Number. Prevents the user from typing non-numeric characters in the Edit Box. The default is False.

BUTTON OBJECT PROPERTIES

You definitely need to know about the Button object property named Default. If True, pressing Enter has the same effect as clicking the button. The only exception occurs when the focus is at a Multi-line Edit Box with Want Return set to True.

CHECK BOX OBJECT PROPERTIES

The Check Box object has the following important properties:

◆ Auto. If True, the object automatically switches between checked and unchecked states when selected by the user. The default is True.

◆ Tri-State. Creates a three-state check box that can be grayed as well as checked or not checked. A grayed check box indicates that the state represented by the control is undetermined. The default is False.

LIST BOX OBJECT PROPERTIES

The List Box object has two properties you should know about:

◆ Selection. Determines how items in the List Box can be selected. The Single setting permits only one item to be selected at a time. Multiple permits more than one item to be selected but disables the Ctrl and Shift keys (click or double-click an item to select or deselect it). Extended is like Multiple but with the Ctrl and Shift keys enabled to be used with the mouse in selecting groups of items and non-adjacent items.

◆ Sort. If True (the default), the items in the List Box are sorted alphabetically.

COMBO BOX OBJECT PROPERTIES

The Combo Box has one property, Type, that determines the object's operation. The three possible settings for the Type property are:

◆ Simple. Creates a simple Combo Box that combines an Edit Box object with a List Box object. The list is displayed at all times. The user can enter text in the Edit Box or select an item from the list.

◆ Dropdown. This type is the same as a Simple Combo Box, except that the list is not displayed unless the user clicks a drop-down arrow. This is the default type.

◆ Drop List. This type is similar to the Dropdown style, but the Edit Box is replaced by a static text object. Thus, users must select from the list and cannot enter their own text.

Running The Resource Wizard

After creating your resources (menus are covered later in this chapter) you must use the Resource Wizard to convert the Windows resource file to Java code. The procedure is quite simple:

1. Select Java Resource Wizard from the Tools menu.

2. Enter the resource template file name in the dialog box, or use the Browse button to find it.

3. Click the Next button and the Wizard will show you a list of the resources defined in the template file. If this is incorrect, you can click Back to select another template file, or click Cancel to abort the Wizard.

4. Click Finish. The Wizard processes the template file and displays a list of the Java files it created.

Using A Dialog Box

Creating a dialog box with the Dialog Editor is one thing, but how do you use it in your program? In the broad sense, this involves two parts. One section involves displaying the dialog box, a task that is made easy by the code generated by the Resource Wizard. The other part is interacting with the dialog box components—detecting user actions, such as clicking a button, and retrieving information, such as the text entered in an Edit Box. This second part involves interacting with the individual objects—their methods and/or properties—and is primarily independent of whether or not the object is in a dialog box. You'll learn all the details of the individual graphical objects in the later chapter on the Abstract Window Toolkit.

Let's run through an example. In the code samples that follow, we will assume that we have created a dialog box class named NewDialog. The first step is to use the **import** statement to make the dialog class available to the Java program:

```
import NewDialog;
```

Next, declare a variable of the appropriate type to refer to the instance of NewDialog that we will be creating:

```
NewDialog dlg;
```

The next two steps are typically done in the applet's **Init()** method. First, use the **new** keyword to create an instance of the NewDialog class:

```
dlg = new NewDialog( this );
```

Then, call the **CreateControls()** method to create the dialog's controls and display them:

```
dlg.CreateControls();
```

If you do not want the dialog box displayed right away, you will place the call to **CreateControls()** elsewhere; for example, in the event handler for a menu command.

Now let's run through an example. To start the dialog box demonstration project, use the Applet Wizard to create a new project called dialogdemo. Specify "Applet Only" and select "No" for animation support. All other Wizard items should be left at their default settings.

Once the basic project has been created, select Resource from the Insert menu, then select Dialog. The Dialog Editor will open with the basic dialog box displayed. In turn, select the OK and Cancel buttons and delete them. Next, add two new Button controls and one Static Text control, leaving their captions and other properties at their default values. At this point, your dialog box will resemble Figure 4.4. You may want to change the dialog object's Font property to something larger than the default 8 point size; we used 12 point. This is not necessary for the demonstration to run, but we have found that 8 point text can be difficult to read.

Close the Dialog Editor, and use the File Save command to save the resource template file. Assign any name you like, and place it in the dialogdemo project directory. Next, start the Resource Wizard and locate the template file that you just saved. When you run the Resource Wizard on this file, you'll see that the dialog box class is called IDD_DIALOG1, the default name assigned by the Dialog Editor.

Once the Resource Wizard has finished, use the Add Files to Project command (on the Insert menu) to add the two files created by the Wizard to your project. They are named IDD_DIALOG1.JAVA and DIALOGLAYOUT.JAVA.

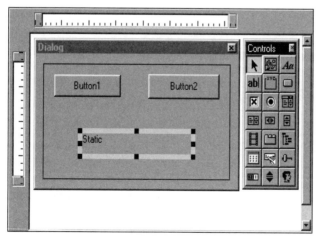

Figure 4.4   The demonstration dialog box in the Dialog Editor.

The dialog box class is now complete. The next step is to add code to the project to display the dialog and respond to user input. Open the file dialogdemo.java for editing. Add the following line of code near the start of the file, just after the other **import** statements:

```
import IDD_DIALOG1;
```

Now, scroll down about 12 lines and add this line, just after the line of code that declares m_dialogdemo and initializes it to **null**:

```
IDD_DIALOG1 dlg;
```

Next, scroll down to the class's **Init**() method and find the line that reads:

```
resize(320,200);
```

Delete this line (or comment it out) and replace it with the following:

```
dlg = new IDD_DIALOG1( this );
dlg.CreateControls();
```

Now, scroll down to the **paint**() method and delete or comment out the following line of code:

```
g.drawString("Running: " + Math.random(), 10, 20);
```

The project is not complete, but you can now build and execute it. You'll see the dialog box displayed in the browser, complete with the two buttons and one text control. They won't do anything, however, because we have not written the code to respond to user actions. That's our next task.

Events that happen to objects cause the **action**() function to be called. Note that this is different from the **mouseDown**() and similar functions that respond to general mouse actions within the applet's screen area. This function looks like this:

```
public boolean action(Event evt, Object what)
```

The two arguments identify the event that happened and the object to which it happened. Using these arguments, code in the **action**() function can determine exactly what happened and where, and take action accordingly. Note that the **action()** procedure is not placed in your code by the Applet Wizard; you must add it yourself. Here's the full code for our project's **action()** function. Place it in the file dialogdemo.java just before the final closing brace.

```
public boolean action(Event evt, Object what)
{
    if (evt.target instanceof Button)
    {
        dlg.IDC_STATIC1.setText((String)what);
        return true;
    }

    return super.handleEvent(evt);
}
```

Let's take a look at what this code does. The first line asks if the event happened to a Button object. We are not interested in exactly what event happened or which Button was involved—all we care about is that one of the two buttons received an event (which, in this applet, would be a mouse click).

If the event did happen to a Button object, the next two lines of code are executed. The first one uses the Static Text object's **setText()** method to display the identity of the clicked object. This information was passed to the function in the **what** argument, and we use the **String** statement to convert the **what** argument to the string form required by the **setText()** method. The results: When the user clicks one of the buttons, the text changes to display the button's identifier, either Button1 or Button2.

The second line of code returns the value **true**. This signals that the event was successfully handled in the function. If the event was not handled—if the event did not happen to one of the buttons—the final line of code in the function passes the event to the next object in the object hierarchy.

The project is now complete. You can build and execute it. The dialog box will display in the browser and clicking one of the buttons will display its caption in the text control, as shown in Figure 4.5.

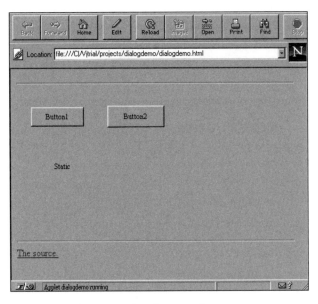

Figure 4.5   The dialog box demonstration in operation.

Now that you have seen how to create and use dialog boxes, it's time to move on to menus. Keep in mind that you'll be earning a great deal more about visual interface objects in the chapter on the Abstract Window Toolkit.

Menus

A Java menu is organized as a hierarchy of objects. At the top level is the MenuBar class that displays the top-level menu commands. The MenuBar class has only one property (its ID) that you use to refer to the menu in code. At the next level down is the Menu class. A MenuBar will contain one or more Menu objects, each corresponding to a command displayed on the MenuBar. At the bottom level is the MenuItem class. As you have probably guessed, a MenuItem object corresponds to a command on a menu. Using the Visual J++ menus as an example, the entire menu across the top of the screen corresponds to a MenuBar object; the File menu, Edit menu, and so on correspond to a Menu object; and the Open command on the File menu corresponds to a MenuItem object.

In the simplest and most common situation, a MenuBar will contain several Menu objects, and each Menu object will contain several MenuItem objects. Each MenuItem object will correspond to a particular program action. Things can become a bit more complicated, however. A Menu object can itself initiate an action instead of displaying a list of MenuItem objects. In addition, a Menu object can contain other Menu objects, with the result being a cascade menu (where selecting a menu command displays an additional menu).

Java menus do not exist in isolation. A MenuBar must be displayed within a Frame or Window, and each Java Frame or Window can have at most one MenuBar. When you create a menu, you must also create a Frame in which to display it. You'll learn the details of creating a Java menu from scratch in a later chapter. Fortunately, the Menu Editor and Resource Wizard automate most of the process. Let's see how it's accomplished.

Creating A Menu With The Menu Editor

A menu resource is stored in a resource template file, just like a dialog box resource. Information on using resource template files was presented earlier in this chapter. To create a new menu, select Resource from the Insert menu, then select Menu in the dialog box and click OK. The Menu Editor starts and displays a blank menu for you to work with, as shown in Figure 4.6.

The empty box with the thick dotted border is the first Menu on your MenuBar. Start typing the menu's caption (the text that will be displayed), and the Menu object's property sheet will open automatically. This is shown in Figure 4.7.

Note that the caption you started to type is being entered in the Caption property. For a Menu object, this is the only property that you need to set.

Figure 4.6   The Menu Editor displays a blank menu when it starts.

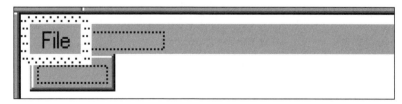

Figure 4.7   Entering the Menu object's Caption property.

Complete typing in the caption, then press Enter to close the property sheet. Assuming you typed in "File" for the caption, the menu editor will now appear as shown in Figure 4.8.

Note that blank boxes are now displayed both below and to the right of the new Menu that you just defined. The box to the right represents a new Menu object waiting to be defined, and the box below represents a new MenuItem object. Click the box you want to work with and start typing in its caption. As before, the object's property sheet will open. If you are adding a second Menu object, proceed as described above. Remember, for a Menu object, the only property you need to define is the Caption.

When defining a MenuItem object, the property choices are not as simple. The MenuItem property sheet is shown in Figure 4.9. The relevant properties are explained here:

◆   ID. The MenuItem object's identifier, used to refer to it in code. You do not need to enter anything here, because the Menu Editor will automatically generate an ID based on the Caption property and the caption of the parent Menu object.

◆   Separator. If this property is checked, the menu item displays as a horizontal separator line. All other properties become unavailable, as they are not meaningful for a separator.

Figure 4.8   The Menu Editor, after creating the first Menu object.

Figure 4.9 Setting properties for a MenuItem object.

◆ Checked. This property causes a check mark to be displayed to the left of the menu item's caption.

◆ Popup. If True, changes the MenuItem object to a Menu object that can contain a sub-menu (cascade menu).

◆ Inactive. If this property is True, the menu item is inactive and cannot be selected by the user.

◆ Grayed. If this property is True, the menu item is displayed in "grayed-out" text and is also inactive.

The procedure for creating an entire menu bar is basically a repetition of these steps. Each time you add a Menu to the MenuBar, a new blank Menu object is created to the right. Likewise, each time you add a MenuItem to a Menu, a new blank MenuItem is added below. If you want to insert a new Menu or MenuItem within the existing structure, just click to select the item that's currently in the desired position and press Ins. Likewise, to delete a Menu or MenuItem, select it and press Del.

Responding To Menu Commands

The code that responds to selection of menu commands is similar to that used to detect user actions in a dialog box. You write an **action()** function and include code that checks to see if the event was a menu item being selected and then branches accordingly. The **action()** function must be part of the menu's container class, which is often a Frame object. If the container has both dialog components and a menu, you'll use the same **action()** function to respond to both. Here's a sample **action()** function to detect menu selections:

```
public boolean action( Event evt, Object obj )
    {
```

```
    Object target = evt.target;
    if (target instanceof MenuItem)
    {
        //Use (String)obj to obtain the caption
        //of the selected menu command.
        return true;
    }
    return false;
}
```

A Menu Demonstration

Now, it's time to see all this in action. In the following program, we will create a menu and write the code to respond when the user selects a command from the menu. It will be rather simple—all that will happen is a screen display of the selected menu caption, but it still demonstrates the basics. Let's get started.

1. Use the Applet Wizard to create a new project called MENUDEMO. Select "As an Applet Only" and "No Animation", leaving other Wizard settings at their default values.

2. Add a Menu resource to the project using the techniques described in this chapter. Place two Menu objects on the MenuBar and two MenuItem objects on each Menu. We used the following names, but you can use whatever you like:

```
Main1
Main1Item1
Main1Item2
Main2
Main2Item1
Main2Item2
```

3. Close the Menu Editor, saving the resource template file under the default name in the MENUDEMO project folder.

4. Open the Resource Wizard and process the resource template file that you just created. It will contain one class with the name IDR_MENU1.

5. Use the Add Files to Project command to add the file IDR_MENU1. JAVA to your project.

6. Open the file MENUDEMO.JAVA for the following edits. Start by adding this line of code near the beginning of the file, just after the other **import** statements:

```
import IDR_MENU1;
```

7. A few lines further down, just after the declaration of the **Thread** variable, add these two lines of code. This code declares one variable to refer to an instance of the menu we just created and another variable for the frame to hold the menu (we'll define the frame soon).

```
IDR_MENU1 menu;
MenuFrame frame;
```

8. In the class's **Init()** method, delete or comment out the **resize()** method; in the same location, add the following code. The comments explain what the code does.

```
//Create a new MenuFrame object with the specified title.
frame = new MenuFrame( "Menu demonstration" );
//Size it to 300 by 200.
frame.resize( 300, 200 );
//Create a new IDR_MENU1 object in the frame we just created.
menu = new IDR_MENU1( frame );
//Create the menu components and display the frame.
menu.CreateMenu();
frame.show();
```

9. At the very end of the file, after the final closing brace, we will now add the definition of the MenuFrame class. Here's the code to add, complete with comments explaining what's going on. Don't worry about the layout statements—they are used to automate the process of arranging objects on the screen, and you'll learn about them in a later chapter.

```
class MenuFrame extends Frame
{
    Label lab1;

    MenuFrame(String title)
    {
        //Display the window title.
```

```
        super(title);

        //Create a new label with the specified text.
        lab1 = new Label("Waiting for a selection");
        //Create a layout and add the label to it.
        setLayout( new FlowLayout());
        add(lab1);
        //Display it.
        show();
    }

    public boolean action( Event evt, Object obj )
    {
        //Get the target ID.
        Object target = evt.target;

        //If a MenuItem object was clicked...
        if (target instanceof MenuItem)
        {
            //Set the label object to the menu item text.
            lab1.setText((String)obj);
            return true;
        }
        return false;
    }
}
```

When you run the program, you'll see your menu displayed in its own little window (or frame). When you select a command from the menu, its caption is displayed in the label, as shown in Figure 4.10.

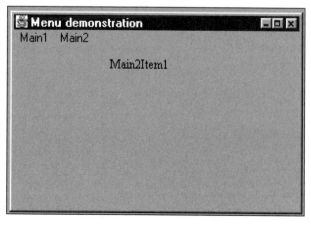

Figure 4.10   Running the menu demonstration program.

Java Language Fundamentals 5

Anthony Potts

The language building blocks of Java are similar to those found in C++, but keep a close eye out because there are some subtle differences.

You should now have a basic understanding of the J++ development environment and how it works with the Java language. In this chapter and the ones that follow, we'll uncover the key Java language features that you'll need to know to write useful programs with J++. In particular, we'll explain the basic Java language components in this chapter—everything from comments to variable declarations. Then we'll move ahead and cover operators, expressions, and control structures in Chapter 6.

For those of you who are already familiar with programming, especially C or C++ programming, this chapter and Chapter 6 should serve as a good hands-on review. As we discuss Java, we'll point out the areas in which Java differs from other languages. If you don't have much experience using structured programming languages, this chapter will give you a good overview of the basic components required to make programming languages like Java come alive.

The actual language components featured in this chapter include:

- ◆ Comments
- ◆ Identifiers
- ◆ Keywords
- ◆ Data types
- ◆ Variable declarations

What Makes A Java Program?

Before we get into the details of each Java language component, let's stand back ten steps and look at how many of the key language components are used in the context of a Java program. Figure 5.1(shown later) presents a complete visual guide. Here we've highlighted components such as variable declarations, Java keywords, operators, literals, expressions, and control structures. As we work our way through the next two chapters, you'll learn how these components are defined and used.

In case you're wondering, the output for this program looks like this:

```
Hello John my name is Anthony
That's not my name!
Let's count to ten....
1 2 3 4 5 6 7 8 9 10
Now down to zero by two.
10 8 6 4 2 0
Finally, some arithmetic:
10 * 3.09 = 30.9
10 * 3.09 = 30 (integer cast)
10 / 3.09 = 5.23625
10 / 3.09 = 3 (integer cast)
```

Lexical Structure

The lexical structure of a language refers to the elements of code that make the code easy for us to understand, but have no effect on the compiled code. For example, all the comments you place in a program to help you understand how it works are ignored by the Java compiler. You could have a thousand lines of comments for a twenty line program and the compiled *bytecodes* for the program would be the same size if you took out all the comments. This does not mean that *all* lexical structures are optional. It simply means that they do not effect the bytecodes.

The lexical structures we will discuss include:

◆ Comments

◆ Identifiers

◆ Keywords

◆ Separators

Comments

Comments make your code easy to understand, modify, and use. But adding comments to an application only after it is finished is not a good practice. More often than not, you won't remember what the code you write actually does after you get away from it for a while. Unfortunately, many programmers follow this time-honored tradition. We suggest you try to get in the habit of adding comments as you write your code.

Java supports three different types of comment styles. The first two are taken directly from C and C++. The third type of comment is a new one that can be used to automatically create class and method documentation.

COMMENT STYLE #1

```
/* Comments here... */
```

This style of commenting comes to us directly from C. Everything between the initial slash-asterisk and ending asterisk-slash is ignored by the Java compiler. This style of commenting can be used anywhere in a program, even in the middle of code (not a good idea). This style of commenting is useful when you have multiple lines of comments because your comment lines can wrap from one line to the next, and you only need to use one set of the /* and */ symbols. Examples:

```
/*
 This program was written by Joe Smith.
 It is the greatest program ever written!
 */
```

```
while (i <= /* comments can be placed here */ maxnum)
{
    total += i;
    i++;
}
```

In the second example, the comment line is embedded within the program statement. The compiler skips over the comment text, and thus the actual line of code would be processed as:

```
while (i <= maxnum)
...
```

Programmers occasionally use this style of commenting while they are testing and debugging code. For example, you could comment out part of an equation or expression:

```
sum = i /* + (base - 10) */ + factor;
```

COMMENT STYLE #2

```
// Comment here...
```

This style of commenting is borrowed from C++. Everything after the double slash marks is ignored by the Java compiler. The comment is terminated by a line return, so you can't use multiple comment lines unless you start each line with the double-slash. Examples:

```
// This program was written by Joe Smith.
// It is the greatest program ever written!

 while (i <= // this won't work maxnum)
{
    total += i;
    i++;
}

base = 20;
// This comment example also won't work because the Java
// compiler will treat this second line as a line of code
value = 50;
```

The comment used in the second example won't work like you might intend because the remainder of the line of code would be commented out (everything after **i** <=). In the third example, the second comment line is missing the starting **//** symbols, and the Java compiler will get confused because it will try to process the comment line as if it were a line of code. Believe it or not, this type of commenting mistake occurs often—so watch out for it!

Comment Style #3

```
/** Doc Comment here... */
```

This comment structure may look very similar to the C style of commenting, but that extra asterisk at the beginning makes a huge difference. Of course, remember that only one asterisk must be used as the comment terminator. The Java compiler still ignores the comment; but another program called JAVADOC.EXE that ships with the Java Development Kit uses these comments to construct HTML documentation files that describe your packages, classes, and methods as well as all the variables they use.

Let's look at the third style of commenting in more detail. If implemented correctly and consistently, this style of commenting can provide you with numerous benefits. Figure 5.2 shows what the output of the JAVADOC program looks like when run on a typical Java source file.

If you have ever looked at the Java API documentation on Sun's Web site, Figure 5.2 should look familiar to you. In fact, the entire API documentation was created with JAVADOC.

JAVADOC will work if you have created comments or not. Figure 5.3 shows the output from this simple application:

```
class HelloWorld {
    public static void main(String args[]) {
        System.out.println("Hello World");
    }
}
```

To add a little more information to our documentation, all we have to do is add this third style of comments. If we change the little HelloWorld application and add a few key comments, the code will look like this:

```
/**
 * Sample Java Application
 * @author Anthony Potts
 * @version 1.0
 */
class Test extends Object { // Begin Test class
  // Define class variables
  static int i = 10;
  static final double d = 3.09;

  /*
  The main() method is automatically called when
  the program is run. Any words typed after the program
  name when it is run are placed in the args[] variable
  which is an array of strings.
  For this program to work properly, atleast one word must
  be typed after the program name or else an error will occur.
  */
  public static void main(String args[]) {
    Test thisTest = new Test(); // Create instance (object) of
 class
    String myName = "Anthony";
    boolean returnValue;

    System.out.println("Hello " + args[0] + " my name is " +
 myName);

    if(thisTest.sameName(args[0], myName)) {
      System.out.println("Your name is the same as mine!");
    } else {
      System.out.println("That's not my name!");
    }

    System.out.println("Let's count to ten....");

    for (int x = 1; x < 11; x++) {
      System.out.print(x + " ");
    }
```

unique Java style comment
superclass
standard C++ style comment
variable declarations
standard data type
variable
literal
declaration and assignment
assignment operator
string data type
if-then-else control structure
increment operator
expression

Continued

Figure 5.1 A visual guide to the key Java language components.

```
        System.out.println("\nNow down to zero by two.");
                                    ┌──────── logical expression
        while ( i > -1) {
            System.out.print(i + " ");
            i -= 2;
        }

        System.out.println("\nFinally, some arithmetic:");

        thisTest.doArithmetic(); ──── method call
    }

    // This method compares the two names sent to it and
    // returns true if they are the same and false if they are not
    public boolean sameName(String firstName, String secondName) {
        if (firstName.equals(secondName)) {
            return true; ─┐
        } else {          ├──── returns value to
            return false; ─┘      calling class
        }
    }

    // This method performs a few computations and prints the result
    public void doArithmetic(){
        i = 10; ──────────────────── assignment expression
        System.out.println(i + " * " + d + " = " + (i * d));
        System.out.println(i + " * " + d + " = " +
                        (int)(i * d) + " (Integer)");
        System.out.println(i + " / " + d + " = " + (i / d));
        System.out.println(i + " / " + d + " = " +
                        (int)(i / d) + " (Integer)");
    }
} // End of class
```

while control statement — (points to while block)

method modifier — (points to `public`)

Figure 5.1   A visual guide to the key Java language components (Continued).

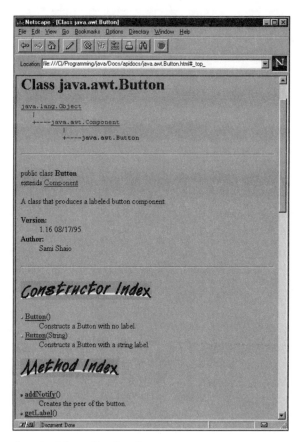

Figure 5.2   Sample output from the JavaDoc program.

```
/**
 * Welcome to HelloWorld
 * @author Anthony Potts
 * @version 1.1
 * @see java.lang.System
 */
class helloworld {
   /**
    * Main method of helloworld
    */
   public static void main(String args[]) {
      System.out.println("Hello World!");
   }
}
```

If you now run JAVADOC, the browser will display what you see in Figure 5.4. As you can see, this gives us much more information. This system is great for producing documentation for public distribution. Just like all comments though, it is up to you to make sure that the comments are accurate and plentiful enough to be helpful. Table 5.1 lists the tags you can use in your class comments.

Identifiers

Identifiers are the names used for variables, classes, methods, packages, and interfaces to distinguish them to the compiler.

Identifiers in the Java language should always begin with a letter of the alphabet, either upper or lower case. The only exceptions to this rule are the underscore symbol (_) and the dollar sign ($), which may also be used. If you try to use any other symbol or a numeral as the initial character, you will receive an error.

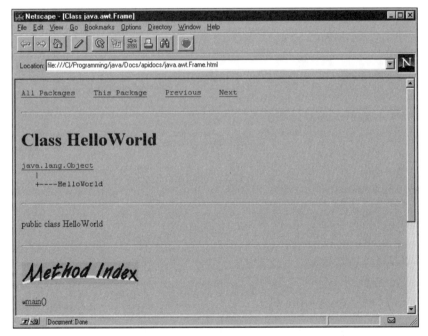

Figure 5.3   Simple output from the JavaDoc program.

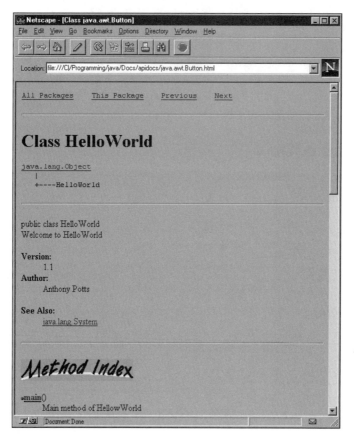

Figure 5.4   The new JavaDoc output.

After the initial character you are allowed to use numbers, but not all symbols. You can also use almost all of the characters from the Unicode character set. If you are not familiar with the Unicode character set or you get errors, we suggest that you stick with the standard alphabetic characters.

The length of an identifier is basically unlimited. We managed to get up to a few thousand characters before we got bored. It's doubtful you will ever need nearly that many characters, but it is nice to know that the Java compiler won't limit you if you want to create long descriptive names. The only limit you may encounter involves creating class names. Since class names are also used as file names, you need to create names that will not cause problems with your operating system or anyone who will be using your program.

Table 5.1   Tags used in class comments.

Tag	Description
@see classname	Adds a hyperlinked "See Also" to your class. The classname can be any other class.
@see fully-qualified-classname	Also adds a "See Also" to the class, but this time you need to use a fully qualified class name like "java.awt.window."
@see fully-qualified-classname #methodname	Also adds a "See Also" to the class, but now you are pointing to a specific method within that class.
@version version-text	Adds a version number that you provide. The version number can be numbers or text.
@author author-name -	Adds an author entry. You can use multiple author tags.

The tags you can use in your method comments include all of the "@see" tags as well as the following:

@param paramter-name description...	Used to show which parameters the method accepts. Multiple "@param" tags are acceptable.
@return description...	Used to describe what the method returns.
@exception fully-qualified-classname description...	Used to add a "throw" entry that describes what type of exceptions this method can throw. Multiple "@exception" tags are acceptable. (Don't worry about exceptions and throws too much yet.)

You must also be careful not to use any of the special Java keywords listed in the next section. The following are examples of valid identifiers:

```
HelloWorld      $Money    TickerTape
_ME2      Chapter3    ABC123
```

And here are some examples of invalid identifiers:

```
3rdChapter      #Hello     -Main
```

COMMON ERRORS WITH USING IDENTIFIERS

As you are defining and using identifiers in your Java programs, you are bound to encounter some errors from time-to-time. Let's look at some of the more common error messages that the Java compiler displays. Notice that we've included the part of the code that is responsible for generating the error, the error message, as well as a description of the message so that you can make sense of it.

Code Example:
```
public class 1test {
}
```

Error Message:
```
D:\java\lib\test.java:1: Identifier expected.
```

Description:
An invalid character has been used in the class identifier. You will see this error when the first character is invalid (especially when it is a number).

Code Example:
```
public class te?st {
}
```

Error Message:
```
D:\java\lib\test.java:1: '{' Expected
```

Description:
This is a common error that occurs when you have an invalid character in the middle of an identifier. In this case, the question mark is invalid, so the compiler gets confused where the class definition ends and its implementation begins.

Code Example:
```
public class #test {
}
```

Error Message:
```
D:\java\lib\test.java:1: Invalid character in input.
```

Description:
Here, the error stems from the fact that the initial character is invalid.

Code Example:
```
public class catch {
}
```

Error Message:
```
D:\java\lib\test.java:1: Identifier expected.
```

Description:
This error shows up when you use a protected keyword as an identifier.

Keywords

In Java, like other languages, there are certain *keywords* or "tokens" that are reserved for system use. These keywords can't be used as names for your classes, variables, packages, or anything else. The keywords are used for a number of tasks such as defining control structures (*if*, *while*, and *for*) and declaring data types (*int*, *char*, and *float*). Table 5.2 provides the complete list of the Java keywords.

The words marked with an asterisk (*) are not currently used in the Java language, but you still can't use them to create your own identifiers. More than likely they will be used as keywords in future versions of the Java language.

Literals

Literals are the values that you assign when entering explicit values. For example, in an assignment statement like this

```
i = 10;
```

the value 10 is a literal. But do not get literals confused with types. Even though they usually go hand in hand, literals and types are not the same.

Types are used to define what type of data a variable can hold, while literals are the values that are actually assigned to those variables.

Literals come in three flavors: numeric, character, and boolean. Boolean literals are simply True and False.

Table 5.2   Java language keywords.

Keyword	Description
abstract	Class modifier
boolean	Used to define a boolean data type
break	Used to break out of loops
byte	Used to define a byte data type
byvalue *	Not implemented yet
cast	Used to translate from type to type
catch	Used with error handling
char	Used to define a character data type (16-bit)
class	Used to define a class structure
const *	Not implemented yet
continue	Used to continue an operation
default	Used with the switch statement
do	Used to create a do loop control structure
Double	Used to define a floating-point data type (64-bit)
else	Used to create an else clause for an if statement
extends	Used to subclass
final	Used to tell Java that this class can not be subclassed
finally	Used with exceptions to determine the last option before exiting. It guarantees that code gets called if an exception does or does not happen
float	Used to define a floating-point data type (32-bit)
for	Used to create a for loop control structure
future *	Not implemented yet
generic *	Not implemented yet
goto *	Not implemented yet
if	Used to create an if-then decision-making control structure
implements	Used to define which interfaces to use
import	Used to reference external Java packages
inner	Used to create control blocks
instanceof	Used to determine if an object is of a certain type
int	Used to define an integer data type (32-bit values)
interface	Used to tell Java that the code that follows is an interface
long	Used to define an integer data type (64-bit values)

Continued

Table 5.2   Java language keywords (Continued).

Keyword	Description
native	Used when calling external code
new	Operator used when creating an instance of a class (an object)
null	Reference to a non-existent value
operator *	Not implemented yet
outer	Used to create control blocks
package	Used to tell Java what package the following code belongs to
private	Modifier for classes, methods, and variables
protected	Modifier for classes, methods, and variables
public	Modifier for classes, methods, and variables
rest *	Not implemented yet
return	Used to set the return value of a class or method
short	Used to define an integer data type (16-bit values)
static	Modifier for classes, methods, and variables
super	Used to reference the current class' parent class
switch	Block statement used to pick from a group of choices
synchronized	Modifier that tells Java that only one instance of a method can be run at one time. It keeps Java from running the method a second time before the first is finished. It is especially useful when dealing with files to avoid conflicts
this	Used to reference the current object
throw	Statement that tells Java what exception to pass on an error
transient	Modifier that can access future Java code
try	Operator that is used to test for exceptions in code
var *	Not implemented yet
void	Modifier for setting the return value of a class or method to nothing
volatile	Variable modifier
while	Used to create a while loop control structure

NUMERIC LITERALS

Numeric literals are just what they sound like—numbers. We can subdivide the numeric literals further into *integers* and *floating-point* literals.

Table 5.3   Summary of integer literals.

Integer Literals Ranges	Negative Minimum	Positive Maximum
int data type	-2,147,483,648	2,147,483,648
long data type	-9.223372036855e+18	9.223372036855e+18

Integer literals are usually represented in *decimal* format although you can use the *hexadecimal* and octal format in Java. If you want to use the hexadecimal format, your numbers need to begin with an 0x or 0X. Octal integers simply begin with a zero (0).

Integer literals are stored differently depending on their size. The **int** data type is used to store 32-bit integer values ranging from -2,147,483,648 to 2,147,483,648 (decimal). If you need to use even larger numbers, Java switches over to the **long** data type, which can store 64 bits of information for a range of - 9.223372036855e+18 to 9.223372036855e+18. This would give you a number a little larger than 9 million trillion—enough to take care of the national debt! To specify a **long** integer, you will need to place an "l" or "L" at the end of the number. Don't get confused by our use of the terms **int** and **long**. There are many other integer data types used by Java, but they all use **int** or **long**literals to assign values. Table 5.3 provides a summary of the two integer literals.

Here are some examples of how integer literals can be used to assign values in Java statements:

```
int i;
i = 1;   // All of these literals are of the integer type
i= -9;
i = 1203131;

i = 0xA11;   // Using a hexadecimal literal
i = 07543;   // Using an octal literal

i = 5.5;     // This would be illegal because a floating-point
             // literal can't be assigned to an integer type
long lg;
lg = 1L;     // All of these literals are of the long
             // integer type
lg = -9e15;
lg = 7e12;
```

The other type of numeric literal is the floating-point literal. Floating-point values are any numbers that have anything to the right of the decimal place. Similar to integers, floating-point values have 32-bit and 64-bit representations. Both data types conform to IEEE standards. Table 5.4 provides a summary of the two floating-point literals.

Here are some examples of how floating-point literals can be used to assign values in Java statements:

```
float f;
f = 1.3;  // All of these literals are of the floating-point
          // type float (32-bit)
f = -9.0;
f = 1203131.1241234;
double d;
d = 1.0D;  // All of these literals are of the floating-point
           // type double(32-bit)
d = -9.3645e235;
d = 7.0001e52D;
```

CHARACTER LITERALS

The second type of literal that you need to know about is the *character literal*. Character literals include single characters and strings. Single character literals are enclosed in single quotation marks while string literals are enclosed in double quotes.

Single characters can be any one character from the Unicode character set. There are also a few special two-character combinations that are non-printing characters but perform important functions. Table 5.5 shows these special combinations.

The string character literal are any number of characters enclosed in The character combinations from Table 5.5 also apply to strings. Here are some examples of how character and string literals can be used in Java statements:

Table 5.4   Summary of floating-point literals.

Floating-Point Ranges	Negative Minimum	Positive Maximum
float data type	1.40239846e-45	5.40282347e38
double data type	5.94065645841246544e-324	1.79769313486231570e308

```
char ch;
ch = 'a';    // All of these literals are characters
ch = \n;     // Assign the newline character
ch = \';     // Assign a single quote
ch = \x30;   // Assign a hexadecimal character code

String str;
str = "Java string";
```

Operators

Operators are used to perform computations on one or more variables or objects. You use operators to add values, comparing the size of two numbers, assigning a value to a variable, incrementing the value of a variable, and so on. Table 5.6 lists the operators used in Java. Later in this chapter, we'll explain in detail how each operator works; and we'll also explain operator precedence.

Separators

Separators are used in Java to delineate blocks of code. For example, you use curly brackets to enclose a method's implementation, and you use parentheses to enclose arguments being sent to a method. Table 5.7 lists the separators used in Java.

Table 5.5   Special character combinations in Java.

Character Combination	Standard Designation	Description
\	\<newline\>	Continuation
\n	NL or LF	New Line
\b	BS	Backspace
\r	CR	Carriage Return
\f	FF	Form Feed
\t	HT	Horizontal Tab
\\	\	Backslash
\'	'	Single Quote
\"	"	Double Quote
\xdd	0xdd	Hex Bit Pattern
\ddd	0ddd	Octal Bit Pattern
\uddd	0xdddd	Unicode Character

Table 5.6   Operators used in Java.

Operator	Description
+	Addition
-	Subtraction
*	Multiplication
/	Division
%	Modulo
++	Increment
—	Decrement
>	Greater than
>=	Greater than or equal to
<	Less than
<=	Less than or equal to
==	Equal to
!=	Not equal to
!	Logical NOT
&&	Logical AND
||	Logical OR
&	Bitwise AND
^	Bitwise exclusive OR
|	Bitwise OR
~	Bitwise complement
<<	Left shift
>>	Right shift
>>>	Zero fill right shift
=	Assignment
+=	Assignment with addition
-=	Assignment with subtraction
*=	Assignment with multiplication
/=	Assignment with division
%=	Assignment with modulo
&=	Assignment with bitwise AND

Continued

Table 5.6   Operators used in Java (Continued).

Operator	Description
|=	Assignment with bitwise OR
^=	Assignment with bitwise exclusive OR
<<=	Assignment with left shift
>>=	Assignment with right shift
>>>=	Assignment with zero fill right shift

Table 5.7   Separators used in Java.

Separator	Description
( )	Used to define blocks of arguments
[ ]	Used to define arrays
{ }	Used to hold blocks of code
,	Used to separate arguments or variables in a declaration
;	Used to terminate lines of contiguous code

Types And Variables

Many people confuse the terms *types* and *variables*, and use them synonymously. They are, however, not the same. Variables are basically buckets that *hold information*, while types *describe what type of information* is in the bucket.

A variable must have both a type and an identifier. Later in this chapter we will cover the process of declaring variables. For now, we just want to guide you through the details of how you decide which types to use and how to use them properly.

Similar to literals, types can be split into several different categories including the numeric types—**byte**, **short**, **int**, **long**, **float**, and **double**—and the **char** and **boolean** types. We will also discuss the string type. Technically, the string type is not a type—it is a class. However, it is used so commonly that we decided to include it here.

All of the integer numeric types use signed 2's-complement integers for storing data. Table 5.8 provides a summary of the ranges for each of the key Java data types.

byte

The **byte** type can be used for variables whose value falls between -256 and 255. **byte** types have an 8-bit length. Here are some examples of byte values:

```
-7 5      238
```

short

The **short** numeric type can store values ranging from -32768 to 32767. It has a 16-bit depth, as in the following examples:

```
-7 256     -29524
```

int

The **int** data type takes the **short** type to the next level. It uses a 32-bit signed integer value that takes our minimal and maximal value up to over 2 billion. Because of this tremendous range, it is one of the most often used data types for integers.

Often, unskilled programmers will use the **int** data type even though they don't need the full resolution that this data type provides. If you are using smaller integers, you should consider using the **short** data type. The rule of

Table 5.8 Summary of the Java data types.

Data Type	Negative Minimal	Positive Maximal
byte	-256	255
short	-32768	32767
int	-2147483648	2147483647
long	-9223372036854775808	9223372036854775807
float	1.40239846e-45	5.40282347e38
double	5.94065645841246544e-324	1.79769313486231570e308
boolean	False	True

thumb to follow is *if you know exactly the range of values a certain variable will store, use the smallest data type possible*. This will let your program use less memory and therefore run faster, especially on slower machines or machines with limited RAM.

Here are some examples of **int** values:

```
-7 256      -29523234      1321412422
```

long

The **long** data type is the mother of all integer types. It uses a full 64-bit data path to store values that reach up to over 9 million trillion. But be extremely careful when using variables of the **long** type. If you start using many of them or God forbid, an array of **long**s, you can quickly eat up a ton of resources.

The danger of using long.

Java provides useful garbage collection tools, so when you are done with these large data types, they will be disposed of and their resources reclaimed. But if you are creating large arrays of long integers you could really be asking for trouble. For example, if you created a two-dimensional array of long integers that had a 100x100 grid, you would be using up about 100 kilobytes of memory.

Here are some examples of **long** values:

```
-7 256      -29523234      1.835412e15      -3e18
```

float

The **float** data type is one of two types used to store floating-point values. The **float** type is compliant with the IEEE 754 conventions. The floating-point types of Java can store gargantuan numbers. We do not have enough room on the page to physically show you the minimal and maximal values the **float** data type can store, so we will use a little bit of tricky sounding lingo taken from the Java manual.

"The finite nonzero values of type **float** are of the form s * m * 2e , where s is +1 or -1, m is a positive integer less than 2^24 and e is an integer between -149 and 104, inclusive."

Whew, that's a mouthful. Here are a few examples to show you what the **float** type might look like in actual use:

```
-7F      256.0  -23e34    23e100
```

double

As if the **float** type could not hold enough, the **double** data type gives you even bigger storage space. Let's look again at Sun's definition of the possible values for a **double**.

"The finite nonzero values of type **float** are of the form s * m * 2e , where s is +1 or -1, m is a positive integer less than 2^53 and e is an integer between -1045 and 1000, inclusive."

Again, you can have some truly monstrous numbers here. But when you start dealing with hard core programming, this type of number becomes necessary from time to time, so it is wise to understand its ranges. Here are a few examples:

```
-7.0D   256.0D  -23e424 23e1000
```

boolean

In other languages, the **boolean** data type has been represented by an integer with a nonzero or zero value to represent True and False, respectively. This method works well because it gives the user the ability to check for all kinds of values and perform expression.

```
x=2;
if x then...
```

This can be handy when performing parsing operations or checking string lengths. In Java, however, the **boolean** data type has its own True and False literals that do not correspond to other values. In fact, as you will learn later in this chapter, Java does not even allow you to perform casts between the **boolean** data type and any others. There are ways around this limitation that we will discuss in a few pages when we talk about conversion methods.

char

The **char** data type is used to store single characters. Since Java uses the Unicode character set, the **char** type needs to be able to store the thousands of characters, so it uses a 16-bit signed integer. The **char** data type has the ability to be cast or converted to almost all of the others, as we will show you in the next section.

string

The **string** type is actually not a primitive data type; it is a class all its own. We decided to talk about it a little here because it is used so commonly that it might as well be considered a primitive. In C and C++, strings are stored in arrays of chars. Java does not use the **char** type for this but instead has created its own class that handles strings. In Chapter 5, when we get into the details of declaring variables within classes, you will see the difference between declaring a primitive variable and declaring an instance of a class type.

One big advantage to using a class instead of an array of **char** types is that we are more or less unlimited in the amount of information we want to place in a string variable. In C++, the array of chars was limited, but now that limitation is taken care of within the class, where we do not care how it is handled.

Variable Declarations

Declaring variables in Java is very similar to declaring variables in C/C++ as long as you are using the primitive data types. As we said before, almost everything in Java is a class—except the primitive data types. We will show you how to instantiate custom data types (including strings) in Chapter 6. For now, let's look at how primitive data types are declared.

Here is what a standard declaration for a primitive variable might look like:

```
int i;
```

We have just declared a variable "i" to be an integer. Here are a few more examples:

```
byte i, j;
int a=7, b = a;
float f = 1.06;
String name = "Tony";
```

These examples illustrate some of the things you can do while declaring variables. Let's look at each one individually.

```
int i;
```

This is the most basic declaration, with the data type followed by the variable you are declaring.

```
byte i, j;
```

In this example, we are declaring two byte variables at one time. There is no limit to the number of variables you can declare this way. All you have to do is add a comma between each variable you wish to declare of the given type, and Java takes care of it for you.

You also have the ability to assign values to variables as you declare them. You can even use a variable you are declaring as part of an expression for the declaration of another variable in the same line. Before we confuse you more, here is an example:

```
int i = 1;
int j = i, k= i + j;
```

Here we have first declared a variable **i** as **int** and assigned it a value of 1. In the next line, we start by declaring a variable **j** to be equal to **i**. This is perfectly legal. Next, on the same line, we declare a variable **k** to be equal to **i** plus **j**. Once again, Java handles this without a problem. We could even shorten these two statements to one line like this:

```
int i = 1, j = i, k= i + j;
```

One thing to watch out for is using variables *before* they have been declared. Here's an example:

```
int j = i, k= i + j;  // i is not defined yet
int i = 1;
```

This would cause an "undefined variable" error because Java does not know to look ahead for future declarations. Let's look at another example:

```
float f = 1.06;
```

Does this look correct? Yes, but it's not. This is a tricky one. By default, Java assumes that numbers with decimal points are of type **double**. So, when you try and declare a **float** to be equal to this number, you receive the following error:

```
Incompatible type for declaration. Explicit cast needed to convert
    double to float.
```

Sounds complicated, but all this error message means is that you need to explicitly tell Java that the literal value 1.06 is a **float** and not a **double**. There are two ways to accomplish this. First, you can *cast* the value to a **float** like this:

```
float f = (float)1.06;
```

This works fine, but can get confusing. Java also follows the convention used by other languages of placing an "f" at the end of the literal value to indicate explicitly that it is a float. This also works for the double data type, except that you would use a "d." (By the way, capitalization of the f and d does not make a difference.)

```
float f = 1.06f;
double d = 1.06d;
```

You should realize that the "d" is not needed in the **double** declaration because Java assumes it. However, it is better to label all of your variables when possible, especially if you are not sure.

We will cover variables and declarations in more detail in Chapter 6, but you should have enough knowledge now to be able to run a few basic programs and will delve deeper into the Java fundamentals and look at operators, expressions, and control statements.

Using Arrays

It's difficult to imagine creating any large application or applet without having an array or two. Java uses arrays in a much different manner than other languages. Instead of being a structure that holds variables, arrays in Java are actually objects that can be treated just like any other Java object.

The powerful thing to realize here is that because arrays are objects that are derived from a class, they have methods you can call to retrieve information about the array or to manipulate the array. The current version of the Java language only supports the **length** method, but you can expect that more methods will be added as the language evolves.

One of the drawbacks to the way Java implements arrays is that they are only one dimensional. In most other languages, you can create a two-dimensional array by just adding a comma and a second array size. In Java, this does not work. The way around this limitation is to create an array of arrays. Because this is easy to do, the lack of built-in support for multi-dimensional arrays shouldn't hold you back.

Declaring Arrays

Since arrays are actually instances of classes (objects), we need to use constructors to create our arrays much like we did with strings. First, we need to pick a variable name and declare it as an array object and also specify which data type the array will hold. Note that an array can only hold a single data type—you can't mix strings and integers within a single array. Here are a few examples of how array variables are declared:

```
int intArray[];
String Names[];
```

As you can see, these look very similar to standard variable declarations, except for the brackets after the variable name. You could also put the brackets after the data type if you think this approach makes your declarations more readable:

```
int[] intArray;
String[] Names;
```

Sizing Arrays

There are three ways to set the size of arrays. Two of them require the use of the **new** operator. Using the **new** operator initializes all of the array elements to a default value. The third method involves filling in the array elements with values as you declare.

The first method involves taking a previously declared variable and setting the size of the array. Here are a few examples:

```
int intArray[];          // Declare the arrays
String Names[];

intArray[] = new int[10];         // Size each array
Names[] = new String[100];
```

Or, you can size the array object when you declare it:

```
int intArray[] = new int[10];
String Names[] = new String[100];
```

Finally, you can fill in the array with values at declaration time:

```
String Names[] = {"Tony", "Dave", "Jon", "Ricardo"};
int[] intArray = {1, 2, 3, 4, 5};
```

Accessing Array Elements

Now that you know how to initialize arrays, you'll need to learn how to fill them with data and then access the array elements to retrieve the data. We showed you a very simple way to add data to arrays when you initialize them, but often this just is not flexible enough for real-world programming tasks. To access an array value, you simply need to know its location. The indexing system used to access array elements is zero-based, which means that the first value is always located at position 0. Let's look at a little program that first fills in an array then prints it out:

```
public class powersOf2 {

    public static void main(String args[]) {
        int intArray[] = new int[20];
        for (int i = 0; i < intArray.length; i++) {
            intArray[i] = 1;
            for(int p = 0; p <  i; p++) intArray[i] *= 2 ;
        }
        for (int i = 0; i < intArray.length; i++)
            System.out.println("2 to the power of " + i + " is " +
                intArray[i]);
    }
}
```

The output of this program looks like this:

```
2 to the power of 0 is 1
2 to the power of 1 is 2
2 to the power of 2 is 4
2 to the power of 3 is 8
2 to the power of 4 is 16
2 to the power of 5 is 32
2 to the power of 6 is 64
2 to the power of 7 is 128
2 to the power of 8 is 256
2 to the power of 9 is 512
2 to the power of 10 is 1024
2 to the power of 11 is 2048
2 to the power of 12 is 4096
2 to the power of 13 is 8192
2 to the power of 14 is 16384
2 to the power of 15 is 32768
2 to the power of 16 is 65536
2 to the power of 17 is 131072
2 to the power of 18 is 262144
2 to the power of 19 is 524288
```

So, how does the program work? We first create our array of integer values and assign it to the **intArray** variable. Next, we begin a loop that goes from zero to **intArray.length**. By calling the **length** method of our array, we find the number of indexes in the array. Then, we start another loop that does the calculation and stores the result in the index specified by the **i** variable from our initial loop.

Now that we have filled in all the values for our array, we need to step back through them and print out the result. We could have just put the **print** statement in the initial loop, but the approach we used gives us a chance to use another loop that references our array.

Here is the structure of an index call:

```
arrayName[index];
```

Pretty simple. If you try and use an index that is outside the boundaries of the array, a run-time error occurs. If we change the program to count to an index of 21 instead of the actual array length of 20, we would end up getting an error message like this:

```
java.lang.ArrayIndexOutOfBoundsException: 20
        at powersOf2.main(powersOf2.java:10)
```

This is a pretty common error in any programming language. You need to use some form of exception handling to watch for this problem unless you are positive you can create code that never does this (in your dreams). See Chapter 7 for additional information on exception handling.

Multidimensional Arrays

Multidimensional arrays are created in Java in using arrays of arrays. Here are a few examples of how you can implement multidimensional arrays:

```
int intArray[][];
String Names[][];
```

We can even do the same things we did with a single dimension array. We can set the array sizes and even fill in values while we declare the arrays:

```
int intArray[][] = new int[10][5];
String Names[][] = new String[25][3];

int intArray[][] = {{2, 3, 4} {1, 2, 3}};
String Names[][] = {{"Jon", "Smith"}{"Tony", "Potts"}{"Dave",
 "Friedel"}};
```

We can also create arrays that are not "rectangular" in nature. That is, each array within the main array can have a different number of elements. Here are a few examples:

```
int intArray[][] = {{1, 2} {1, 2, 3} {1, 2, 3, 4}};
String Names[][] = {{"Jon", "Smith"} {"Tony","A", "Potts"} {"Dave",
 "H", "Friedel", "Jr."}};
```

Accessing the data in a multidimensional array is not much more difficult than accessing data in a single-dimensional array. You just need to track the values for each index. Be careful though, as you add dimensions, it becomes increasingly easy to create out of bounds errors. Here are a few examples of how you can declare multidimensional arrays, assign values, and access array elements:

```
int intArray[][] = new int[10][5];            // Declare the arrays
String Names[][] = new String[25][3];

intArray[0][0] = 5;       // Assign values
```

```
intArray[7][2] = 37;
intArray[7][9] = 37;      // This will cause an out of bounds error!
Names[0][0] = "Bill Gates";
// Access an array element in a Java statement
System.out.println(Names[0][0]);
```

We will cover variables and declarations in more detail in Chapter 5, but you should have enough knowledge now to be able to run a few basic programs and get the feel for Java programming.

Using Command-Line Arguments

Programming with command-line arguments is not a topic you'd typically expect to see in a chapter on basic data types and variable declarations. However, because we've been using command-line arguments with some of the sample programs we've been introducing, we thought it would be important to discuss how this feature works in a little more detail.

Command-line arguments are only used with Java applications. They provide a mechanism so that the user of an application can pass in information to be used by the program. Java applets, on the other hand, read in parameters using HTML tags. Command-line arguments are common with languages like C and C++, which were originally designed to work with command-line operating systems like UNIX.

The advantage of using command-line arguments is that they are passed to a program when the program *first* starts, which keeps the program from having to query the user for more information. Command-line arguments are great for passing custom initialization data.

Passing Arguments

To pass arguments to a J++ application, you have two options. One, you can use DOS command line arguments, or two, you can use J++'s Project Settings dialog box to tell J++ what arguments to pass.

If you want to use the J++ option, just click on the **Build|Settings** menu option. This will bring up the Project Settings dialog box as shown in Figure 5.5. In this dialog box is a drop down menu field called **Category**, under

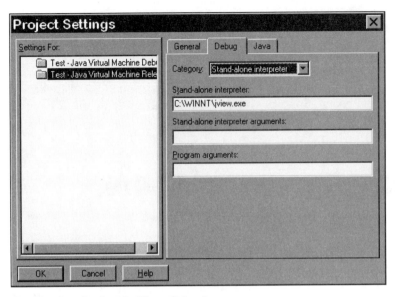

Figure 5.5   The J++ Project Settings dialog box.

the **Debug** tab, where you can enter arguments in the program Arguments field.

The J++ option will only work when you are testing your application from within J++. When you compile your application outside of J++, you will need to use command-line options, so let's cover those in detail.

The syntax for passing arguments to a program is extremely simple. Just start your programs as you usually would and add any number of arguments to the end of the line with each one separated by a space. Here is a sample call to a program named "myApp":

```
Java myApp open 640 480
```

In this case, we are calling the Java run-time interpreter and telling it to run he class file "myApp." We then are passing in three arguments: "open," "640," and "480."

If you wanted to pass in a longer string with spaces as an argument, you could. In this case, you enclose the string in quotation marks and Java will treat it as a single argument. Here is an example:

```
Java myApp "Nice program!" "640x480"
```

Once again the name of the program is "myApp." However, this time we are only sending it two arguments: "Nice program!" and "640×480." Note that the quotes themselves are not passed, just the string between the quotes.

Reading In Arguments

Now that we know how to pass arguments, where are they stored? How can we see them in our application? If you'll recall, all applications have a **main**() method. You should also notice that this method has an interesting argument structure:

```
public static void main(String args[]) {
    ...
}
```

Here, **main**() indicates that it takes an array named **args**[] of type **String**. Java takes any command-line arguments and puts them into the **args**[] string array. The array is dynamically resized to hold just the number of arguments passed, or zero if none are passed. Note that the use of the **args** identifier is completely arbitrary. You can use any word you want as long as it conforms to the Java naming rules. You can even get a little more descriptive, like this:

```
public static void main(String commandLineArgumentsArray[]) { ...
```

That may be a bit much, but you will never get confused as to what is in the array!

Accessing Arguments

Once we've passed in the arguments to an application and we know where they are stored, how do we get to them? Since the arguments are stored in an array, we can access them just like we would access strings in any other array. Let's look at a simple application that takes two arguments and prints them out:

```
class testArgs {
    public static void main(String args[]) {
        System.out.println(args[0]);
        System.out.println(args[1]);
    }
}
```

If we use this command line statement to run the application:

```
java testArgs hello world
```

we'd get this output:

```
hello
world
```

Now, try this command line:

```
java testArgs onearg
```

Here is the result:

```
onearg
java.lang.ArrayIndexOutOfBoundsException: 1
        at testArgs.main(testArgs.java:4)
```

What happened? Since we only were passing a single argument, the reference to **args[1]** is illegal and produces an error.

So, how do we stop from getting an error? Instead of calling each argument in line, we can use a **for** loop to step through each argument. We can check the **args.length** variable to see if we have reached the last item. Our new code will also recognize if no arguments have been passed and will not try and access the array at all. Enough talking, here is the code:

```
class testArgs {
    public static void main(String args[]) {
        for (int i = 0; i < args.length; i++) {
            System.out.println(args[i]);
        }
    }
}
```

Now, no matter how many arguments are passed (or none) the application can handle it.

Indexing command-line arguments.

Don't forget that Java arrays are zero based, so the first command-line argument is stored at position 0 not position 1. This is different than some other languages like C where the first argument would be at position 1. In C, position 0 would store the name of the program.

Dealing With Numeric Arguments

One more thing we should cover here is how to deal with numeric arguments. If you remember, all arguments are passed into an array of strings so we need to convert those values into numbers.

This is actually very simple. Each data type has an associated class that provides methods for dealing with that data type. Each of these classes has a method that creates a variable of that type from a string. Table 5.9 presents a list of those methods.

Table 5.9   Classes and their associated methods for handling data types.

Class	Method	Return
Integer	parseInt(String)	An integer value
Integer	valueOf(String)	An Integer object initialized to the value represented by the specified String
Long	parseLong(String)	A long value
Long	valueOf(String)	A long object initialized to the value represented by the specified String
Double	valueOf(String)	A Double object initialized to the value represented by the specified String
Float	valueOf(String)	A Float object initialized to the value rep resented by the specified String

Make sure you understand the difference between the **parse*()** methods and the **valueOf()** methods. The parsing methods return just a value that can be plugged into a variable or used as part of an expression. The **valueOf()** methods return an *object* of the specified type that has an initial value equal to the value of the string.

Operators, Expressions, And Control Structures 6

Anthony Potts

Operators, expressions, and control structures give you power to manipulate your data and steer your program.

*N*ow that you know about the types of data you can use in Java, you need to learn how to manipulate your data. The tools for manipulating data fall into three categories—operators, expressions, and control structures—each playing a more powerful role as you move up the ladder. In this chapter, we'll discuss each of the key Java operators—everything from assignment statements to bitwise operators. Although Java operators are very similar to C/C++ operators, there are a few subtle differences which we'll point out. Next, we'll show you the basics for creating expressions with Java. Finally, in the last part of the chapter, we'll investigate the world of Java control structures.

Using Java Operators

Operators allow you to perform tasks such as addition, subtraction, multiplication, and assignment. Operators can be divided into three main categories: *assignment, integer,* and *boolean* operators. We'll explore each Java operator in detail by examining each of the three categories. But first, let's cover operator precedence.

Operator Precedence

As you are writing your code, you need to keep in mind which operators have precedence over the others—the order in which operators take effect. If you are an experienced programmer or you can remember some of the stuff you learned in your high school algebra classes, you shouldn't have any problem with understanding the principles of operator precedence. The basic idea is that the outcome or result of an expression like this:

```
x = 5 * (7+4) - 3;
```

is determined by the *order in which the operators are evaluated* by the Java compiler. In general, all operators that have the same precedence are evaluated from left to right. If the above expression were handled in this manner, the result would be 36 (multiply 5 by 7, add 4, and then subtract 3). Because of precedence, we know that some operators, such as (), are evaluated before operators such as *. Therefore, the real value of this expression would be 52 (add 7 and 4, multiply by 5, and then subtract 3).

Table 6.1 Operator precedence with Java.

Operators	Operator Type
() [].	Expression
++ -- ! - ~	Unary
* / %	Multiplicative
+ -	Additive
<< >> >>>	Shift
< <= > >=	Relational (inequality)
== !=	Relational (equality)
&	Bitwise ADD
^	Bitwise XOR
|	Bitwise OR
&&	Logical AND
||	Logical OR
?:	Conditional
= *= /= %= += -= <<= >>= &= |= ^=	Assignment

The actual rules for operator precedence in Java are nearly identical to those found in C/C++. The only difference is that C/C++ includes a few operators, such as ->, that are not used in Java. Table 6.1 lists the major operators in order of precedence. Notice that some operator symbols such as (-) show up twice. The reason for this is because the operator has different meanings depending on how it is used in an expression. For example, in an expression like this

```
x = 7 + -3;
```

the (-) operator is used as a unary operator to negate the value 3. In this case, it would have a higher precedence than a standard additive operator (+ or -). In an expression like this, on the other hand,

```
x = 7 - 3 + 5;
```

the (-) operator is used as a binary additive operator, and it shares the same precedence with the (+) operator.

Which operators are missing?

If you are an experienced C/C++ programmer, you're probably wondering what operators used in C/C++ are not available in Java. The ones missing are the four key data access and size operators shown in Table 6.2. These operators are not needed because Java does not support pointers and does not allow you to access memory dynamically.

Table 6.2   C/C++ operators missing from Java.

Operator	Description
*	Performs pointer indirection
&	Calculates the memory address of a variable
->	Allows a pointer to select a data structure
sizeof	Determines the size of an allocated data structure

Assignment Operators

The most important and most often used operator is the assignment operator (=). This operator does just what it looks like it should do; it takes whatever variable is on the left and sets it equal to the expression on the right:

```
i = 35;
```

The expression on the right can be any valid Java expression—a literal, an equation with operands and operators, a method call, and so on. When using an assignment operator, you must be careful that the variable you are using to receive the expression is the correct size and type to receive the result of the expression on the right side. For example, statements like the following could cause you a lot of headaches:

```
short count;
// This number is way too big for a short type!
count = 500000000000;

char ch;
// Oops! We should be assigning a character here
ch = 100;
```

In the first example, the variable count is declared as a **short**, which means that the variable can only hold a number as large as 32767. Obviously, the number being assigned to the variable is way too large. In the second example, the variable ch expects to receive a character but in reality is assigned something else entirely.

If you look closely at the last line in Table 6.1, you'll see that Java offers a number of variations of the standard assignment statement. They are all borrowed from the C language. An assignment statement like this:

```
num *= 5;
```

would be equivalent to this expression:

```
num = num * 5;
```

The combination assignment operators turn out to be very useful for writing expressions inside loops that perform counting operations. Here's an example:

```
While (i <= count)
{
    i += 2;    // Increment the counting variable
    ...
}
```

In this case **i** is used as the loop "counting" control variable, and it is incremented by using a combination assignment statement.

Integer Operators

In the category of integer operators, there are two flavors to choose from: *unary* and *binary*. A unary operator performs a task on a single variable at a time. Binary operators, on the other hand, must work with two variables at a time. Let's start with the unary operators.

UNARY OPERATORS

There are four integer unary operators: negation, bitwise complement, increment, and decrement. They are used without an assignment operation. They simply perform their operation on a given variable, changing its value appropriately.

Negation (-)

Unary negation changes the sign of an integer. You must be careful when reaching the lower limits of integer variables because the negative limit is always one greater than the positive limit. So, if you had a variable of type **byte** with a value of -256 and you performed a unary negation on it, an error will occur because the **byte** data type has a maximum positive value of 255. Here are some examples of how this operator can be used:

```
- k;
-someInt;
x = -50 + 10;
```

As we learned earlier, the negation operator is at the top end of the precedence food chain; thus, you can count on operands that use it to be evaluated first.

Bitwise Complement (~)

Performing a bitwise complement on a variable flips each bit of the variable—all 1s become 0s and all 0s become 1s. For strict decimal calculations, this operator is not used very often. But if you are working with values that represent bit settings, such as an index into a color palette, this type of operator is invaluable. Here is an example of the unary complement operator in action:

```
// input: byte type variable bitInt = 3 (00000011 in binary)
~bitInt;
// Output: bitInt = 252 (11111100 in binary)
```

Increment (++) And Decrement (- -)

The increment and decrement operators are very simple operators that simply increase or decrease an integer variable by 1 each time they are used. These operators were created as a shortcut to saying x=x+1. As we've already mentioned, they are often used in loops where you want a variable incremented or decremented by one each time a loop is completed. Here is an example of how each operator is used:

```
++intIncrement;
--intDecrement;
```

BINARY OPERATORS

When you need to perform operations that involve two variables, you will be dealing with binary operators. Simple addition and subtraction are prime examples of binary operators. These operators do not change the value of either of the operands, instead they perform a function between the two operands that is placed into a third. Table 6.3 lists the complete set of the binary integer operators. Let's look at each of these operators in detail.

Addition, Subtraction, Multiplication, And Division

These operators are the standard binary operators that we have all used since we started programming. We won't explain the theory behind algebra because we assume you already know this stuff. We will, however, give you a few examples:

```
// X=12 and Y=4
Z = X + Y; // Answer = 16
Z = X - Y; // Answer = 8
Z = X * Y; // Answer = 48
Z = X / Y; // Answer = 3
```

Modulus

The modulus operator divides the first operand by the second operand and returns the remainder:

```
// X=11 and Y=4
Z = X % Y; // Answer = 3
```

Bitwise Operators

The bitwise binary operators perform operations at the binary level on integers. They act much like custom *if...then* statements. They compare the respective bits from each of the operands and set the corresponding bit of the return variable to a 1 or 0 depending on which operator is used. The AND operator works as follows: "if both bits are 1 then return a 1, otherwise return a 0." The OR operators works like this: "if either bit is a 1 then return a 1, otherwise return a 0." Finally, the XOR operator works like this: "if the bits are different return a 1, if they are the same return a 0." Table 6.4 provides a set of examples that illustrate how each bitwise operator works.

Table 6.3   The binary integer operators.

Operator	Description
+	Addition
-	Subtraction
*	Multiplication
/	Division
%	Modulus
&	Bitwise AND
		Bitwise OR
^	Bitwise XOR
<<	Left Shift
>>	Right Shift
>>>	Zero-Fill Right Shift

And here are some code examples to show you how to incorporate bitwise operators into your Java statements:

```
// X=3 (00000011)
// Y=2 (00000010)
Z = X & Y; // Answer: Z = 2X 00000011
        //            Y 00000010
        //            Z 00000010

Z = X | Y; // Answer: Z = 3X 00000011
        //            Y 00000010
        //            Z 00000011

Z = X ^ Y; // Answer: Z = 1X 00000011
        //            Y 00000010
        //            Z 00000001
```

Boolean Operators

The boolean data type adds several new operators to the mix. All of the operators that can be used on boolean values are listed in Table 6.5.

Table 6.4   Using the Java bitwise operators.

Operand 1	Operand 2	Bitwise Operator	Return
1	1	AND	True
1	0	AND	False
0	1	AND	False
0	0	AND	False
1	1	OR	True
1	0	OR	True
0	1	OR	True
0	0	OR	False
1	1	XOR	False
1	0	XOR	True
0	1	XOR	True
0	0	XOR	False

Table 6.5   Java boolean operators.

Operator	Operation
!	Negation
&	Logical AND
|	Logical OR
^	Logical XOR
&&	Evaluation AND
||	Evaluation OR
==	Equal to
!=	Not Equal to
&=	And Assignment
|=	OR Assignment
^=	XOR Assignment
?:	Ternary (Conditional)

BOOLEAN NEGATION (!)

Negation of a boolean variable simply returns the opposite of the boolean value. As you might have guessed, boolean negation is a unary operation. Here's an example:

```
// Bool1 = True
!Bool1; // Answer: Bool1 = False
```

LOGICAL AND (&), OR (|), AND XOR (^)

The AND, OR, and XOR operators work identically to the way they do with integer values. However, they only have a single bit to worry about:

```
Bool2 = true;
Bool3 = true;
Bool4 = False;
Bool5 = False;
Bool1 = Bool2 & Bool3; // Answer: Bool1 = True
Bool1 = Bool2 & Bool4; // Answer: Bool1 = False
Bool1 = Bool2 | Bool3; // Answer: Bool1 = False
Bool1 = Bool2 | Bool4; // Answer: Bool1 = True
Bool1 = Bool3 ^ Bool4; // Answer: Bool1 = False
Bool1 = Bool4 ^ Bool5; // Answer: Bool1 = True
```

EVALUATION AND (&&) AND OR (||)

The evaluation AND and OR are a little different than the logical versions. Using these operators causes Java to avoid evaluation of the righthand operands if it is not needed. In other words, if the answer can be derived by only reading the first operand, Java will not bother to read the second. Here are some examples:

```
// op1 = True op2 = False
result = op1 && op2; // result=False-both ops are evaluated
result = op2 && op1; // result=False-only first op is evaluated

result = op1 || op2; // result=True-only first op is evaluated
result = op2 || op1; // result=True-both ops are evaluated
```

EQUAL TO (==) AND NOT EQUAL TO (!=)

These operators are used to simply transfer a boolean value or transfer the opposite of a boolean value. Here are a few examples:

```
op1 = True;
if (result == op1); // Answer: result = true
if (result != op1); // Answer: result = false
```

ASSIGNMENT BOOLEAN OPERATORS (&=), (|=), (^=)

Boolean assignment operators are a lot like the assignment operators for integers. Here is an example of an assignment being used on both an integer and a boolean so that you can compare the two:

```
i    += 5;      // Same as int = int + 5
bool &= true;   // Same as bool = bool & true
bool |= true;   // Same as bool = bool | true
bool ^= false;  // Same as bool = bool ^ false
```

TERNARY OPERATOR

This powerful little operator acts like an extremely condensed *if...then* statement. If you look at the example below you will see that if the operand is True, the expression before the colon is evaluated. If the operand is False, the expression after the colon is evaluated. This type of coding may look a little strange at first. But once you understand the logic, you'll begin to see just how useful this operator can be. In the following example, the parentheses are not actually needed, but when you use more complicated expressions they will make the code much easier to follow:

```
// op1 = True op2 = False
op1 ? (x=1):(x=2); // Answer: x=1
op2 ? (x=1):(x=2); // Answer: x=2
```

Floating-Point Number Operators

Almost all of the integer operators work on floating-point numbers as well, with a few minor changes. Of course, all the standard arithmetic operators (+, -, *, /) work as well as the assignment operators (+=, -=, *=, /=). Modulus (%) also works; however, it only evaluates the integer portion of the operands. The increment and decrement operators work identically by adding or subtracting 1.0 from the integer portion of the numbers. Be careful when using relational operators on floating-point numbers. Do not make assumptions about how the numbers will behave just because integers behave a certain way. For example, just because an expression like a==b may be true for two floating-point values, don't assume that an expression like a<b || a>b will be true. This is because floating-point values are not ordered like integers. You also have to deal with the possibility of a floating-point variable being equal to negative or positive infinity, **-Inf** and **Inf**, respectively. You can get a positive or negative **Inf** when you perform an operation that returns an overflow.

Using Casts

In some applications you may need to transfer one type of variable to another. Java provides us with *casting* methods to accomplish this. Casting refers to the process of transforming one variable of a certain type into another data type.

Casting is accomplished by placing the name of the data type you wish to cast a particular variable into in front of that variable in parentheses. Here is an example of how a cast can be set up to convert a **char** into an **int**:

```
int a;
char b;
b = 'z';
a = (int) b;
```

Since the variable **a** is declared as an **int**, it expects to be assigned an **int** value. The variable **b**, on the other hand, is declared as a **char**. To assign the contents of **b** to **a**, the cast is used on the right side of the assignment statement. The contents of **b**, the numeric value of the character 'z' is safely assigned to the variable **a** as an integer. If you wanted to, you could perform the cast in reverse:

```
short a;
char b;
a = 40;
b = (char) a;  // Convert value 40 into a character
```

Casting is extremely simple when you are using the primitive data types—**int**, **char**, **short**, **double**, and so on. You can also cast classes and interfaces in Java, which we'll show you how to do in Chapter 7.

The most important thing to remember when using casts is the space each variable has to work with. Java will let you cast a variable of one data type into a variable of a different data type if the size of the data type of the target variable is smaller than the other data type, but you may not like the result. Does this sound confusing? Let's explain this a little better. If you had a variable of type **long**, you should only cast it into another variable of type **float** or **double** because these data types are the only other two primitives with at least 64-bits of space to handle your number. On the other hand, if you had a variable of type **byte**, then you could cast it into any of the other primitives except boolean because they all have more space than the lowly **byte**. When you are dealing with **double** variables, you are stuck, since no other data type offers as much space as the **double**.

If you have to cast a variable into another variable having less space, Java will do it. However, any information in the extra space will be lost. On the plus side though, if the value of a larger variable is less than the maximum value of the variable you are casting into, no information will be lost.

Writing Expressions And Statements

So far we've been more or less looking at operators, literals, and data types in a vacuum. Although we've used these components to write expressions, we haven't formally defined what Java expressions are. Essentially, expressions are the Java statements that make your code work; they are the guts of your programs. A basic expressions contains *operands* and *operators*. For example, in this expression

```
i = x + 10;
```

the variable x and the literal 10 are the operands and + is the operator. The evaluation of an expression performs one or more operations that return a result. The data type of the result is always determined by the data types of the operand(s).

When multiple operands are combined, they are referred to as a *compound expression*. The order in which the operators are evaluated is determined by the precedence of the operators that act upon them. We discussed precedence earlier and showed you the relative precedence of each Java operator.

The simplest form of expression is used to calculate a value, which in turn is assigned to a variable in an assignment statement. Here are a couple assignment statements that use expressions that should look very familiar to you by now:

```
i = 2;
thisString = "Hello";
```

Here are a few assignment statements that are a little more involved:

```
Bool1 != Bool2;
i += 2;
d *= 1.9
Byte1 ^= Byte2;
```

An assignment expression involves a variable that will accept the result, followed by a single assignment operator, followed by the operand that the assignment operator is using.

The next step up the ladder is to create expressions that use operators like the arithmetic operators we have already discussed:

```
i = i + 2;
thisString = "Hello";
```

Expressions with multiple operands are probably the most common type of expressions. They still have a variable that is assigned the value of the result produced by evaluating the operands and operators to the right of the equal sign. You can also have expressions with many operators and operands like this:

```
i = i + 2 - 3 * 9 / 3;
thisString = "Hello" + "World, my name is " + myName;
```

The art of programming in Java—with J++ or without it—involves using operators and operands to build expressions, which are in turn used to build *statements*. Of course, the assignment statement is just one type of statement that can be constructed. You can also create many types of control statements, such as while and for loops, if-then decision making statements, and so on. (We'll look at all of the control statements that can be written in Java in the last part of this chapter.)

There are essentially two types of statements you can write in Java: *simple* and *compound*. A simple statement performs a single operation. Here are some examples:

```
int i;      // Variable declaration
i = 10 * 5; // Assignment statement
if (i = 50) x = 200;  // if-then decision statement
```

The important thing to remember about simple statements in Java is that they are *always* completed with a semicolon (;). (Some of the others like class declarations and compound *if...else* statements don't need semicolons, but if you leave it off the end of an expression, you'll get an error.)

Compound statements involve the grouping of simple statements. In this case, the characters ({ }) are used to group the separate statements into one compound statement. Here are a few examples:

```
while (x < 10)
{
    ++x;
    if (sum < x) printline();
}

if (x < 10)
```

```
{
    i = 20;
    p = getvalue(i);
}
```

Notice that the (;) terminating character is not used after the final (}). The braces take care of this for us.

Control Flow Statements

Control flow is what programming is all about. What good are basic data types, variables, and casting if you don't have any code that can make use of them? Java provides several different types of control flow structures. These structures provide your application with direction. They take an input, decide what to do with it and how long to do it, and then let expressions handle the rest.

Let's look at each of these structures in detail. If you have done any programming before, all of these should look familiar. Make sure you study the syntax so that you understand exactly how they work in Java as compared to how they work in other languages.

Table 6.6 lists all of the standard control flow structures, and it shows you what the different parts of their structure represent.

if...else

The **if...else** control structure is probably used more than all the others combined. How many programs have you written that didn't include one? Not very many, we'll wager.

In its simplest terms, the **if...else** structure performs this operation: if *this* is true then do *that* otherwise do *something else*. Of course, the "otherwise" portion is optional. Since you probably already know what **if...else** statements are used for, we will just show you a few examples so you can see how they work in Java.

Here is the structure labeled with standard terms:

```
if (boolean) statement
else statement;
```

Table 6.6 Control flow structures.

Structure	Expression
if...else	if (boolean = true) statement else statement;
while	while (boolean = true) statement;
do...while	do statement while (boolean = true);

switch	switch (expression) {
	case expression: statement;
	case expression: statement;
	...
	default: statement;
	}

for	for (expression1; expression2; expression3) statement;
label	label: statement break label; continue label;

Here is a sample of what an **if...else** statement might look like with actual code:

```
if (isLunchtime) {
    Eat = true;
    Hour = 12;
}
else {
    Eat = False;
    Hour = 0;
}
```

You can also use nested **if...else** statements:

```
if (isLunchtime) {
    Eat = true;
    Hour = 12;
}
else if (isBreakfast) {
        Eat = true;
        Hour = 6;
```

```
    }
    else if (isDinner) {
         Eat = true;
         Hour = 18;
    }
    else {
         Eat = false;
         Hour = 0;
    }
```

The curly braces are used when multiple statements need to take place for each option. If we were only performing a single operation for each part of the **if...else** statement, we would not need the braces. Here is an example of an **if...else** statement that uses curly braces for one part but not the other:

```
if (isLunchtime) {
    Eat = true;
    Hour = 12;
}
else Eat = False;
```

while and do...while

The **while** and **do...while** loops perform the same function. The only difference is that the **while** loop verifies the expression *before* executing the statement, and the **do...while** loop verifies the expression *after* executing the statement. This is a major difference that can be extremely helpful if used properly.

Here are the structures labeled with standard terms:

```
while (boolean) {
    statement;
}

do {
    statement
} while(boolean);
```

while and **do...while** loops are used if you want to repeat a certain statement or block of statements until a certain expression becomes false. For example, assume you wanted to send e-mail to all of the people at a particular Web site. You could set up a **while** loop that stepped through all the people, one-by-one, sending them e-mail until you reached the last person. When the last person is reached, the loop is terminated and the program control flow moves on to the statement following the loop. Here is what that loop might look like in very simple terms:

```
boolean done = false;

while (!done){
    emailUser();
    goNextuser();
    if (noNewuser) done = true;
}
```

switch

The **switch** control flow structure is useful when you have a single expression with many possible options. The same thing can be done using recursed **if...else** statments, but that can get very confusing when you get past just a few options. The **if...else** structure is also difficult to change when it becomes highly nested.

The **switch** statement is executed by comparing the value of an initial expression or variable with other variables or expressions. Let's look at the labeled structure:

```
switch(expression) {
    case expression: statement;
    case expression: statement;
    case expression: statement;
    default: statement;
}
```

Now let's look at a real piece of code that uses the **switch** structure:

```
char age;

System.out.print("How many computers do you own? ");
age = System.in.read();
switch(age) {
    case '0':
        System.out.println("\nWhat are you waiting for?");
        break;
    case '1':
        System.out.println("\nIs that enough these days?");
        break;
    case '2':
        System.out.println("\nPerfect!");
```

```
        break;
    default:
        System.out.println("\nToo much free time on you hands!");
}
```

The **break** statement is extremely important when dealing with **switch** structures. If the **switch** finds a case that is true, it will execute the statements for that case. When it is finished with that case, it will move on to the next one. This process continues until a match is found or the **default** statement is reached. The **break** statement tells the **switch** "OK, we found a match, let's move on."

The **default** clause serves as the "catch-all" statement. If all of the other cases fail, the **default** clause will be executed.

for

for loops are another programming standard that would be tough to live without. The idea behind a **for** loop is that we want to step through a sequence of numbers until a limit is reached. The loop steps through our range in whatever step increment we want, checking at the beginning of each loop to see if we have caused our "quit" expression to become true.

Here is the labeled structure of a **for** loop:

```
for (variable ; expression1 ; expression2);
```

The variable we use can either be one we have previously created, or it can be declared from within the **for** structure. Expression1 from the above example is the expression we need to stay true until the loop is finished. More often than not, this expression is something like x<10 which means that we will step through the loop until x is equal to 10 at which time the expression (x<10) becomse false and drops us out of the loop.

Here is an example of a **for** loop that actually works:

```
for (int x = 0 ; x < 10 ; x++) {
  System.out.println(x);
}
```

If you put this code into an empty **main** method you should get the following output:

```
0
1
2
3
4
5
6
7
8
9
```

For loops are used for many different applications. They are a necessity when dealing with arrays and can really help when creating lookup tables or indexing a database.

labels

Java **labels** provide a means of controlling different kinds of loops. Sometimes, when you create a loop, you need to be able to break out of it before it finishes on its own and satisfies its completion expression. This is where **labels** come in very handy.

The key to **labels** is the **break** statement that you learned to use with the **switch** statement. You can also use the **break** statement to exit out of any loop. It is great for breaking out of **for** loops and **while** loops especially.

However, sometimes you have embedded loops and you need to be able to break out of a certain loop. A great example of this is two embedded **for** loops that are setting values in an array. If an error occurs or you get a strange value, you may want to be able to break out of one loop or another. It gets confusing if you have all these embedded loops and break statements all over with no apparent link to one loop or another. **labels** rectify this situation.

To use a label, you simply place an identifier followed by a colon at the beginning of the line that initiates a loop. Let's look at an example before we go further:

```
outer: for (int x = 0 ; x < 10 ; x++) {
    inner: for (int y = 0 ; y < 10 ; y++) {
   System.out.println(x + y);
       if (y=9) {
```

```
        break outer:
    } else {
        continue outer:
    }
  }
}
```

Labels are probably new to most of you, so you may not see a need for them right away. However, as your programs become more complicated you should think about using lables where appropriate to make your code simple and more readable.

Moving Ahead

We covered a lot of ground in this chapter and the previous one. If you are new to Java programming and have little C or C++ background, make sure you understand these concepts well so that you do not get confused in the upcoming chapters.

Let's now move on to another basic structure of Java programming. In fact, we would have to call it the basic structure of Java programming—the class.

Java Classes And Methods 7

David H. Freidel, Jr.

Classes are the key Java components that give the language its object-oriented personality.

If you have some experience programming in a language like C++, you are probably familiar with the power and flexibility that classes provide. They are ideal for plugging general information into a template-like structure for reusing over and over. For example, if you are developing an interactive drawing package, you could create standard classes for some of the fundamental drawing operations and then use those classes to create more sophisticated drawing tasks. If you are new to the world of object-oriented programming (OOP), you'll soon discover that classes are the essential building blocks for writing OOP applications. At first glance, Java classes look and operate like C++ classes; but there are some key differences which we'll address in this chapter.

We'll start by looking at the basics of classes. You'll quickly learn how classes are defined and used to derive other classes. The second half of the chapter covers *methods*—the components used to breathe life into classes.

Understanding Classes

In traditional structured programming languages like C or Pascal, everything revolves around the concepts of algorithms and data structures. The algorithms are kept separate from the data structures, and they operate on the data to perform actions and results. To help divide programming tasks into separate units, components like functions and procedures are defined. The problem with this programming paradigm is that it doesn't allow you to easily create code that can be reused and expanded to create other code.

To solve this problem, object-oriented programming languages like Smalltalk and C++ were created. These languages introduced powerful components called *classes* so that programmers could combine functions (operations) and data under one roof. This is a technique called *encapsulation* in the world of object-oriented programming. Every language that uses classes defines them in a slightly different way; however, the basics concepts for using them remain the same. The main advantages of classes are:

◆ They can be used to define abstract data types.

◆ Data is protected or hidden inside a class so other classes can't access it.

◆ Classes can be used to derive other classes.

◆ New classes derived from existing classes can inherit the data and methods already defined—a concept called *inheritance*.

As you'll learn in this chapter, the techniques for defining and using Java classes are adapted from techniques found in the C++ language. In some cases, the Java syntax will look very similar to C++ syntax, but in other cases you'll find a number of differences, including new keywords that have been added to Java for declaring classes and methods; restrictions, such as the elimination of pointers; and different scoping rules that determine how classes can be used in an application.

Declaring A Class

Let's take look at the full declaration used to define classes in Java:

```
[Doc Comment] [Modifier] class Identifier
[extends Superclassname]
```

```
[implements Interfaces] {
   ClassBody;
}
```

Of course, keep in mind that you won't always use all of the clauses, such as *Doc Comment*, *Modifier*, **extends**, and so on. For example, here's an example of a very small class definition:

```
class Atom_ant {
   int a = 1;
}
```

This class has an identifier, **Atom_ant**, and a body, **int a = 1;**. Of course, don't try to compile this at home as is because it will only result in an error. Why? Well, even though it is a valid class, it is not capable of standing on its own. (You would need to set it up as an applet or a main program to make it work.)

A class declaration provides all of the information about a class including its internal data (*variables*) and functions (*methods*) to be interpreted by the Java compiler. In addition, class declarations provide:

◆ Programmer comments

◆ Specifications of the other classes that may reference the class

◆ Specifications of the superclass the class belongs to (the class' parent)

◆ Specifications of the methods the class can call

Using A Class

Before we move on and look at all of the other components used to declare classes, let's return to our simple class declaration to see how classes are used in Java programs. Once a class has been declared, you need to use it to create an object. This process is called making an "instance of" a class. In a Java program it requires two steps. First, you declare an object variable using a syntax that looks just like a variable declaration, except the class name is used instead of the name of a primitive data type. For example, this statement would use the **Atom_ant** class we defined earlier to declare an object from the class definition:

```
Atom_ant crazyant;
```

Once the object has been declared, in this case **crazyant**, you then create an instance of it in a Java application by using the **new** operator:

```
crazyant = new Atom_ant();
```

Now the object **crazyant** can access all of the components in a **Atom_ant** class, thus making it an instance of an **Atom_ant** class. To see how this works in context, let's expand our example:

```
class Atom_ant {  // Simple class
   int a = 1;
}
public class Bug {
   int i = 10;
   Atom_ant crazyant;  // Declare an object

   public static void main (String args[]) {
      // Create an instance of Atom_ant called crazyant
      crazyant = new Atom_ant();
      System.out.println("There are " + bug.i + " bugs here but only "
         + crazyant.i + " atom ant.");
   }
}
```

The output produced by this example would be:

```
There are 10 bugs here but only 1 atom ant.
```

The main class, **Bug**, creates an instance of the **Atom_ant** class—the **crazyant** object. Then it uses the object to access the data member, **a**, which is assigned a value in the **Atom_ant** class. Notice that the dot operator (.) is used to access a member of a class.

Object declaration timesaver.

In Java, you can both declare an object variable and create an instance all in one statement. Here's an example of how it is done:

```
Atom_ant crazyant = new Atom_ant();
```

Notice that the class Atom_ant is used to declare the object variable crazyant and then the new operator is used to create an instance of Atom_ant.

Components Of A Class Declaration

Let's look at the components of the class declaration in a little more detail. As you recall from our first example, the only really necessary part of a class declaration is its name or *identifier*. However, whenever you need to reference your class in your program to reuse it, you'll need to reference it by its *fully qualified name*. This name is the package name, or group of classes from which it came, followed by the identifier. For example, if *Atom_ant* is the class name and it belongs to a package named *molecule*, its fully qualified name would be *molecule.Atom_ant*.

Documentation Comment

The *Doc Comment* clause of the class declaration is provided as an aid to help other programmers who might need to use your class. It allows you to write your documentation while you're writing the code. The comments you include as part of this clause can easily be converted into easy to read HTML pages. However, keep in mind that your HTML pages will only be as good as your comments. Let's look at an example to see how the *Doc Comment* feature works. The code snippet below:

```
/**
 * Atom ant is the world's smallest super hero,
    so we gave him a class by himself.
 * @author Dave Friedel
 */
class Atom_ant {
    int i = 1;
}
```

uses *Doc Comment* style comments to produce the HTML page shown in Figure 7.1. Notice how the comments are formatted and used to document the class. In this case, **Atom_ant** is a subclass under the **java.lang.Object** class—the default parent for all classes.

In case you're wondering, the **@author** notation is a special type of comment tag that allows you to personalize your class.

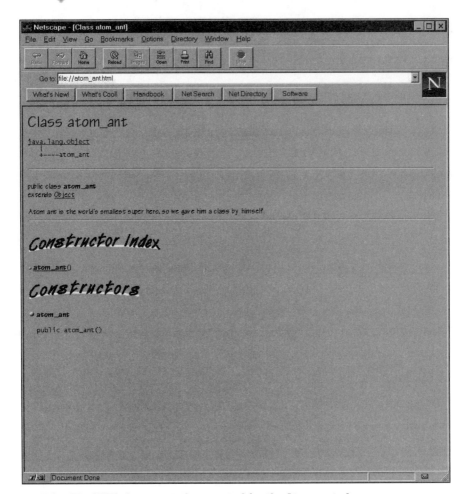

Figure 7.1   The HTML documentation created for the Atom_ant class.

Class Modifiers

Modifiers define the rules for how classes are used in Java applications. They determine how other packages, or classes of other groups can interact with the current class. There are three kinds of modifiers that can be used in a class declaration:

◆   public

◆   abstract

◆   final

If you don't use one of these modifiers when declaring a class, Java will automatically decide that only other classes in the current package may access the class. Let's look at how each of these modifiers are used.

PUBLIC CLASS

The **public** modifier is used to define a class that can have the greatest amount of access by other classes. By declaring a class as **public**, you allow all other classes and packages to access its variables, methods, and subclasses. However, *only one public class is allowed in any single Java applet or a single source code file*. You can think of the one public class in an applet as serving the role that the **main()** function does in a C/C++ program.

The source code for an applet must be saved as *ClassName.java*, where *ClassName* is the name of the single public class defined in the applet. If we created a TickerTape applet, for example, the single public class might be defined as:

```
public class TickerTape extends Applet implements Runnable {...
```

and the name of the file would be TickerTape.java.

Let's look at another example of how the **public** modifier is used to define a Java class:

```
// Filename: Atom_ant.java
public class Atom_ant {
   public static void main (String args[]) {
      System.out.println("Hello World");
   }
}
```

In this case, **Atom_ant** is the name of the class and the filename for the applet is Atom_ant.java.

ABSTRACT CLASS

The **abstract** modifier is used to declare classes that serve as a shell or placeholder for implementing methods and variables. When you construct a hierarchy of classes, your top most class will contain the more general data definitions and method implementations that represent your program's features. As you work your way down the class hierarchy, your classes will start to implement more specific data components and operations. As you build your hierarchy, you may need to create more general classes and *defer* the actual implementation to later stages in the class hierarchy. This is where the abstract class comes in. This approach allows you to reference the operations that you need to include without having to restructure your entire hierarchy.

The technique of using abstract classes in Java is commonly referred to as *single inheritance* by C++ programmers. (By the way, limited multiple inheritance techniques can also be implemented in Java by using interfaces.)

Any class that is declared as an abstract class must follow certain rules:

◆ No objects can be instantiated from an abstract class.

◆ Abstract classes must contain at least one declaration of an abstract method or variable.

◆ All abstract methods that are declared in an abstract class must be implemented in one of the subclasses beneath it.

◆ Abstract classes cannot be declared as final or private classes.

Let's look at an example of how an abstract class is defined and used to help create other classes:

```
abstract class Quark extends Atom_ant {
    ...
    abstract void abstract_method1();
    abstract void abstract_method2();
    void normal_method();
    ...
}

public class Aparticles extends Quark {
    public void abstract_method1() {
        ... // Definition of the method
    }
}

public class Bparticles extends Quark {
    public void abstract_method2() {
    ... // Definition of the method
    }
}
```

Here, the class **Quark** is declared as an abstract class and it contains two methods that are declared as abstract methods. The subclasses **Aparticles** and **Bparticles** are located beneath the class **Quark** in the hierarchy of classes. Each one defines a method based on one of the abstract methods found in the **Quark** class. A compile-time error would occur if we had failed to define both of the abstract methods in the **Quark** class. All abstract methods must be defined in the subclasses that are derived from abstract classes.

Restrictions in declaring abstract classes.

An abstract class cannot be defined as a final class (using the final keyword) because the Java compiler will always assume that the abstract class will be used to derive other classes—other subclasses will follow it. (As you'll see in the next section, a final class defines the end of the line for a class hierarchy.) Furthermore, you cannot used a private modifier in an abstract class's method declarations because this modifier restricts methods from being used by any other classes except the class they are defined in.

FINAL CLASS

The **final** modifier is used to declare a class that will not be used to derive any other classes. The final class is like the last station on a railway line. By its position in a class hierarchy, a final class cannot have any subclasses beneath it. In **final** class declarations, you cannot use the **extends** clause because the Java compiler always assumes that a final class cannot be extended. Here's an example of what would happen if you tried to declare a final class and then use it in another class declaration:

```
final class Molecule extends Element {
    static String neutron = "molecule";
}

class Atom_ant extends Molecule {
    static String proton = "atom_ant";
}

Compiling...
E:\java\jm\element.java
E:\java\jm\element.java:12: Can't subclass final classes: class
 Moleculeclass Atom_ant extends Molecule {       ^1 errorsCompile Ended.
```

In this case, **Molecule** has been defined as a final class. But notice that the second class definition, **Atom_ant**, attempts to use **Molecule** as its parent. The Java compiler catches this illegal declaration and provides the appropriate warning.

Class Identifiers

Each class you define in a Java program must have its own unique identifier. The class's identifier or name directly follows the **class** keyword. The rules for naming classes are the same as those used to name variables. To refresh your memory, identifiers should always begin with a letter of the alphabet, either upper or lower case. The only exception to this rule is the underscore symbol (_) and the dollar sign ($), which may also be used. The rest of the name can be defined using characters, numbers, and some symbols.

Since class names are also used as file names, you need to create names that will not cause problems with your operating system or anyone who will be using your program.

Extending Classes

In most Java applets and programs you write, you will have a number of classes that need to interact each other—in many cases classes will be derived from other classes creating hierarchies. The keyword that handles the work of helping you extend classes and create hierarchies is named appropriately enough, **extends**.

In a class hierarchy, every class must have a parent—except the class that is at the top. The class that serves as a parent to another class is also called the superclass of the class it derives—the class that takes the position immediately above the class. Let's look at an example. As Figure 7.2 indicates, the classes *911*, *944*, and *928* all belong to the superclass *Porsche*. And *Porsche* belongs to the superclass *sportscar*, which in turn belongs to the superclass *automobile*.

When you derive a class from a superclass, it will inherit the superclass's data and methods. (For example, *911* has certain characteristics simply because it is derived from *Porsche*.) To derive a class from a superclass in a

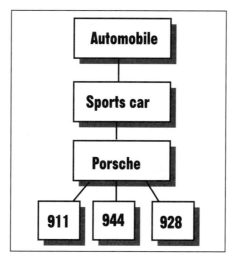

Figure 7.2 A sample class hierarchy.

class declaration hierarchy, you'll use the **extend** clause followed by the name of the superclass. If no superclass is defined, the Java compiler assumes you are deriving a class using Java's top-level superclass named **Object**.

```
public class Element extends Object {
    public static void main() {
      Atom_ant ATOMOBJ = new Atom_ant();
      Molecule MOLEOBJ = new Molecule();
      System.out.println(ATOMOBJ.proton);
    }
}

class Molecule extends Element {
    static String neutron = "molecule";
}

class Atom_ant extends Molecule {
    static String proton = "atom_ant";
}
```

In this class declaration section, the top-level class defined is **Element**. Notice that it is derived or "extended" from **Object**—the built-in Java class. The first line of the declaration of **Element** could have also been written as:

```
public class Element {
...
```

since the Java compiler will assume that a class is automatically derived from the **Object** class if the **extends** clause is omitted. The second class, **Molecule**, is derived from **Element** and the third class, **Atom_ant**, is derived from **Molecule**. As Figure 7.3 shows, both **Molecule** and **Atom_ant** inherit the components of the **Element** class.

Using The Implements Clause To Create Class Interfaces

When classes are used to derive other classes, the derived classes can access the data and methods of the classes higher up in the hierarchy chain. Fortunately, Java provides a mechanism called *interfaces* so that classes that are not part of a hierarchy can still access components of other classes. An interface is created for a class by using the **implements** clause. A class can implement as many interfaces as it wishes, but all the interfaces introduced must have all their methods defined in the body of the class implementing it. Thus, all the subclasses that follow from that point on will inherit the methods and variables defined.

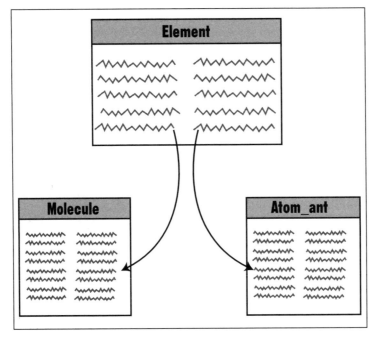

Figure 7.3 Using the extends keyword to derive a series of classes.

Let's develop the **Atom_ant** class we introduced in the previous section to see how an interface can be coded:

```
class Atom_ant extends Molecule implements Protons, Neutrons,
  Electrons {
    static int proton = 45378444;
    void Proton_function() {
        ... // definition of the Proton_function()
    }

    void Neutron_function() {
        ... // definition of the Neutron_function()
    }

    void Electron_function() {
        ... // definition of the Electron_function()
    }
}
```

Here we are making the assumption that the interfaces **Protons, Neutrons,** and **Electrons** only have one method declared in each of the interfaces. For example, **Protons** may be set up as follows:

```
Public interface Protons {

    void Proton_function(); // declares the method that will be used
}
```

As you can see, setting up the interface is a two step process. The class where the methods are defined uses the **implements** clause to indicate which interfaces can have access to the methods. Then, **interface** statements are used to declare the method that will be used.

In the source below, the **TickerTape** class implemented the interface **Runnable** from the package java.lang. The **Runnable** interface has only one method declared in it, which is **run**(). This method is then defined in the class that is implementing it. In this case, the applet TickerTape has defined **run**() to instruct the thread to sleep, call the **setcoord**() method, and rerun the **paint**() method every time the applet calls the **run**() method. This happens in situations where the screen is resized or, in this case, where the applet is instructed to move the text across the screen and the **run**() method is called.

```
// TickerTape Applet

import java.applet.*;
import java.awt.*;
// TickerTape Class
public class TickerTape extends Applet implements Runnable {
   ...
   public void run() {
      while(ttapeThread != null){ // verifies thread still active
         try {Thread.sleep(50);} catch (InterruptedException e){}
         setcoord();         // changes the placement of the text
         repaint();          // repaints the screen by activating the
paint()
// method
      }
   }
   ...

} // End TickerTape
```

This allows the ability to effectively encapsulate(hide) the classes and all its methods that actually support the **run**() method. Interfaces allow for distinct behaviors, defined by the programmer, to be used without exposing the class(es) to everyone.

Class Body

The class body contains the code that implements the class. This is where you provide the detail for the actions the class needs to perform (methods) and the data it needs to use (variables). The body can also contain constructors (special methods) and initializers. The basic format for a class body is:

```
{
   Variable-declarations;
   Method-declarations;
}
```

The variable declarations can be any standard Java declaration. Later in this chapter we'll discuss how methods are declared and used. Here's an example of a class with a body:

```
public class TickerTape extends Applet implements Runnable {
// Beginning of class body
   String inputText;
```

```
    String animSpeedString;
    Color color = new Color(255, 255, 255);
    int xpos;
    ...
    // Methods
    public void paint(Graphics g) {
        paintText(osGraphics);
        g.drawImage(im, 0, 0, null);
    }
    ...
// End of Class Body

}
```

NAME SPACE

Every method and variable defined in a class is recorded into an area called a *name space*. This name space is then inherited by the other classes in a class hierarchy which are derived from the class. If a variable or method has been previously defined elsewhere in the structure with the same name, a *shadowing* effect occurs for that level. To access the value of a variable that supersedes the current value, you need to put the prefix clause **super** in front of the variable name. This clause instructs the expression to take the value of the superclass. To access the value of the current variable, you use the prefix **this**. Let's look at an example:

```
public class House extends Object {    static int tvamount = 8;    //
  Variable
    void main() {
        Room();
    }
}

public class Room extends House {    static int tvamount = 5;    //
  Variable
    int Child = this.tvamount;  // Child equals 5-same as saying
                               // tvamount
    int Parent = super.tvamount;    // Parent equals 8
}
```

In this example the **House** class is derived from the standard **Object** class. Then, the **Room** class is derived from **House**. Now notice that each class defines a variable named **tvamount** and assigns it a value. In the second assignment statement in **Room**, the variable **Child** is assigned the value 5 because **this** is used to access the class's local copy of the **tvamount** variable. In the next assignment statement, notice how **super** is used to access the value **tvamount** was assigned in **House**—the superclass.

Methods

As we've seen, the mechanisms used to implement operations in classes are called *methods*. This terminology is borrowed directly from object-oriented languages like Smalltalk and C++. Methods define the behavior of a class and the objects created from the class. A method can send, receive, and alter information to perform a task in an application. Java requires that every method be defined within a class or interface, unlike C++ where methods (functions) can be implemented outside of classes.

Let's refer to the car class hierarchy we presented earlier in this chapter to get a better understanding of the role methods play. All of the cars we introduced have doors and we could define two methods to operate on these doors: open and close. These same methods could be designed to perform operations on other car components such as windows, trunks, hoods, and so on. A component like a door can be viewed as an object. Of course, a car would be made up of many objects and many methods would be required to process all of the objects. As a programmer, it would be up to you to decide how to arrange the objects you need and what methods must be implemented.

Declaring A Method

Before moving on to the specifics of what Methods can consist of. Let's take a step back and look at the full declaration used to define a Java method:

```
[Modifier] ReturnType Identifier([ParameterList]) [Throws]
{
    MethodBody;
}
```

The *Modifier* and *Throws* clauses are optional. They are used to specify how the method needs to be accessed and which exceptions should be checked for.

Components Of A Method Declaration

If you were to break down the method declaration, you would find it performs three main tasks:

◆ It determines who may call the method.

◆ It determines what the method can receive (the parameters).

◆ It determines how the method returns information.

Method Modifiers

Earlier in this chapter, you learned that a set of modifiers are available for defining how classes can be accessed. Methods also can be defined using modifiers, although the method modifiers only affect how methods are used, not the class they are defined in. Java provides eight modifiers for defining methods, but only one modifier from each of the groups listed next may be used in a method declaration. For example, you cannot use a **public** and **private** modifier in the same declaration. Here is the complete set of method modifiers:

◆ **public, protected, private**

◆ **static**

◆ **abstract, final, native, synchronized**

Keep in mind that it doesn't make sense to use some modifiers in one group with modifiers from another group. For example, a method that is defined using the **private** and **abstract** modifiers contradicts itself. An abstract method is one that requires its actual code to be defined in the subclasses that follow, whereas a private method is one that can only be accessed in the class it is defined in. The rule of thumb when choosing and combining modifiers is that you need to make sure that they are complementary rather than contradictory. If a modifier is not used, the method may be accessed only by the classes that are in the current package.

PUBLIC METHOD

A method declared as public can be accessed by *any* class in the same package. It can also be accessed by other classes from other packages. This modifier gives a method the most freedom.

PROTECTED METHOD

A method declared as protected can only be used by other classes within the same package. All the subclasses beneath the class the method is defined in may access the method unless shadowing occurs. Shadowing involves naming a method using a name that already exists in a superclass above the class the method is defined in.

PRIVATE METHOD

A method declared as private is one that can only be accessed by the class it is defined in. This modifier gives a method the least amount of freedom.

STATIC METHOD

A method declared as static is one that cannot be changed. This type of method is also referred to as a *class method*, because it belongs explicitly to a particular class. When an *instance* of the class that defines the method is created, the static method cannot be altered. For this reason, a static method can refer to any other static methods or variables by name. Limitations of static methods to keep in mind are that they cannot be declared as final, and they cannot be overridden.

ABSTRACT METHOD

A method declared as abstract is one that must be defined in a subclass of the current class. However, an abstract method must be declared in the current class with a (;) semicolon in place of the method's block of code. Methods that are declared abstract are not required to be implemented in every subclass.

FINAL METHOD

A method declared as final is one that ends the hierarchical tree. No methods having the same name can be defined in subclasses that exist below the class that declares the method as final.

NATIVE METHOD

A method declared as native is one that will be implemented using outside code—code that is written in another language, to be used in conjunction with your current program. This limits you to a specific platform and restricts you from creating Java applets. Native methods are declared by leaving out the method body and placing a semicolon at the end of the method declaration.

SYNCHRONIZED METHOD

A method declared as synchronized limits it from being executed by multiple objects at the same time. This is useful when you are creating Java applets and you could have more than one thread running at the same time accessing one central piece of data. If the method is static (e.g., a class method), the whole class would be locked. If you just declare a particular method as synchronized, the object containing the method would only be locked until the method finishes executing.

Return Type Of A Method

Any information that is returned from a method is declared as the *return type*. This assures that the information that is returned from a method call will be of the correct type; otherwise, a compile-time error will be generated. If no information will be returned by a method, the **void** keyword should be placed in front of the method name.

Parameter Lists For A Method

The parameter list consists of the ordered set of data elements passed to a method. You can pass zero, one, or multiple parameters by listing them between the parentheses, with each type and variable name being separated by a comma. If no parameters are passed, the parentheses should be empty. All variables that are passed become local for that instance of the method. Here's an example of how methods can be declared with and without parameters:

```
public static void MyFirstMethod(String Name, int Number) {
    ...
    // the String variable Name is assigned whatever is passed to it
    // the integer variable Number is assigned whatever is passed to
    // it
```

```
    . . .
}

public static void MyFirstMethod() {
    . . .
    // Nothing is passed to it.
    . . .
}
```

Method Throws

The **throws** clause is used to specify the type of error(s) that will be handled within a method. In effect, it is used to help you set up an automatic error-handler. In the event of an error, the error must be assignable to one of the exceptions in either the **Error**, **RunTimeException**, or **Exception** classes. (These are special classes that Java provides for catching compile-time and run-time errors.) Each method you declare does not need to use the **throws** clause in its declaration, but in the event of an error, the omission of this clause will leave the error handling up to the Java compiler or the Java interpreter. Let's look at an example of how the **throws** clause is used.

In the following method declaration, the Java exception named **ArrayOutOfBoundsException** is specified so that in the event an array range error occurs, the method will know how to handle the error:

```
public class Array_check() {
    String arr[5];

    public static void main(void) throws ArrayOutOfBoundsException {
        int i=0;
        char ch;

        // Specify which code should be tested
        try {
            while (i <= 5) ch = arr[i++];
        }
        // An error has occurred—display a message
        catch {
            System.out.println("Array out of bounds");
        }
    }
}
```

At some point **main()** will try to access a location outside the legal range of the array **arr[]**. When this happens, an exception will be "thrown" and the catch clause will handle it. Also notice the use of the **try** clause which is needed to specify which code in the method should be tested. In our case, we want to check each iteration of the **while** loop.

Method Body

All executable code for Java classes is contained in the body of the methods. Unless a method is declared as abstract, native, or is declared in the body of an interface, the code for the method is placed between a pair of curly braces. This code can be any valid Java statements including variable declarations, assignment statements, method calls, control statements, and so on.

Here's an example of how a basic method is defined:

```
public int SimpleMethod(int Number) {

    // The integer variable Number is assigned whatever is passed to
    // it

    int lowrange = 1;  // Local declarations for the method
    int highrange = 10;

    if (Number <= lowrange) return -1;
    if (Number >= highrange) return 100
       else return 50;
}
```

In this case, the method's name is **SimpleMethod**(). Because it is declared as public, it can be used by any class in the package in which the method is defined. The return type for the method is **int** and it accepts one **int** parameter. The method body contains a few local declarations and a set of if-then decision-making statements.

For a method declared as abstract, native, or one that is declared in an interface, the body is left blank and the declaration is terminated with a semicolon. The bodies are then defined elsewhere depending on how they are declared. Here's an example:

```
abstract class Aparticles extends Quark {

    abstract int abstract_method();  // Defined in the subclasses of
                                     // the class
```

```
    native void native_method ();   // Defined in an external process

    public String normal_method() {
       ... // Definition of the method
    }
}
```

Using The this And super Keywords

To access class variables and methods from within an object, you can reference them by using the keywords **this** and **super**. When the Java compiler encounters the **this** keyword in the body of a method, it knows that you are accessing other methods and variables defined within the scope of the class the method is defined in. On the other hand, variables and methods that are available for accessing in the parent class (superclass) to the current class are referenced using the **super** keyword. Here's an example of how each of these keywords can be used:

```
class Atom_ant extends Molecule {
    int Number;
    ...
}

class Quark extends Atom_ant {
    int Proton;
    int Neutron;
    String Electon = "Negative attraction";
    ...
    void Count() {
        System.out.println(this.Proton + " is the number of Protons");
        System.out.println(Neutron + " is the number of Neutrons");
        System.out.println(super.Number + " is the number of Atoms");
        System.out.println(Atom_ant.Number + " is the number of
           Atoms");
        ...
    }
}
```

In this example, this.Proton references the local variable Proton defined in the class Quark. But take a look at the second method call in the Count() method. Here, the variable Neutron, which is also declared in Quark, is referenced without the use of the **this** keyword. What gives? Actually, since both of these variables are defined within Quark, the **this** keyword is not really needed.

As for the two following lines of code, they each reference the **Number** variable declared in the **Atom_ant** class, which serves as the parent to the **Quark** class. Notice that the keyword **super** is placed in front of the variable **Number** to allow it to be accessed. This is the same as using the superclass name in the statement **Atom_ant.Number** to reference the value of **Number**. Superclass names can be referenced further up the hierarchical tree but the **super** keyword can only be used to access class members that reside one level above the current class. If the **Molecule** class contained a variable named **M1**, and we wanted to reference it from the **Quark** class, a statement like this would be required:

```
Proton = Molecule.M1;
```

Here the superclass named **Molecule** is included in the assignment statement. If it was omitted or the **super** keyword was used instead, as in the code line below:

```
Proton = super.M1;
```

the Java compiler would return an error because it would try to locate the **M1** variable in the class that is directly above the **Quark** class.

Overloading And Overriding Methods

A method may be declared with multiple declarations, each specifying different types and arguments that may be passed to the method. *The context in which the method is called will determine which actual method code is used.* The techniques of using a method's name more than once to define an operation in a class involves overloading and overriding methods. As long as you can define each method having the same name so that it can be distinguished from the others sharing the same name, the Java compiler will not give you an error. The technique for creating overridden methods involves using different parameters (types and numbers) and return types. Methods that are inherited from a superclass may be overridden but the overriding method must provide at least the same access.

Let's look at some examples of how we can override methods:

```
class Atom_ant extends Molecule {
    int Number;
    protected void Count(String Astring, int Number) {
```

```
        ...
    }
}

class Quark extends Atom_ant {
    int Proton;
    int Neutron;
    String Electon = "Negative attraction";
    ...
    public void Count(int Number, String Astring) { // Correct
        ...
    }

    protected void Count() {    // Correct
        ...
    }
}
```

Here we've declared two classes: **Atom_ant** and **Quark**. **Atom_ant** serves as the superclass. The method that is overridden is **Count()**. It is first introduced as a protected method in the **Atom_ant** class. Notice that it is declared here as taking two parameters: **Astring** and **Number**. Because **Atom_ant** is declared as a protected method, it is restricted from being called by other classes outside of the package **Atom_ant** is declared in.

The **Quark** class, which is derived from **Atom_ant**, provides two new variations of the **Count()** method, each one being overridden from the base method defined in **Atom_ant**. Notice that each of the overridden methods uses different parameters and/or return types than the original method.

To see how the different versions of the **Count()** method can be called, let's expand the **Quark** class a little:

```
class Atom_ant extends Molecule {
    int Number;
    protected void Count(String Astring, int Number) {
        ...
    }
}

class Quark extends Atom_ant {
    int Proton;
    ...
    public void Count(int Number, String Astring) { // Correct
```

```
   ...
  }

  void check() {
     Atom_ant.Count("Hello", 5);  //Correct refer to superclass
                                  //method
     super.Count("GoodBye", 5);   //Correct same as previous
     Molecule.Count("Hello World"); //Correct as long as it exists
     Count(5, "World");              //Correct same as this.Count
  }
}
```

The first two calls to the **Count**() method result in calling the **Count**() method defined in **Atom_ant**. For the third call, we are making the assumption that the class **Molecule**, which **Atom_ant** is derived from, contains a **Count**() method. If it doesn't, a compiler error will occur. The last call to **Count**() accesses the method of the same name defined in **Quark**.

Constructors—
The Special Methods

Although constructors are identified as special methods, it is important to distinguish between the two. Methods define an object's behavior in terms of what operations the object can perform. A constructor, on the other hand, determines how an object is initialized by creating a new instance of a class with specified parameters.

Methods and constructors actually differ in three ways. First, constructors do not have their own unique names; they must be assigned the same name as their class name. Second, constructors do not have a return type—Java assumes that the return type for a constructor is **void**. And third, constructors are not inherited by subclasses, as are methods.

To understand how constructors work conceptually, let's return to the car analogy we introduced earlier in this chapter. Each car in our hierarchy represents an object and the blueprint for each car is a class structure. Also recall that operations such as opening and closing car doors were considered to be our methods.

Now, imagine that we have a subclass, called *BodyShop*, which defines the body style for a car. This class could be inserted under the general *car* class in the class hierarchy. An object could be created from this class called *FrameCreation*, which is responsible for making body frames for cars. The process of building a frame could involve first calling a constructor to do the dirty work of "setting up the shop" for building a particular car frame. The manner in which the different classes are defined in the hierarchy will determine what frame a particular car gets at the *BodyShop* from the *FrameCreation* team. (The *FrameCreation* team is responsible for initializing an "object" depending on the information passed to a constructor.)

Now let's assume we have three choices for making body frames:

◆ 4 Door(*integer*) Falcon(*String*)

◆ 3 Door(*integer*) Pinto(*String*)

◆ 2 Door(*integer*) Mustang(*String*), which is the default.

We could just say 2, 3, or 4 doors, but the *FrameCreation* team insists on a certain format for each. The Falcon requires (*integer* Doors, *String* Name), the Pinto requires (*String* Name, *integer* Doors), and the Mustang doesn't require any values (). When you pass these values, known as **types** to the *FrameCreation* team, they immediately know which frame to create, or *initialize*, by the arrangement of the information passed to them (data types and number of parameters). By passing the information in a distinct pattern *FrameCreation(Doors, Name)*, *FrameCreation(Name, Doors)*, or *FrameCreation()* to create an object, we are using a *constructor*.

A constructor is a special method that determines how an object is initialized when created. The constructor is named the same as the class it follows. The code for our example could be written like this:

```
class FrameCreation extends BodyShop {
   //  ** Initializing the object newcar **
   FrameCreation newcar = FrameCreation(4 , Falcon);

// ** The Beginning of the Constructor **
   FrameCreation {
   // ** An example of Overloading the Constructor **
     FrameCreation(int, String) {
      // Creates the FALCON
```

```
   }
// ** An example of Overloading the Constructor **
   FrameCreation(String, int) {
 // Creates the Pinto
   }

   FrameCreation() {    // ** An example of Overloading the
 Constructor **
 // Creates the Mustang
   }
// ** The End of the Constructor **
}
```

FrameCreation is the constructor, which is declared multiple times—each taking different parameter configurations. When it is called with a configuration (a number, a word), the constructor with the matching configuration is used.

In calling a constructor, you need to disregard the rules for calling methods. Methods are called directly; constructors are called automatically by Java. When you create a new instance of a class, Java will automatically initialize the object's instance variables, and then call the class's constructors and methods. Defining constructors in a class can do several things, including:

◆ Setting initial values of the instance variables.

◆ Calling methods based on the initial variables.

◆ Calling methods from other objects.

◆ Calculating the initial properties of the object.

◆ Creating an object that has specific properties outlined in the new argument through overloading.

Components Of A Constructor Declaration

The basic format for declaring a constructor is:

```
[ConstructorModifier] ConstructorIdentifier([ParameterList]) [Throws]
  {
    ConstructorBody;
  }
```

As with the other declarations we've introduced in previous sections, only the identifier and body are necessary. Both the modifier and the throws clause are optional. The identifier is the name of the constructor; however, it is important to remember that the name of the constructor must be the same as the class name it initializes. You may have many constructors (of the same name) in a class, as long as each one takes a different set of parameters. (Because the different constructors in a class must have the same name, the type, number, and order of the parameters being passed are used as the distinguishing factors.) For example, all constructors for a class named **Atom_ant**, must be named **Atom_ant**, and each one must have different set of parameters.

In addition to having a unique declaration from that of a method, a special format is used for calling a constructor:

```
Typename([ParameterList]);
```

The only required element is *Typename*, which names the class containing the constructor declaration. Here's an example of a constructor, with the class **Atom_ant** and a constructor that uses the **new** operator to initialize instance variables:

```
class Atom_ant {
   String   superhero;
   int height;

   Atom_ant(String s, int h) {  // Declare a constructor
      superhero = s;
      height = h;
   }

   void printatom_ant() {
      System.out.print("Up and attam, " + superhero);
      System.out.println("!  The world's only " + height +
         " inch Superhero!");
   }

   public static void main(String args[])  {
      Atom_ant a;

      a =  new Atom_ant("Atom Ant" , 1); // Call the constructor
      a.printatom_ant();
```

```
    System.out.println("——");

    a = new Atom_ant("Grape Ape", 5000);
    a.printatom_ant();
    System.out.println("——");
  }
}
```

The output for this program looks like this:

```
Up and attam,  Atom Ant!  The world's only 1 inch Superhero!
——
Up and attam, Grape Ape!  The world's only 5000 inch Superhero!
——
```

Notice that each constructor call is combined with the **new** operator. This operator is responsible for making sure a new instance of a class is created and assigned to the object variable **a**.

USING JAVA'S DEFAULT CONSTRUCTOR

If you decide not to declare a constructor in a class, Java will automatically provide a default constructor that takes no arguments. The default constructor simply calls the superclass constructor **super()** with no arguments and initializes the instance variable. If the superclass does not have a constructor that takes no arguments, you will encounter a compile-time error. You can also set a class's instance variables or call other methods so that an object can be initialized.

Here is an example of a Java class that does not use a constructor but instead allows Java to initialize the class variables:

```
class Atom_ant2 {
  String  superhero;
  int height;
  Boolean villain;
  void printatom_ant() {
    System.out.print("Up and attam, " + superhero);
    System.out.println("!  The world's only " + height +
        " inch Superhero!");
  }

  public static void main(String args[])  {
    Atom_ant2 a;
```

```
        a =  new Atom_ant2();
        a.printatom_ant();
        System.out.println("——") ;
    }
}
```

Because no constructor is defined for this example program, the Java compiler will initialize the class variables by assigning them default values. The variable **superhero** is set to null, **height** is initialized to zero, and **villain** is set to false. The variable **a**, in the **main()** method, could have been initialized at the time the constructor was called by substituting the code **a = new Atom_ant2();** for **Atom_ant2 a = new Atom_ant2();**. Either statement provides an acceptable means of creating an instance of a class—the object **a**. Once this object is in hand, the method **printatom_ant()** can be called.

The output for this program looks like this:

```
Up and attam, The world's only 0 inch Superhero!
——
```

CONSTRUCTOR MODIFIERS

Java provides three modifiers that can be used to define constructors:

◆ **public**

◆ **protected**

◆ **private**

These modifiers have the same restrictions as the modifiers used to declare standard methods. Here is a summary of the guidelines for using modifiers with constructor declarations:

◆ A constructor that is declared without the use of one of the modifiers may only be called by one of the classes defined in the same package as the constructor declaration.

◆ A constructor that is declared as public may be called from any class that has the ability to access the class containing the constructor declaration.

◆   A constructor that is declared as protected may only be called by the subclasses of the class that contains the constructor declaration.

◆   A constructor that is declared as private may only be called from within the class it is declared in.

Let's look at an example of how each of these modifiers can be used:

```
class Atom_ant2 {
    String  superhero;
    int height;
    String  villain;
    int numberofsuperheros;

    Atom_ant2() {
        this("Dudley Do Right", 60);
    }

    public Atom_ant2(String s, int h) {
        superhero = s;
        height = h;
    }

    protected Atom_ant2(int s, int h) {
        numberofsuperheros = s;
        height = h;
    }

    private Atom_ant2(String s, int h, String v) {
        superhero = s;
        height = h;
        villain = v;
        }

    void printatom_ant() {
        System.out.print("Up and attam, " + superhero);
        System.out.println("!  The world's only " + height +
            " inch Superhero!");
    }
    public static void main(String args[]) {
        Atom_ant2 a;

        a =  new Atom_ant2();
        a.printatom_ant();

        a = new Atom_ant2("Grape Ape", 5000);
        a.printatom_ant();
    }
}
```

```
class Molecule_mole extends Atom_ant2 {
    String  superhero;
    int height;

    public static void main(String args[]) {
        Atom_ant2 a;

        a =  new Atom_ant2(); // Compile-time Error
        a.printatom_ant();

        a =  new Atom_ant2("Atom Ant", 1);  // Correct
        a.printatom_ant();

        a =  new Atom_ant2(5, 5); // Correct
        a.printatom_ant();

// Compile-time Error
        a =  new Atom_ant2("Atom Ant", 1 , "Dudley Do Right");
        a.printatom_ant();
    }
}
```

In this example, the **Atom_ant2** class uses constructors with all three of the modifiers: **public**, **protected**, and **private**. In addition, a constructor is declared that does not use a modifier. Notice how the constructors are called from the **Molecule_mole** class. Each constructor type is both defined and called using a different parameter configuration. (This is how the Java compiler knows which constructor to use.)

The first constructor call, **Atom_ant2()**, produces a compiler error because of Java's scoping rules—the declaration of this constructor is outside of the range of the **Molecule_mole** class, and the constructor was not declared as public or protected. Also notice that the call to the fourth constructor produces a compiler error. In this case, the constructor was declared in the **Atom_ant** class as private, which limits the constructor from being called by the class it is declared in.

As this example illustrates, you need to make sure you understand the restrictions that modifiers can place on method declarations. For example, here is an example of a compile-time error you will encounter if you try to access a constructor from another class when its modifier has been declared as private:

```
Compiling...
E:\java\jm\Molecule_mole.java
E:\java\jm\Molecule_mole.java:8: No constructor matching _
   Atom_ant2(java.lang.String, int, java.lang.String) found in class
  Atom_ant2.
               a =  new Atom_ant2("Atom ant",5,"Dudley");
  ^1 error
Compile Ended.
```

Parameter List And Throws Clause

Both the parameter list and throws clause follow the same rules used for declaring and calling methods; after all, a constructor is just a special method. When calling a constructor, different parameter configurations (type of parameters and quantity) can be used as long as you have a matching declaration that uses the same parameter configuration.

Constructor Body

The body of the constructor is essentially the same as the body of a method. The only difference occurs in the first statement. If the constructor is going to call "itself" (an alternate constructor for the same class having the same name) or call the constructor of its superclass, it must do this in the first statement. To access its own class, the **this**() statement is used as a placeholder for the class's identifier. To refer to the class's superclass, the **super**() statement is used. Following each of the clauses are parentheses containing the parameter list to be passed to the constructor, identified by the keyword. Here is an example of how both the **this**() and **super**() statements are used within the constructors defined for **Atom_ant2**:

```
class Atom_ant2 extends Quark {
   String  superhero;
   int height;
   String  villain;
   int numberofsuperheros;

   Atom_ant2() {
   this("Atom Ant", 1);   // Call another Atom_ant2() constructor
   }

   public Atom_ant2(String s, int h) {
      superhero = s;
      height = h;
   }
```

```
Atom_ant2(String s, int h, String v) {
super(s, h);    // Call the superclass's constructor
}

protected Atom_ant2(int s, int h) {
   numberofsuperheros = s;
   height = h;
}

synchronized void printatom_ant() {
   System.out.print("Up and attam, " + superhero);
   System.out.println("!  The world's only " + height +
      " inch Superhero!");
System.out.print("\n—\n");
}

public static void main (String args[ ])  {
   Atom_ant2 a;

   a =  new Atom_ant2();
   a.printatom_ant();
   System.out.println ("——") ;
}
}
```

When the program runs, the call to **Atom_ant2**() results in the first constructor defined in the **Atom_ant2** class being called. Then, the first constructor calls the second constructor defined in the class. This process is illustrated in Figure 7.4.

In the first constructor, **this**() is used so that the constructor can directly call one of **Atom_ant2**'s other constructors. How does the compiler know

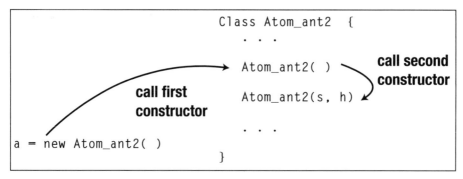

Figure 7.4   **The chain of constructor calls in the Atom_ant2 example.**

which one to use? It looks for a match between the parameters based on **this**("Atom Ant", 1) and one of the other **Atom_ant2**(...) constructors. Since the **this**() statement passes a string and an integer, the actual constructor that is called is the second one defined in the **Atom_ant2** class.

In the third constructor declaration, the **super**() statement performs a similar operation except this time it searches the immediate superclass's constructor for a match. It is important to remember that when using either of these statements, you may not directly call instance variables of the object being created. Furthermore, an instance variable cannot be dependent upon another variable that has not yet been defined, or is defined after it.

Here's an example:

```
class Foo {
    int variableNow = variableLater + 10;
    int variableLater = 20;
}
```

As you can see, **variableNow** is trying to initialize itself before **variableLater** is assigned a value.

Object Creation

There are two ways to create an instance of a class: use a literal, specific to the **String** class or use the **new** operator. The **new** operator is placed in front of the constructor. The parameter list of the constructor determines what constructor is used to create an instance of an object.

```
...
public static void main(String args[])  {
    Atom_ant2 a;

    a =  new Atom_ant2();
    a.printatom_ant() ;
    System.out.println ("——");
}
...
```

Here, the **new** operator initializes **Atom_ant2** with an empty parameter list, initializes the variable to create an instance of the class **Atom_ant2**, and assigns it to **a**.

Variables For Classes

Before moving on, let's refresh your memory with some Java basics: A variable is a named storage location that can hold various values, depending on the data type of the variable. The basic format for declaring a variable is as follows:

```
VariableModifiers Type Indentifier = [VariableInitializer];
```

Only the *Type* and *Identifier* components are necessary. The modifiers are optional.

As with all the identifiers we've used throughout this chapter, the variable identifier simply names the variable. However, you can name any number of variables in the declaration by naming them in the identifier position and separating them with commas. If you decide to declare multiple variables, also realize that the modifiers and *Type* apply to all the variables that are named. For example, in these declarations

```
int paul, david, kelly;
static String henry, diana;
```

the variables **paul**, **david**, and **kelly** are declared as integers, and the variables **henry** and **diana** are declared as static strings.

VARIABLE MODIFIERS

Java provides seven different modifiers for declaring variables within classes. However, you can only use two of them—one from each group—in a declaration. Also, you can't use two modifiers that contradict each other in the same declaration. The two groups of modifiers are:

◆ public, protected, private

◆ static, final, transient, volatile

The **public**, **protected**, and **private** modifiers are discussed under the modifiers sections of class, method, and constructors.

STATIC MODIFIERS

A static variable is also known as a class variable. This is because there is only one variable of that name, no matter how many instances of the class are created. Here's an example of how the **static** modifier can be used:

```
Atom_ant2() {
   static int Doug = 9;
   this("Atom Ant", 1);
}

...
public static void main(String args[])  {
   Atom_ant2 a, b, c, d;

   a =  new Atom_ant2();
   b =  new Atom_ant2();
   c =  new Atom_ant2();
   d =  new Atom_ant2();
   a.printatom_ant() ;
   System.out.println("——") ;
}
...
```

Here, no matter how many objects we create, there is exactly one variable **Doug** for every instance of **Atom_ant()**.

FINAL MODIFIER

When a variable is assigned final, it acts as a constant throughout the instance of the class. They must be declared at time of initialization of the class or method.

TRANSIENT MODIFIER

This is a modifier that has been reserved by Java virtual machine language for low level segments that do not pertain to the persistent state of an object. Other implementations will follow for this modifier in future versions.

VOLATILE MODIFIER

These are modifiers that are processed through the multi-processor in an asynchronous manner. The variables are reloaded from and stored to memory every time the variables are used.

The Art Of Casting With Classes

In previous chapters, we showed you how to use casting techniques to convert the values assigned to variables of predefined data types to other data types. For example, in a set of statements like this

```
int i;
short s;

s = 10;
i = (int) s;
```

the contents of the variable s—originally defined to be of the **short** type—is converted to an **int** type by using a cast in the assignment statement. When casting variable types from one to another, no information will be lost as long as the receiver is larger than the provider. Java also allows you to cast instances of a class, known as objects, to instances of other classes. The declaration for an explicit cast to a class is as follows:

`(Classname)reference`

The *Classname* is the name of the class you wish to cast to the receiving object. The reference specifies the object that is to receive the cast. When applying a narrowing effect to a class, as you will read about later, this type of cast is required by the Java compiler. Figure 7.5 illustrates this concept.

If a superclass attempts to cast an instance of itself to a subclass beneath it, a runtime error will occur even though this type of cast will be accepted by the Java compiler. The technique of passing object references down a class hierarchy is referred to as *widening*. As a class is located at lower levels in a hierarchy it becomes more specific and thus it contains more information than the classes above it. Superclasses, on the other hand, are usually more general than the classes beneath them. Conversions that occur when you pass the references up the hierarchy are thus referred to a narrowing because not all the information is passed along to the receiving object. Furthermore, all instance variables of the same name in the receiving object are set to the class variables that are being cast.

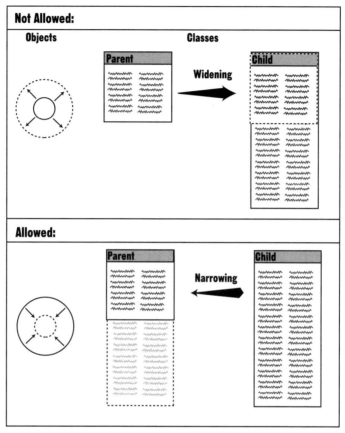

Figure 7.5   Widening and narrowing an instance of a class by using casts.

Casting an object vs. creating an object.

When casting between instances of a class, an object only assumes reference of the class. A new instance of the class is not created; the object merely points to the methods and variables of the casting class. It is important not to confuse the process of casting a object with the process of creating an object. Just as you pass the value of a variable through different types (e.g, int, float, double, and so on), you can pass an object through different classes, as long as the class is in the current hierarchy.

Here is an example of how you can cast references to objects between class types:

```
public class atom_ant {
    String  superhero = "Atom Ant";
    int height = 10;

    atom_ant() {
    }

    void print() {
        System.out.print (superhero + " is " + height + "\n");
    }

    public static void main(String arg[]) {

        atom_ant a1;
        a1 = new atom_ant();
        a1.print();

        proton_pal p1, p2;
        p1 = (proton_pal) a1; // Runtime error due to casting error
        p1.print();  // Unable to execute because of the previous line

        electron_enemy e1;
        e1 = (electron_enemy) p2; // Compile-time error due to casting
                                  // to a sibling class
    e1.print();  // Unable to execute because of the previous line

        atom_ant a2;
        a2 = (atom_ant) p2;
        a2.print();
    }
}

class proton_pal extends atom_ant {

    String  superhero = "Proton Pal";
    int height = 1;

    proton_pal() {
    }

    void print() {
        System.out.print (superhero + " is " + height + "\n");
    }
}
```

```
class electron_enemy extends atom_ant{

    String   superhero = "Electron Enemy";
    int height = -1;

    electron_enemy() {
    }

    void print() {
        System.out.print (superhero + " is " + height + "\n");
    }
}
```

Here we've modified our previous **atom_ant** class to illustrate the basics of casting. Notice that two of the casts used will produce a runtime and compile-time error, respectively. (Thus, don't try to compile the code unless you remove the two illegal casts.) The first cast used in the **main()** method, **p1 = (proton_pal) a1**, produces a *widening* effect. Although this statement will compile, it produces a runtime error because the object **a1** cannot be expected to *grow* to accommodate the new variables and methods it references in **proton_pal**. The second casting statement used is a sibling cast: **e1 = (electron_enemy) p2**. It generates a compile-time error because an illegal reference to a *sibling* class, **electron_enemy** is used. This is due to the fact that the classes can have completely different variables and methods not related to each other. The last form of casting that is addressed in the **atom_ant** class produces a *narrowing* effect. In the statement, (**a2 = (atom_ant) p2**), the object **p2** references variables that are defined in the class, **atom_ant**, that is being cast. The reference is then passed to the variable **a2**.

Interfaces And Packages

David H. Friedel, Jr.

You'll find that Java's flexible interfaces and packages provide a welcome boost to your programming productivity.

*A*fter writing a few applets and applications, you'll probably notice that the directory to which your classes are written will start to become obscenely large. This is the downside of the way Java processes classes; but the good news is that Java provides two key features called *interfaces* and *packages* to help you organize your code. We put these two topics in a chapter by themselves to emphasize how important they are. (Many Java books simply lump interfaces and packages in with classes, or they just skim over them—shameful!) As you start to work more with interfaces and packages, you'll discover a myriad of important program design issues that come into play which you'll need to master to use interfaces and packages effectively.

In this chapter you'll learn about:

◆ The basics of interfaces

◆ Techniques for implementing interfaces

◆ The hierarchical structure related to interfaces themselves

◆ Techniques for using casts with interfaces

◆ The basics of packages

◆ Techniques for creating packages

◆ Techniques for using Java's predefined packages

The underlying goal of this chapter is to help you transition from writing small standalone Java applications and applets to creating classes that can be used over and over. As you start to adopt this style of programming, you'll need the flexibility that interfaces and packages provide.

Understanding Interfaces

An *interface* is a collection of methods and variables that are declared as a unit but they are not implemented until a later stage. Basically this means that the code declarations placed in an interface serve as a shell so that you can create a truly *abstract class*. The goal behind an abstract class is to provide a mechanism so that you can define the *protocols* for a class—how a class should essentially communicate with other classes—early on in the development cycle. The upshot is that when you create your interfaces or abstract classes, you don't have to specify all of the details of how they will be implemented. This is saved for a later stage.

Before we jump in and start writing Java code for declaring interfaces, let's explore a few conceptual examples. The concept of abstract classes and interfaces is tricky to grasp at first. In fact, many experienced object-oriented programmers will tell you that they didn't quite master the concepts until they had written a number of programs. Fortunately, we can help you understand and use the techniques much quicker by providing the background information and conceptual models you'll need to apply them.

The simplest form of an interface involves adding methods and/or variables that are necessary to a particular class, but would disrupt the hierarchy of the class structure you are currently building for an application. If you chose to actually implement these elements in your class, they could limit how you planned to use the class to derive other classes. To make your classes more flexible, you can add interfaces to your classes in your hierarchy early on, so that the interfaces can be used in multiple ways to help construct the "behavior" of other classes that appear elsewhere in your class hierarchy. (If this discussion sounds like we are talking in circles—welcome to the world of interfaces! Hopefully these fine points will start to make sense to you in a moment when we look at a specific example.)

Let's assume that we need to develop an application that processes information about different forms of transportation. Figure 8.1 shows the hierarchy that could be used along with the list of components that could be implemented as interfaces.

As with typical class hierarchies, the classes shown in Figure 8.1 become more specific as they appear further down in the hierarchy tree. The interface components are advantageous when you have operations that are to be performed in one section of the hierarchy and not in the other areas. For example, the class *Car* has two subclasses: *Solar* and *Gas*. Let's assume you need to calculate the liters of gas that a gas car will use. You could include the methods and variables for performing this operation in the *Car*

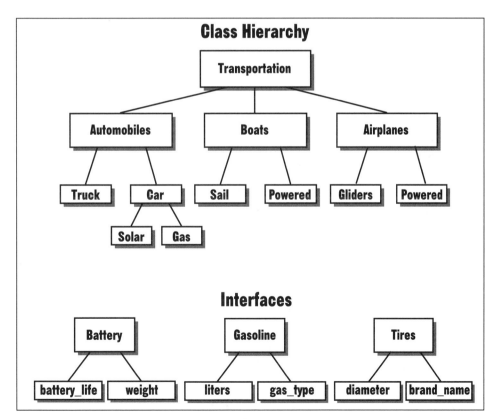

Figure 8.1   The hierarchy of classes for the transportation example.

superclass, or even better, up two levels in the *Transportation* class, so that the *Powered\Boats* and *Powered\Airplanes* classes could use this code also.

Unfortunately, when you consider the scope of the application and all of the subclasses that inherit this useless information, you'd probably agree that this design approach is flawed. After all, the *Solar\Car* class would never calculate the liters of gas used and neither would the *Sail\Boats* or *Gliders\Airplanes* classes. A class that handles the gas calculating operation would be an incredible pain to incorporate at the *Transportation* level so that it could be designed into the hierarchy, and thus forcing all the subclasses to inherit all of its methods. If we were creating a small application that only required a few classes, this approach could be used. But if you are building an application that uses lots of classes from the beginning or you are expecting to expand the application in the future, this approach could quickly become a programmer's nightmare because limitations could arise from placing such restrictions early on.

In applications that have class hierarchies like our transportation example, interfaces become priceless because they allow us to "mix-in" classes into the application, adding them only where they become absolutely necessary. Another feature that enhances the interface's capabilities is the use of multiple implementations of interfaces per class. For example, in our transportation application, theoretically the *Car* class would be interested in the *Gasoline* interface, but the *Tire* interface could also be of use. An abstract class could incorporate both of these interfaces (the methods and variables that define them) at the *Transportation* level, but the *Boat* class would also be forced to inherit them. The *Boat* class never would have any use for the *Tire*'s methods or variables.

Design issues with interfaces.

Interfaces will usually fall into a class hierarchy without any problems when you are creating small scale applications. They also help separate the design process from the implementation process because they keep you from having to combine the more abstract design issues with implementation details in one component. They also allow you to derive classes without relying on the more limited technique of SINGLE INHERITANCE. A single inheritance model requires you to create class hierarchy trees by deriving one class from a single parent or superclass. Each class in the tree is created by using only data and operations that were defined in the levels above the current class.

Interfaces help you build class hierarchies that use more powerful object-oriented techniques like MULTIPLE INHERITANCE. With interfaces, you can define classes that have multiple parents. You can incorporate interfaces into a hierarchical class tree to include new methods and variables without having to worry about disrupting your current implementation tree.

Declaring An Interface

Let's look at the basic declaration for an interface and then we'll show you the syntax for implementing an interface. After that, we'll introduce some code to illustrate how the transportation example we presented in the previous section could be set up. The basic syntax for declaring an interface looks similar to the syntax used for defining a Java class:

```
public interface InterfaceName {
   StaticVariables;
   AbstractMethods;
}
```

In this case, however, the **class** keyword is not used; the keyword **interface** takes its place. The *InterfaceName* serves as the interface identifier name and the rules for specifying this name are the same as those used to name classes. The body of the interface declaration simply consists of the declaration of static variables and the names of one or more methods. Here's an example of an interface declaration:

```
public interface Gasoline {
// This variable is  defined as a constant
   public static final int Feet_in_Miles = 7245;

// A Method that is to be defined in a class
   void gas_type(String Name);
// Another method to be defined later
   void liters(int Amount);
}
```

Note that the variable **Feet_in_Miles** is declared as both static and final. This is required because all variables in interfaces *cannot* be changed. This type of declaration essentially turns the variable into a constant. If you leave out the **static** and **final** keywords, Java will force the variable to be declared as a constant. The two methods listed include both the method name and the method's parameter list. The actual code for the method will come when the interface is implemented.

Implementing An Interface

Declaring an interface is only half of the work. At some point, the interface must be implemented. This is accomplished by using the interface definition (or abstract class) to create a class. In a sense, a class can be "derived" using the interface shell. The syntax for implementing an interface is:

```
modifier class Identifier extends Superclass
implements InterfaceName [, InterfaceList ] {
    ClassBody;
}
```

In implementing an interface, you are essentially defining a special type of class. First, the class *modifier* is needed, followed by the **class** keyword. Then, the name of the class is provided. Next, the **extends** keyword is used followed by a superclass name to indicate that the class being defined is derived from a parent class. The **implements** keyword followed by the name of one or more interfaces, tells the Java compiler which interfaces will be used to implement the class. It is important to keep in mind that a class can implement more than one interface.

The class body consists of all of the variables and method definitions for the class. This is where all of the code must be placed for the methods that are listed in the interface declarations that are used. Using the **Gasoline** interface we declared earlier, here is a class called **Gas** that "implements" the **Gasoline** interface:

```
public class Gas extends Car implements Gasoline {
    int Miles;   // Variable declarations
    ...
    void gas_type(String Name) {
    ... // Add code for this method
```

```
    }
    void liters(int Amount) {
    ... // Add code for this method
    }
}
```

Notice that this class is derived from a superclass named **Car.**

Now that we've covered the basics of declaring and implementing an interface, let's return to the transportation example we presented earlier. The first thing we need to do is declare the interfaces for the ones listed in Figure 8.1—**Gasoline, Battery,** and **Tire:**

```
public interface Gasoline {
// This variable is now a constant
    public static final int Feet_in_Miles = 7245;

// A Method that is to be defined in a calling class
    void gas_type(String Name);
// Another method to be defined later
    void liters(int Amount);
}

public interface Batteries {
// A Method that is to be defined in a calling class
    void battery_life(int Time);
// Another method to be defined later
    void weight(int Amount);
}

public interface Tires {
// A Method that is to be defined in a calling class
    void diameter(int Distance);
// Another method to be defined later
    void brand_name(int Name);
}
```

With these interfaces in hand, we're ready to create the two classes—**Gas** and **Powered**—each one will implement some of the interfaces in different ways. They will also show you how multiple interfaces can be used in a class definition:

```
public class Gas extends Car implements Gasoline, Batteries, Tires {

    int Feet_Traveled;
    int Miles_Traveled = 20;
```

```
        Feet_Traveled = Miles_Traveled * Feet_in_Miles;

        public static gas_type(String Name) {
           ... // Any functions that are to be performed with gas_type
           if(Name.equals("Diesel"))
             System.out.println("Ah, good power");
           if(Name.equals("Unleaded"))
             System.out.println("ok power");
           if(Name.equals("Leaded"))
             System.out.println("eh, clogged injectors");
        }

        public static liters(int Amount) {
           ... // Any functions that are to be performed with liters
        }

        public static battery_life(int Time) {
           ... // Any functions that are to be performed with battery_life
        }

        public static weight(int Amount) {
           ... // Any functions that are to be performed with weight
        }

        public static diameter(int Distance) {
           ... // Any functions that are to be performed with diameter
        }

        public static brand_name(int Name) {
           ... // Any functions that are to be performed with brand_name
        }
    }

    public class Powered extends Boat implements Gasoline, Batteries {

        int Feet_Traveled;
        int Miles_Traveled = 20;

        Feet_Traveled = Miles_Traveled * Feet_in_Miles;

        public static gas_type(String Name) {
           ... // Any functions that are to be performed with gas_type
           if(Name.equals("Diesel"))
             System.out.println("Required");
           if(Name.equals("Unleaded"))
             System.out.println("Not applicable");
           if(Name.equals("Leaded"))
             System.out.println("Not applicable");
        }
```

```
public static liters(int Amount) {
    ... // Any functions that are to be performed with liters
}

public static battery_life(int Time) {
    ... // Any functions that are to be performed with battery_life
}

public static weight(int Amount) {
    ... // Any functions that are to be preformed with weight
}
}
```

Notice that the **Gas** class is extended from the superclass **Car** and implements the interfaces **Gasoline**, **Batteries**, and **Tires**. In the class body of **Gas**, the methods declared for these interfaces are coded as well as other variables that the class needs, such as **Feet_Traveled** and **Miles_Traveled**. The **Boat** class, on the other hand, only implements two interfaces: **Gasoline** and **Batteries**. Notice that the **Boat** class implementation for the **gas_type**() method (declared in the **Gasoline** interface) differs from the version implemented in the **Gas** class.

Tips on using interfaces.

The implements clause lists all of the interfaces that are to be included in the class definition. By referencing the interface, the class implementing it must restate the methods and their definitions in the body of the class. Constructors—the special methods that initialize new objects—may not be included in the interface declaration because interfaces can not instantiate new objects. Interfaces reference an object that is an instance of a class. By doing this they state that the object being referenced includes all the methods in the class that created the object.

The Art Of Casting With Interfaces

A cast can be used to change a reference to an object and not the actual object itself. Moreover, instance variables can be created and initialized to reflect the current reference to an object. This occurs when the names of the variable are the same in two classes—the one casting the object and the object the variable references.

Let's return to our **Gas** class example to see how we can use casts with interfaces. This time around **Gas** will reference the interfaces **Gasoline**, **Tires**, and **Batteries**; and **Gas** will create objects that reference the interfaces in different ways. Some of the references are correct and some of them will produce compile-time errors. We've included line numbers at the start of each line of code so that you can easily refer to the example in the discussion that follows:

```
1 public class Gas extends Car implements Gasoline, Tires, Batteries {
2
3 Gas      aCar   = makeGasCar();
4 Gasoline aGasCar= (Gasoline) makeGasCar();    // Use cast
5 Tires    aTireCar = (Tires) makeGasCar();     // Use cast
6
7 aGasCar.gas_type(Diesel);               // Valid
8 aGasCar.liters(5.8);                    // Valid
9
10                              aTireCar.diameter(6.9);
                                // Valid
11                              aTireCar.gas_type(Unleaded);
                                // Not Valid
12
13                              aCar.gas_type(Diesel);// Valid
14                              aCar.weight(12.7);  // Valid
15                              aCar.diameter(6.9); // Valid
16                              aCar.brand_name(Bridgestone);
                                // Valid
17
18      . . .    // Any functions that you would perform on the Cars
                 // created
19 }
```

Let's break down what is going on here so that you can better understand some of the important and subtle Java programming techniques that are being used. Our example is only missing one thing that is not shown in the code—a method named **makeGasCar()** that creates and returns an object. Line 3 shows that an object is returned from the **makeGasCar()** method and is named **aCar** of type **Gas**. By assigning the returned value of **makeGasCar()** to an object variable of the type **Gas**, the object inherits all the methods pertaining to the **Gas** class. This means it acquires all the methods relating to the class, its superclass, and *the interfaces the class implements*. In line 4, we acquire an object from the **makeGasCar()** method, but this time we cast it as type **Gasoline** from the interface **Gasoline**. This means that the object, **aGasCar**, inherits all the methods that relate to the **Gas** class, its superclass, and *only the methods and variables declared in the interface Gasoline*. As we'll see in a second, this means no methods or variables from the other interfaces are available for the object to reference. The next line does the same as the previous line, but the **Tires** interface is used in place of **Gasoline**.

Lines 7 and 8 both have the object **aGasCar** call the methods **gas_type**() and **liters**(), which were originally declared in the **Gasoline** interface. These method calls are valid because the correct parameters are used and the object **aGasCar** has access to both of these methods because of the cast that was used. In line 10, the **aTireCar** object references the **diameter**() method which is also valid because this object was created using the (**Tires**) cast and the **diameter**() method is declared within the **Tires** interface. But in line 11, the **aTireCar** object tries to call a method that is declared in the **Gasoline** interface. This produces a compile-time error because the object does not implement the interface **Gasoline**. Only the methods declared in the **Tires** interface are available from the object.

In the last section of the **Gas** class, lines 13 through 16, the object **aCar** may call any of the methods available to the interfaces because this object is an instance of the class **Gas** and is not cast to any particular class. This shows you the versatility possible in creating objects using interfaces.

Tips On Implementing Interfaces

You'll notice that most applets that utilize the thread feature implement an interface named **Runnable** for the explicit function of moving (actually redrawing) text across the screen. When the applet is loaded into a browser, the browser checks to see if the object **ttapeThread**, which is an instance of the class **Thread** from a package that is imported into our class **TickerTape**, implements the **Runnable** interface. In this case, the browser detects the interface and uses the **run**() method declared in the class **Thread** during the operation of the applet:

```
// TickerTape Class
public class TickerTape extends Applet implements Runnable{
```

```
...
// Change coordinates and repaint
public void run(){
    while(ttapeThread != null){
        try {Thread.sleep(50);} catch (InterruptedException e){}
        setcoord();
        repaint();
    }
}
...
}
```

This is a powerful feature for creating methods and variables in classes that can be set up with interfaces for future use, as long as the interface explains how information will be transferred to and from it. You don't need to allow others access to your original classes.

Using the INSTANCEOF operator.

To detect if an object implements an interface, you can use the INSTANCEOF operator. This operator allows you to look at a group of objects to pick out which ones can perform certain operations. Here's an example:

```
if (ttapeThread iinstanceof Runnable) {
((Runnable)ttapeThread).run(); // performs this function only
                               // if the object ttape implements
                               // the Runnable interface
}
```

In this case the IF statement checks to see if the object TTAPETHREAD is an instance of the RUNNABLE interface. If it is, the RUN() method defined in the RUNNABLE interface is called.

Creating And Using Packages

As you begin to design and code Java applications and applets that use multiple classes and interfaces, you'll need a way to organize your code so that you can easily update and reuse your growing library of classes and interfaces. Because the Java language is specifically designed to allow you to use classes and interfaces over and over, it's likely that you'll end up getting some of your class and interface names mixed up.

Furthermore, another programmer may design an excellent class that performs operations that you may want to use. Incorporating this class into one of your applications that already uses a number of classes could become difficult, especially if the class name conflicts with the name of a class you are already using. For example, you may have a custom print class named *Print* that performs certain functions for printing to the screen. After you've developed the class, another programmer might provide you with a class having the same name that prints a certain format to a printer that you need to support. You could actually use both of these classes even if they shared the name "Print"; however, they must be packaged in different groups so that the Java compiler can easily determine which one you want to use.

To help us combine classes into unique groups, Java supports the concept of *packages*. A package is essentially a device for grouping classes that you want to be labeled as a unit. You can actually combine any classes that you want into a single group. Usually, classes that share a common goal are combined in a class. For example, if you were creating a set of classes to handle drawing-related functions for a design application, you might create a package called *Draw* and place all of the related classes in this package.

One of the packages used for almost every applet that is created is the **Applet** package—a package that Java provides, which contains all the necessary classes for creating an applet. A package is introduced to a class by using the **import** keyword in the beginning of a source code file. This will be covered in more detail later in the chapter. As you will see, classes and packages are segregated according to the functions they perform. This reduces the risk of having methods that share the same name interfere with each other. Here is a simple example of how you can implement methods that belong to different packages into a common class:

```
// TickerTape Applet

import java.applet.*;
import java.awt.*;
```

```
// TickerTape Class
public class TickerTape extends Applet implements Runnable {
   ...
   public void init(){
      ...
   }
   public void start(){
      ...
   }
   public void run(){
...
   }
   public void graphics() {
...
   }
   public void stop(){
      ...
   }
   ...
} // End TickerTape
```

All of the methods declared in this example come from somewhere other than the current class. They have been *overridden* to perform a certain function specific to the operation of this applet. For example, the methods **init**(), **start**(), and **stop**() are defined in the **Applet** class that is contained in the java.applet package. The **run**() method is defined in the **Runnable** interface contained in the package java.lang.

Naming And Referencing Packages

Besides the fact that you may want to repeat a simple class name over and over, you'll want to create packages so that you can distribute your classes to other Java programmers. As with files on your computer, you list the directories in which they are contained to reference them. This creates a "path" for the Java compiler to follow so that it can locate designated classes and interfaces in your packages. Figure 8.2 shows an example of the directory hierarchy used to reference the package java.awt.image.

By convention, the first level of the hierarchy has been reserved for the name of the company that develops it. An example of this is

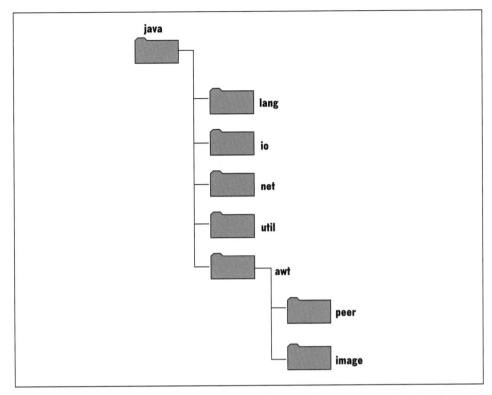

Figure 8.2   Graphical image of the hierarchy of java.awt.image and a call to the (import) java.awt.image on the other side.

sun.audio.AudioData—a package developed by Sun Microsystems. (Of course, as with every programming language, Java provides certain exceptions—one being the guideline for naming and referencing packages. For example, **java**.io.File was developed by Sun Microsystems, but this package is intended to be implemented by other companies as a foundation for building additional I/O packages.) The sections listed beneath the company name reference subdirectories that further specify where the class is located. For example java.**io**.File is a subdirectory that contains classes that relate to the input/output functions of Java. The extension **.class** has been omitted from the reference to the **File** class because interfaces and classes are the only format contained in a package and both end in the **.class** extension.

Uppercase vs. lowercase package names.

A specific format should be followed for naming packages and the classes that are contained within them. All package names and the directories that follow them should be specified using lowercase letters. On the other hand, the class and interface names you wish to reference within a package should be specified using an uppercase letter as the first character. This allows other programmers who use your packages to easily determine which components are directory names and which ones are class and interface names.

Declaration For Creating Packages

To create a package, the following statement should be placed at the beginning of a source file that contains a set of class definitions:

```
package PackageName;
```

Each class defined in the source file will automatically be added to the package having the name specified by *PackageName*. The *PackageName* will be created under the subdirectory you have defined in the CLASSPATH variable set in your environment. (The instructions for setting this environment variable are presented in the sidebar, *Setting Your CLASSPATH Environment Variable*.) As an example, assume that you have a source file that contains a set of classes that implement different types of airplanes. These classes could be combined into a single package named **airplanes** by placing the package statement at the beginning of each source file that defines a public class:

```
package airplanes;  // This statement must come first

// Provide source code for Glider class

public class Glider {
    ...    // Class definition
}
// The end of this source file

package airplanes;  // This statement must come first

// Provide source code for Single_engine class
```

```
public class Single_engine {
    ...    // Class definition
}
// The end of this source file


package airplanes;  // This statement must come first

// Provide source code for Twin_engine class

public class Twin_engine {
    ...    // Class definition
}
// The end of this source file
```

The actual *PackageName* is extended by the Java compiler by preceding it with the *CLASSPATH*. (Each subdirectory included in the path name is separated by a period.) The nice part is that you don't need to create the path for the package you define yourself; it is generated by the compiler at compile-time automatically.

Interfaces and public classes.

Only one public class can be declared in any one source file. Only classes defined as public may be referenced from outside the current package. Otherwise, the classes not defined as public are used to support the public classes in the package.

In another example, if the package CORIOLIS.BOOKS.PROGRAMMING.JAVA is declared, the directory structure will turn out like this:

```
c:\java\lib\coriolis\books\programming\java
```

Essentially, what the Java compiler does when it encounters a statement like PACKAGE CORIOLIS.BOOKS.PROGRAMMING.JAVA is create a new directory structure for CORIOLIS.-BOOKS.PROGRAMMING.JAVA using the directory path specified by the CLASSPATH environment variable. It then places all of the compiled class code defined in the source file in the JAVA directory. As the example above illustrates, the CLASSPATH would be:

```
c:\java\lib;
```

When the package is later referenced by a Java application, the compiler will know exactly where to look for each class that is referenced in the package.

Saving Java source code files.

It is wise to save your Java source code in the directories containing your compiled class. This will allow you to later edit your source code if you wish, but more importantly, you won't have to worry about your class definitions being overwritten with identical names in the default directory where you create and save your source code (.java extension). You'll want to save the different versions of your source files because as you create more and more classes, the chance for repeating a class name becomes more common. For example, assume you have a SPREADSHEET class that contains two classes; one that prints a graph and the other that prints a data sheet. Both classes perform very different operations, but both of them could be assigned the name PRINT.CLASS. In doing so, you must take two steps in generating source code with identical class names because the classes will share the same working directory in most instances. If you placed a statement like this in the beginning of your source code:

```
package acme.spreadsheet.graph;
```

The Java compiler would automatically place the PRINT.CLASS in the directory graph but the original source file (Print.java) would still be paced in the working directory. The next step would be to place the source file in the same directory. This is because the next Print.java source file created (for example, the class responsible for printing the data sheet) will be saved in the working directory, causing the old file to be overwritten. If you later need to modify the class file, you will still have the original source code. At the beginning, the next source file should provide the statement :

```
package acme.spreadsheet.datasheet;
```

Remember, you are required to manually move the source file to the appropriate directory.

Using Packages

The one feature that makes the Java language very powerful is that it lets you use the same code (classes) over and over countless times. This is accomplished by referencing classes that are contained in packages. To use classes that have already been created by you or other Java programmers, you need to reference the package(s) the classes are grouped in. You can do this in one of three ways:

◆ Specify the full package reference each time a class is used that is defined in an outside package. This approach is the most cumbersome and least often used. Here's an example:

```
airplanes.Twin_engine twin = new airplanes.Twin_engine("Beach", 1100);
```

In this case, the object variable **twin** is declared and initialized as an instance of a **Twin_engine** class which is included in the **airplanes** package. With this approach, each time a *Twin_engine* class is accessed, its corresponding package name must also be included.

◆ Import the actual class needed from the package it is defined in. As an example, we could rewrite the previous example by using this code:

```
import airplanes.Twin_engine;
...
Twin_engine twin = new Twin_engine("Beach", 1100);
```

Notice that once the desired class is imported, the name of the **airplanes** package is not needed to reference the **Twin_engine** class.

◆ Import all of the classes defined in a package. The syntax for doing this is illustrated with this statement:

```
import airplanes.*;
```

In this case, all of the public classes combined in the airplanes class, such as **Glider**, **Single_engine**, and **Twin_engine**, would be included.

Importing packages is like including C/C++ header files.

If you are an experienced C / C++ programmer, you can think of the technique of importing a package as you would the technique of using an include file. Typically, you would use an include file to specify the names of function prototypes you wish to call that are defined in external files.

Every class defined in an external package that you want to reference by a class in your Java application or applet must be called directly or with a wild card (*) in the immediate directory. For example, if you look at an example of a ticker tape applet, we called an instance of the class FONTMETRICS that is contained in the java.awt package (directory). The APPLET class imports the java.awt package with a wild card in the beginning of the code (e.g., IMPORT JAVA.AWT.*;). The wild card tells the Java compiler to import ALL of the public classes in the java.awt directory into the TICKERTAPE class. The compiler won't, however, import any of the classes that are contained in the peer or image directories beneath java.awt. To include the classes in those directories, you must reference the directories directly (e.g., IMPORT JAVA.AWT.PEER.*; or IMPORT JAVA.AWT.IMAGE.*;).

```
// TickerTape Applet

import java.applet.*;
import java.awt.*;

// TickerTape Class
public class TickerTape extends Applet implements Runnable {

    // Draw background and text on buffer image
    public void paintText(Graphics g){
        ...
        FontMetrics fmetrics = g.getFontMetrics();
        ...
    }
}
```

Declaration For Importing Packages

When importing a package into a class, the declaration must appear before any class declarations. The format for declaring a package is as follows:

```
import PackageName;
```

The *PackageName* represents the hierarchy tree separating the directories of the package with decimals. The java.lang package is automatically imported into every class that is created. If you look at an example ticker tape applet, you will notice that it does not import the java.lang package but uses many of the classes that are contained in the package. The classes **String**, **Integer**, and **Thread** are just a few of the classes that are called from this package.

```
// TickerTape Class
public class TickerTape extends Applet implements Runnable {
    // Declare Variable
    String inputText;
    String animSpeedString;
```

```
    int xpos;
    int fontLength;
    int fontHeight;
    int animSpeed;
    boolean suspended = false;
      . . .
}
```

Standard Java Packages

Since we created our first applet, we have been using packages already defined by other developers including Sun Microsystems. These packages have been arranged by their category of usage. Table 8.1 shows the packages currently being distributed with the JDK.

Hiding Classes Using The Wild Card

We mentioned before that the Java wild card (*) will only allow you to bring in the public classes from an imported package. The benefit of this feature is that you can hide the bulk of your classes that perform support operations for your public classes. Users who use the public classes won't be able to look at the code or directly access the internal support classes.

Table 8.1   JDK packages included with J++.

Package	Description
java.lang	Contains essential Java classes for performing basic functions. This package is automatically imported into every class that is created in Java.
java.io	Contains classes used to perform input/output functions to different sources.
java.util	Contains utility classes for items such as tables and vectors.
java.net	Contains classes that aid in connecting over networks. These classes can be used in conjunction with java.io to read/write information to files over a network.
java.awt	Contains classes that let you write platform-independent graphics applications. It includes classes for creating buttons, panels, text boxes, and so on.
java.applet	Contains classes that let you create Java applets that will run within Java-enabled browsers.

Java Exceptions 9

David H. Freidel, Jr.

Are you tired of writing applications that mysteriously crash, leaving the user to give up in frustration? If so, you'll be glad to learn that Java provides a powerful feature called *exceptions* that automates the work of catching and handling compile-time and runtime errors.

One of the most difficult and time-consuming tasks of developing software involves finding and fixing bugs. Fortunately, Java provides some built-in features that lend a hand in the debugging process. As errors occur in a Java program, and we all know they will, you can use Java exceptions to provide special code for handling them.

Java programs can detect certain errors on their own and instruct the Java run-time system to take some predefined action. If you don't like the default operations that Java performs when it encounters certain errors, you can write your own custom error handling routines.

In this chapter we'll start by explaining the basics of exceptions. Then, we'll show you

◆ Why exceptions are important

◆ How to use **try** clauses to setup exceptions

◆ How to use **catch** clauses to trap exceptions

◆ When and how to use your own exceptions

Understanding Exceptions

Exceptions catch your errors and handle them gracefully so that your programs can continue to operate. In Java, this process is called *throwing an error.* This type of error handling can greatly benefit both you and the user of your application. After all, nobody likes an application that just crashes out of the blue. Unlike other languages, such as C, C++, and Pascal, where error detection and reporting can often double and even triple the size of an application, Java provides the means to detect and handle errors and at the same time reduce the overall size of your applications. The best part is that error handling in Java replaces the multiple "**if** this occurs **then** do this" statements so often found in programs written in languages like C.

Java's exceptions allow you to effectively code the main sections of your applications without you having to spend too much time writing code to detect and handle potential errors. As you'll learn in this chapter, exceptions create an object when an error occurs. The exception, which is a subclass of the *Throwable* class, *throws* an object, which is passed up through the hierarchy of the calling classes. The object will continue up through the classes until an *exception handler*—a method that deals with the exception— *catches* the object. This process is illustrated in Figure 9.1. If no exception handler is defined, a default exception handler is used to handle the error. This causes the error to be printed to the command line and the program will cease running.

Using Java's Throwable class.

For a class to throw an error or catch one, it must be declared as a subclass of the Java Throwable class. All of the classes in the java package have incorporated the Throwable class in the package. This is why you don't see the Throwable class imported at the beginning of Java source code files. Although if you wish to refer to this class, you can directly import it into an application by including the statement:

```
import java.lang.Throwable;
```

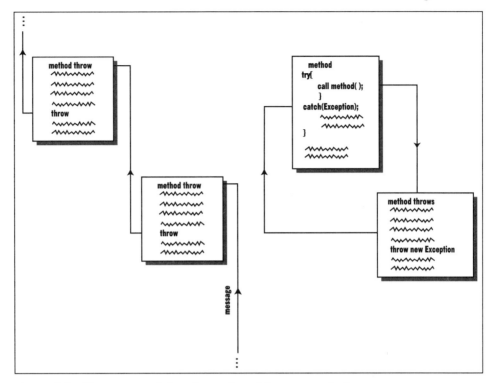

Figure 9.1   The process of throwing and catching an error in Java.

Having error checking and error handling features in Java is important because Java programs, especially applets, run in multitasking environments. Often when an applet is executed in a Web browser like Netscape 2, other applets will be running at the same time. Each applet will have its own *thread* that the system will control. If one applet causes a fatal error, the system could crash. With exceptions, on the other hand, critical errors are caught; and the Java runtime environment will know how to handle each thread that it must manage.

Do You Really Need Exceptions?

Even the smallest program can quickly evolve into a programmer's nightmare when you are trying to locate and fix a troublesome error. Why should you waste your time handling the possible errors that can occur? The fact is, you should only handle errors that you can do something useful with. Grabbing every little error in a program is useless if you do nothing intelligent with them. The best reason to declare exceptions is to provide a means for you and others that follow to understand where your code is having problems during critical operations.

For example, assume you have created a class to write data to a disk file. As your program is running, a number of errors could occur such as your hard disk being full, a file being corrupted, and so on. If you didn't have a way to catch errors like these at some point, the program might crash, leaving the user with nothing except a cryptic error message. Here's a Java program that performs a critical file operation but doesn't provide any error handling:

```
// This program will not compile because an IOException handler is
// expected by the Java compiler
import java.io.*;

public class WriteAFile extends Object {

    WriteAFile(String s) {
        write(s);
    }

    // Writes to a file
    public void write(String s) {          // I/O errors could occur here
        FileOutputStream writeOut = null;
        DataOutputStream dataWrite = null;

        // Begin to Write file out
        writeOut = new FileOutputStream(s);
        dataWrite = new DataOutputStream(writeOut);
        dataWrite.writeChars("This is a Test");
        dataWrite.close();
    }

    // Where execution begins in a stand-alone executable
    public static void main(String args[]) {
        new WriteAFile(args[0]);
    }
}
```

(Actually, this program won't compile just yet because the Java compiler expects to find an exception named *IOException*. We'll explain this in a moment.) The part of the code that could get you into trouble is the **write()** method. This method creates a new file output stream and attempts to write a character string to the stream. If the operation fails for one reason or another, a runtime error would occur, although an exception has not been setup to handle such an error.

To catch potential I/O problems, Java provides a built-in exception called *IOException*. This exception gets "thrown" whenever an I/O error occurs during a transfer to a device, such as a printer, disk drive, and so on. In our sample program, the Java compiler knows you must declare the exception because the **write()** method calls other methods that have declared an *IOException* to be *thrown* to calling methods. To remedy this, we could alter the **write()** method as shown here:

```
// Begin to Write file out
try {
  writeOut = new FileOutputStream(s);
  dataWrite = new DataOutputStream(writeOut);
  dataWrite.writeChars("This is a Test");
  dataWrite.close();
}
  catch(IOException e) {
}
```

Notice that two changes have been made. First, the entire block of code has been placed in a **try** { } clause. Essentially, this tells the Java environment to be on the "lookout" for errors that might occur as each method call is executed. The second change is the addition of the **catch()** method. This block of code performs the job of handling an I/O error that could occur with any of the calls contained in the **try** section. In our example, we are letting Java handle the work of processing an I/O error on its own by using the built-in *IOException,* and that's why no other code is provided with the **catch** statement.

These changes allow the code to compile and run. Unfortunately, they do not address any problems that could arise from actually writing a file to disk. In a perfect world, this code would be sufficient for our needs, but we don't live in a perfect world. For example, what if an error occurred while we were opening the file to be written because the disk is full or not even present? And even if the file could be opened, what would happen if an error occurred while we were writing the data to the file. All of these conditions are valid *exceptions* to writing a file to a disk. Unfortunately, you or others who use your classes might not detect them until it is too late. Remember, the advantage of using a language like Java or other flexible object-oriented languages is the ability to create robust code that can be reused by others.

Now, let's change the **WriteAFile** class once more to make it more robust. Don't worry about the syntax right now, we will discuss the details of implementing exceptions in the sections to follow.

```
// Writes to a file
public void write(String s) {
    FileOutputStream writeOut = null;
    DataOutputStream dataWrite = null;

    try {
        writeOut = new FileOutputStream(s);
        dataWrite = new DataOutputStream(writeOut);
    }
    catch (Throwable e) {
        System.out.println("Error in opening file");
        return;
    }
    try {
        dataWrite.writeChars("This is a Test");
        dataWrite.close();
    }
     catch(IOException e)  {
        System.out.println("Error in writing to file");
     }
}
```

This time around, we've included two **try** clauses. The first one checks the methods used to open the file, and the second one tests the methods used to write to the file and close the file. Notice how each of the **catch** statements specifies the type of object that it will *catch* or the exception that is thrown. We'll show you how to create custom error-handling routines later when we discuss the topic of *catching*. For now it is important to realize that we have separated the possible errors we want to *catch* into two separate cases, opening and writing. By catching these errors, we have prevented the program from crashing as a result of not being able to open or write to a file. If errors like these are found, we could possibly ask the user to change disks or try again instead of having the user loose his or her data. In our case, we have simply written a message to the command-line telling the user where the operation has failed if an error occurs.

Defining A try Clause

The **try** statement is responsible for indicating which section of code in a Java applet or application will most likely throw an exception. The syntax for using this statement is as follows:

```
try {
  statement;
  statement;
}
catch (Throwable-subclass e) {
  statement;
  statement;
}
```

For every **try** section, you must include at least one **catch** block that follows the **try** section. If an exception is thrown in the **try** section during the execution of the code, control flow is transferred to the matching section defined in the **catch** statement. If no match is found, the exception is passed up through the hierarchy of method calls. This allows each level to either handle the exception or pass it on. We'll cover this more when we present exception *throws*.

Using The catch Statement

If an exception is thrown during the execution of a **try** section, the flow of the program is immediately transferred to the corresponding **catch** block. The object, which is a reference to an instance of the exception class being thrown, is compared to the **catch**'s parameter type, also known as an *Exception Handler*. Here is the declaration for the **catch** block:

```
catch (ExceptionType ExceptionObject) {
  statement;
  statement;
}
```

The *ExceptionObject* reference parameter is a subclasses of the *Throwable class*. In most code, this reference is declared as **e** to distinguish it as a reference to an exception. In the event of an error, a subclass of the *Throwable* class is thrown, which is triggered by a violation of one of the procedures. This violation creates an object of the class type that the error originated from and is compared to the *Exception Handler* listed in each of the **catch** blocks that immediately follow the **try** section. The following code example illustrates how this process works:

```
import java.io.*;

// Reads from a file
public class  ReadAFile extends Object {

    ReadAFile(String s) {
        String line;
        FileInputStream fileName  = null;
        BufferedInputStream bufferedInput = null;
        DataInputStream dataIn = null;

        try {
            fileName = new FileInputStream(s);
            bufferedInput = new BufferedInputStream(fileName);
            dataIn = new DataInputStream(bufferedInput);
        }

        catch(FileNotFoundException e) {
            System.out.println("File Not Found");
            return;
        }
        catch(Throwable e) {
            System.out.println("Error in opening file");
            return;
        }

        try {
            while ((line = dataIn.readLine()) != null) {
                System.out.println(line + "\n");
            }
            fileName.close();
        }
        catch(IOException e) {
            System.out.println("Error in reading file");
        }
    }
```

```
    // Where execution begins in a stand-alone executable
    public static void main(String args[]) {
        new ReadAFile(args[0]);
    }
}
```

Here, the **try** block instructs the code to watch for an exception to be
thrown from one of the methods contained in the block. The initializer
that creates an instance of the class type **FileInputStream** named **fileName**
is capable of throwing an exception in the event of an error. More specifically,
the method contained in the class **FileInputStream** declares that an exception
is to be thrown to the calling method. The topic of *throwing* exceptions
will be covered later in the chapter, but for now you just need to know that
you are required to address all exceptions thrown by handling them or
passing them on. You *handle* the exception being thrown by placing *exception
handlers*, declared in **catch** statements that the errors are then compared to.
In the event of an error, the code will break from the normal flow of the
code and immediately jump to the first *exception handler* that matches the
class type defined in the **catch**. In the **ReadAFile()** method, the first **catch**
identifies the **FileNotFoundException** class as a type that may be thrown
upon instance of an error. This is followed by another **catch** identifying the
Throwable class, which will act as a "catch all" for the exceptions being
thrown. This match occurs because all exception classes are derived from
the **Throwable** parent class.

When To Use The finally Statement

When an exception is "thrown," the compiler does not necessarily return
to the exact spot it left off. The developers of Java realized that some
procedures need to perform additional routines after an exception is handled,
so they defined a **finally** statement. This statement instructs the Java Virtual
Machine to return and finish any code after handling the exception before
moving on. Here is the syntax required for using the **finally** statement:

```
try {
  statement;
  statement;
  }
  catch (Exception Handler) {
  statement;
```

```
   statement;
 }
 finally {
  statement;
  statement;
 }
```

The **finally** statement is not necessary to handle an exception, but it can be useful when you wish to handle an operation specific to a class. To see how it is used, let's expand our **WriteAFile** class to incorporate a **finally** statement that will create a backup file whether or not an exception occurs:

```
import java.io.*;

public class WriteAFile {

WriteAFile(String s) {
   write(s);
}

// Writes to a file
public void write(String s) {
   FileOutputStream writeOut = null;
   DataOutputStream dataWrite = null;

   try {
      writeOut = new FileOutputStream(s);
      dataWrite = new DataOutputStream(writeOut);
      dataWrite.writeChars("This is a Test");
      dataWrite.close();
   }
   catch(IOException e)  {
      System.out.println("Error in writing to file");
    }
   catch(Throwable e)  {
      System.out.println("Error in writing to file");
    }
   finally {
      System.out.println("\n\n.....creating a backup file.");
      try {
         writeOut = new FileOutputStream("MyBackup.sav");
         dataWrite = new DataOutputStream(writeOut);
         dataWrite.writeChars("This is a Test");
         dataWrite.close();
      }
```

```
        catch (IOException e) {
            System.out.println("Error in writing backup file");
        }
    }
}
    // Where execution begins in a stand-alone executable
    public static void main(String args[]) {
        new WriteAFile(args[0]);
    }
}
```

The Hierarchy Of Exceptions

Like any other built-in Java classes you use in your applications, the standard exceptions are designed around a class hierarchy. Every exception is derived from the superclass **Throwable** as shown in Figure 9.2. The first subdivision is where the class splits into two categories: *Errors* and *Exceptions*. The *Exceptions* category consists of the more common exceptions that you will want to "catch." The *Errors* category, on the other hand, consists of the low level exceptions that most programmers won't need to deal with.

The next major split occurs with the *Run-Time Exception* category, which is a subclass of *Exception*. Sun has arranged the hierarchy like this because they realized that by separating commonly used exceptions from specific exceptions, programmers would not be forced to include tons of handlers in their code.

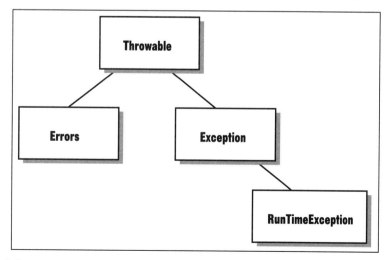

Figure 9.2   The hierarchy of the Throwable class.

ERROR CLASS

The exceptions included in the **Error** class are problems such as Linkage Error, ThreadDeaths, and other catastrophes that result in fatal errors. For the most part, these exceptions will not be handled by most applications. They are reserved for lower level programming tasks that require you to get into the internal workings of the language. For that reason, it is not a good idea to derive your own exception classes from **Error** unless you have a good working knowledge of Java. Table 9.1 provides a list of the key exceptions that are provided. All of the exceptions are defined in the Java Language Package java.lang, expect for **AWTError**, which is defined in the Advanced Windowing Toolkit Package, java.awt.

Table 9.1   Exceptions included in the Error class.

Exception	Description
AbstractMethodError	This exception is thrown when your code attempts to call an abstract method.
AWTError	This exception is thrown when an error occurs in the Advanced Windowing Toolkit.
ClassCircularityError	This exception is thrown when a class hierarchy tries to establish a circle by linking itself to a parent class and the parent links itself to the child class or one of the children classes beneath it.
ClassFormatError	This exception is thrown as a result of an invalid file format being implemented.
IllegalAccessError	This exception occurs when an illegal access has been triggered.
IncompatibleClassChangeError	This exception is thrown when a class of incompatible types is changed.
InstantiationError	This exception occurs when a program attempts to instaniate an object from an abstract class or interface.
InternalError	This exception is thrown when an internal error occurs in the Java Virtual Machine.

Continued

Table 9.1   Exceptions included in the Error class (Continued).

Exception	Description
LinkageError	This exception is thrown when the current class is dependant on anotherclass, but the other class is not compatible with the current class.
NoClassDefFoundError	This exception is thrown when a class cannot be found by checking the path specified by the CLASSPATH environment variable or the current directory.
NoSuchFieldError	This exception is thrown when a specific field cannot be found.
NoSuchMethodError	This exception is thrown when a particular method cannot be found in the current class or one of its superclasses.
OutOfMemoryError	This exception is thrown in the event that no more memory can be allocated.
StackOverflowError	This exception signals that the stack has overflowed.
ThreadDeath	This exception is thrown in the thread that is being terminated. It should be handled when additional procedures are needed to be carried out before the stop() method has finished executing. If the exception is caught, it must be "rethrown" to actually finish killing off the thread. Because the exception is not required to be caught, it will not produce a command line message when it cycles up to the base class.
UnknownError	Bearing a close relation to mystery meat, this exception is triggered when a seriously unknown error occurs.
UnsatisfiedLinkError	This exception is thrown when a link to a library is unsuccessful.
VerifyError	This exception is thrown when the Java compiler is unable to verify if a linkage between classes is valid.
VirtualMachineError	This exception is thrown when the Virtual Machine has depleted its resources.

EXCEPTION CLASS

The exceptions included in the **Exception** class represent the most common errors that a programmer will want to deal with. For the most part, these exceptions can effectively be handled in the average program, to address problems between the user and the program. This class makes an obvious choice to derive your own personal classes from. Table 9.2 provides a list of the key exceptions that are provided in the **Exception** class.

Table 9.2   Exceptions included in the Exception class.

DEFINED IN THE LANGUAGE PACKAGE (JAVA.LANG)

Exception	Description
ClassNotFoundException	This exception is thrown when the compiler is unable to locate a class in the current directory or the directory path specified by the environment variable CLASSPATH.
CloneNotSupportedException	This exception is thrown when an object attempts to clone an object that does not want to be cloned.
IllegalAccessException	This exception is thrown when a method is called from a class that does not have permission to do so. The access is determined by the modifiers used for the class and methods, resulting in the compiler being able to see or not see the calling method.
IllegalMonitorStateException	This exception is thrown in the event that a monitor is accessed that you do not own.
InstantiationException	This exception is thrown because of an attempt to create an instance of an abstract class or interface.
InterruptedException	This exception is thrown when a thread has interrupted the currently runningthread.
NoSuchMethodException	This exception is thrown when a method can't be found in the calling class.

Continued

Table 9.2   Exceptions included in the Exception class (Continued).

DEFINED IN THE UTILITY PACKAGE (JAVA.UTIL)

Exception	Description
EmptyStackException	This exception is thrown in the event of an empty stack.
NoSuchElementException	This exception is thrown in the event that an enumeration is empty.

DEFINED IN THE INPUT/OUTPUT PACKAGE (JAVA.IO)

Exception	Description
EOFException	This exception is thrown when an EOF is reached unexpectedly during input.
FileNotFoundException	This exception is thrown when a file is not found.
IOException	This exception is thrown in the event of an I/O error.
InterruptedIOException	This exception is thrown when an I/O operation has been interrupted.
UTFDataFormatException	This exception is thrown when a malformed UTF-8 string has been read in a DataInput stream.
MalformedURLException	This exception is thrown in the event of a bad URL.
ProtocolException	This exception is thrown when connect receives an EPROTO. This exception is specifically caught in the Socket class.
SocketException	This exception is thrown when an error occurs during the use of a socket.
UnknownHostException	This exception is thrown when there is an error in the connection to server from the client.
UnknownServiceException	This exception is thrown when a service is not identified.

DEFINED IN THE ADVANCED WINDOWING TOOLKIT PACKAGE (JAVA.AWT)

Exception	Description
AWTException	This exception is thrown in the event of an error with the Advanced Windowing Toolkit.

RUNTIME CLASS

The exceptions included in the **Runtime** class are thrown during the execution of Java code. All of these exceptions are exempt from the restrictions of handling the exception at compile time. These exceptions are optional because of the need to keep Java code compact and easy to read. Table 9.3 provides a list of the key exceptions that are provided in the **Runtime** class. These exceptions are defined in the Language Package (java.lang).

Table 9.3   Exceptions included in the Runtime class.

Exception	Description
ArithmeticException	This exception is thrown when an integer is divided by zero.
ArrayIndexOutOfBounds Exception	This exception is thrown when an array is referenced outside the legal range.
ArrayStoreException	This exception is thrown when you attempt to store an incompatible class or type in an array.
ClassCastException	This exception occurs when you attempt to cast an instance of a class to a subclass or a sibling class.
IllegalArgumentException	This exception is thrown when an invalid parameter is passed to a method that is outside the legal range or value.
IllegalThreadStateException	This exception occurs when a thread state is changed to an invalid state or one that the thread is currently in.
IndexOutOfBoundsException	This exception is thrown when an index to an array is outside the legal range.
NegativeArraySizeException	This exception occurs when an array of negative size is to allocated.
NullPointerException	This exception is thrown in the event that an object contains a null reference.
NumberFormatException	This exception is thrown when an invalid string to a number or a number to a string is encountered.
SecurityException	This exception is thrown when an applet attempts to breach the security defined by the browser.
StringIndexOutOfBounds Exception	This exception occurs when a string is accessed outside the legal length of a string.

Declaring A Method Capable Of Throwing Exceptions

All methods capable of throwing an exception to a calling method must declare the exception in the method declaration. The type of exception being thrown to the calling method must be declared so that it understands how to handle the object it is receiving. The format for a method capable of throwing an exception is as follows:

```
[Modifier] Return-type Identifier ([Parameter List]) [throws
  ExceptionName]
{
    Body;
}
```

The **throws** clause may list as many exceptions as will be thrown to it by separating each of them with a comma. For an example, let's take our **ReadAFile** class to the next level and introduce a **throws** method:

```
import java.io.*;

public class wordProcessor extends Object {

    String fileName;

    void save(String fileName) {
     System.out.print ("Saving File Procedure\n");
     try {
            System.out.print ("Saving File " + fileName + "\n");
            ReadAFile aFile = new ReadAFile(fileName );

     }
     catch(FileNotFoundException e) {
        System.out.print ("Procedure to get another name and try
again\n");
        // Procedure to get another name and try again
     }
     catch(IOException e) {
        System.out.print ("Procedure to try again\n");
        // Procedure to try again
     }
     finally {
        System.out.print ("Perform any cleanup\n" );
        // Perform any cleanup
       }
     }
```

```
    // Where execution begins in a stand-alone executable
    public static void main(String args[]) {
        wordProcessor myProgram = new wordProcessor();
        myProgram.save(args[0]);
    }
}


// Reads from a file
class  ReadAFile extends wordProcessor {

    ReadAFile(String s) throws  FileNotFoundException, IOException {
        String line;
        FileInputStream fileName  = null;
        BufferedInputStream bufferedInput = null;
        DataInputStream dataIn = null;

        try {
            fileName = new FileInputStream(s);
            bufferedInput = new BufferedInputStream(fileName);
            dataIn = new DataInputStream(bufferedInput);
        }
        catch(FileNotFoundException e) {
            System.out.println("File Not Found");
            throw e;
        }
        catch(Throwable e) {
            System.out.println("Error in opening file");
        }

        try {
            while ((line = dataIn.readLine()) != null) {
                System.out.println(line + "\n");
            }
        fileName .close();
        }
        catch(IOException e) {
            System.out.println("Error in reading file");
            throw e;
        }
    }
}
```

Notice that we didn't need to make many changes to the **ReadAFile** class
used in this application. This class can quickly be made to pass exceptions
as well as handle the ones that apply specifically to the class. The object
myProgram, which is an instance of the class **wordProcessor**, calls the
method **save()**. This method then calls the **ReadAFile()** method which

declares that it will pass an exception to the calling method in the event of an error. Because the **ReadAFile()** method declares that it throws an exception, **save()** is required to address the exception that is being passed to it. If the method will not handle the exception, it must declare that it passes the particular exception on to the method that derived it:

```
ReadAFile(String s) throws  FileNotFoundException, IOException {
...
```

In our example, this line of code tells the method, **ReaAFile()**, that two exceptions, **FileNotFoundException** and **IOException**, can be thrown from the **try** block. This requires the **save()** method to handle them or declare the exceptions to be passed on to the method **main()** to deal with them.

Throwing Exceptions

The **throw** operator declares a particular exception may be thrown from the current method on to the calling method. This effectively passes the exception to the next method for it to deal with. In our previous example, the **ReadAFile** class declared that the method **save()** would pass two exceptions. In the code that follows, the example identifies which exceptions will be thrown.

```
try {
        fileName = new FileInputStream(s);
        bufferedInput = new BufferedInputStream(fileName);
        dataIn = new DataInputStream(bufferedInput);
    }
    catch(FileNotFoundException e) {
        System.out.println("File Not Found");
        throw e;
    }
    catch(Throwable e) {
        System.out.println("Error in opening file");
    }

    try {
        while ((line = dataIn.readLine()) != null) {
            System.out.println(line + "\n");
        }
    fileName .close();
    }
```

```
catch(IOException e) {
    System.out.println("Error in reading file");
    throw e;
}
```

The statement **throw e** specifies that the exception will be passed on for the calling method to deal with. Furthermore, much like error codes in other languages, messages can be passed along with the object to identify particular details to help process the exception. The following line of code shows how to throw an exception with a message attached:

```
throw new FileNotFoundException("MyFile.txt");
```

To reference the message in the calling method, you could simply call a **getMessage**() method to read the message attached to the file. The following code presents an example of this method:

```
catch(FileNotFoundException e) {
    System.out.println("The file " + e.getMessage +
      " was unable to be located.");
}
```

When To Catch And When To Throw

The issue of knowing when to catch an exception versus when to throw it to the calling method is typically a factor of what the exception does. If you refer back to our WriteAFile example, you'll see that we deal with a couple of exceptions. One of them caught an error that occurs in the event of an **IOException** by printing a message to the command line. This notifies the user of an error when writing to a file; but suppose **WriteAFile** class was a subclass in the hierarchy of the class **wordProcessor**. Here is a new version of our example that has been expanded to handle this:

```
import java.io.*;

public class WriteAFile extends wordProcessor{

WriteAFile(String s) throws IOException {
    write(s);
}

// Writes to a file
```

```
public void write(String s) throws IOException {
   FileOutputStream writeOut = null;
   DataOutputStream dataWrite = null;

   try {
      writeOut = new FileOutputStream(s);
      dataWrite = new DataOutputStream(writeOut);
   }
   catch (Throwable e) {
      System.out.println("Error in opening file");
      return;
   }
   try {
      dataWrite.writeChars("This is a Test");
      dataWrite.close();
   }
    catch(IOException e)  {
      System.out.println("Error in writing to file");
      throw e;
    }
}

}

import java.io.*;

public class wordProcessor extends Object {
   wordProcessor(String s) {
      new WriteAFile(s);
   }

   wordProcessor() {
      System.out.println("Create a backup file");
   }

   // Where execution begins in a stand-alone executable
   public static void main(String args[])  throws IOException {
      new wordProcessor(args[0]);
   }
}
```

Now, let's suppose we pass a filename to the **write()** method and it triggers the **IOException**. The **IOException** again writes a message to the command line, but notice it re-throws the exception to the calling method **wordProcessor()**. This method then allows for an additional message to be printed, in this case "Create a backup file." In place of the message, we could write an additional file to another location or do some other operation specific to the class **wordProcessor**. In addition, any other class could call the method and use it to fit its needs without being forced to perform an operation specific to **wordProcessor**.

Knowing When To Create Your Own Exceptions

The process of creating your own exceptions in Java is similar to creating other types of classes. Knowing when to create an exception is sometimes trickier than writing the exception itself. Here are some guidelines to help you create your own exceptions:

◆ Make sure you derive your new exception from the correct class. For example, if you create an exception that detects the corruption of a file, you'd want to subclass it beneath an **IOException**. Deriving the new exception from an exception like **ArrayOutOfBoundsException** would be pointless.

◆ If your code generates an error condition, you should handle it unless there is an obvious exception already created. For example, in the **ReadAFile** class we coded in this chapter, we used an exception to detect if a file cannot be found. On the other hand, if you created a class that determines whether a file has a virus or not, an **IOException** wouldn't necessarily be a wise choice. This would be a good place to subclass, however.

◆ Exceptions created in most applications should be derived from the **Exceptions** class. Only specific (lower-level) situations should require exceptions that need to be derived from the **Errors** or **RunTime** classes.

To create and use your exception classes, follow the same rules as standard classes. If you need a refresher, refer to Chapter 7. Here is a basic example of an exception:

```
public class AVirusDetectedException extends Exception {

   AVirusDetectedException(String fileName) {
 //perform some actions like read in libraries of virus types
      while(viruslibrary != null) {
```

```
        if (virus(fileName)) {
           throw new AVirusDetected(NameofVirus);
           //code after the throw operator is never executed
        }
    }
//this code is only executed if no virus is found
  }

  int virus(String fileName) {

//perform some actions like read in libraries of virus types
//test the byte code against patterns associated to viruses
      if (fileName = viruspattern) {
          return 1;
      }
  return 0;
  }
}
```

Trying to compile the source code will only result in an error. We subclassed the **AVirusDetectedException** from the **Exception** class because it will be triggered in the event of an I/O operation, but it does not fall under one of the predefined exceptions. This is used to demonstrate how an exception would look if it were created by you. To call this exception in your code, place the following code in your program:

```
try {
   if (file is questioned) {
      throw new AVirusDetectedException(fileName);
   }
} catch (AVirusDetectedException e) {
   System.out.println(e.getMessage + " has been found in " +
 fileName);
}
```

This tests whether a file was read from a disk drive, downloaded, and so on. An exception is then thrown in the event of a virus, as declared in the exception code above.

Threads

10

David H. Freidel, Jr.

To create Java applets and applications that won't turn into system resource hogs, you'll need to arrange your programs into separate processes, which are called threads.

*I*magine what our lives would be like if we could only do one thing at a time. You wouldn't be able to listen to music and program at the same time; and you definitely couldn't cook dinner, watch TV, and carry on a conversation with a friend. Although programming languages don't need to perform tasks like these, newer operating systems and environments like the Web are placing greater demands on programs, requiring them to handle multiple processes at the same time.

Java offers an advantage over most other languages because it was designed from the ground up to support multiple processes. When a Java applet runs in an environment like a Web browser, the browser can determine which parts of the program are separate processes and manage them to keep the program from draining the available system resources. As you gain more experience writing Java programs, you'll learn how to structure your programs to take advantage of the flexibility that multiple processes provide.

In this chapter we'll examine how threads are used to create multiple processes in Java programs. You'll learn how to create threads using either the pre-defined **Thread** class or the **Runnable** interface.

What Is A Thread?

One of the key jobs performed by the Java runtime system is to be able to handle programs that contain multiple processes called *threads*. If you've done any programming for an operating system such as Windows 95 or Windows NT, you've probably come across the concept called *multithreading*. The idea is to create applications that can handle different tasks at the same time, or at least be able to convince the user that multiple tasks are being performed. For example, a multithreaded version of an application that monitors the stock market would be able to download data from a central computer network, perform calculations in the background, and accept input from the user. Although only one thread can be executed at a time, the operating system that runs the program expertly divides up the different processes or threads, runs pieces of them, and jumps from thread to thread.

If you have ever loaded a Web page that contains multiple applets, you can see the process of multithreading at work. Assuming each applet is coded properly, your Web browser will make it look like each one is running at the same time. Of course, since most computers have only a single processor, the Web browser must be able to juggle each process so that each one gets its share of processing time.

To better understand how threads are coded, let's start with a simple example that contains a single process. Then we'll add to it so that you can see the effect that using threads has on the execution of the program. In the following **Hi3Person** class, the code executes in a linear fashion until the last line is reached, and the process ends:

```
public class Hi3Person {

    public static void main(String args[]) {
        Hi3Person people = new Hi3Person();

        people.hi("Person");
        people.hi("Person 2");
        people.hi("Person 3");
```

```
        System.out.println("Hello Everyone");
    }

    void hi(String who) {
        System.out.println("Hi " + who);
    }
}
```

Code execution begins by creating an instance of the class **Hi3Person.** Next, the three **hi()** methods are called. Each of these is executed one at a time, returning control back to the main body of the code. The final statement in **main()** writes the text "Hello Everyone" before the program ends.

As we introduce the concept of threads to **Hi3Person**, the linear path of execution will be disrupted. The program will be split into multiple processes, each responsible for writing to the screen. Let's look at the new version of our code to see what is going on behind the scenes:

```
public class Hi3People implements Runnable {

    public static void main(String args[]) throws InterruptedException
    {

        int i = 0;

        Hi3People person = new Hi3People();
        // Create thread #1
        Thread aThread = new Thread(person, "Person 1");
        // Create thread #2
        Thread anotherThread = new Thread(person, "Person 2");

        aThread.start();              // Start the first thread
        anotherThread.start();        // Start the second thread

        // Body of main program
        while ((aThread.isAlive()) || (anotherThread.isAlive())) {
          i++;
        }

        // Executes after both threads have finished
        System.out.println(i + "\n");
        System.out.println("Hello Everyone");
```

```
        aThread.stop();              // Stop the first thread
        anotherThread.stop();        // Stop the second thread
    }

    public void run() {
        System.out.println("Hi " + Thread.currentThread().getName());
    }
}
```

(For now, don't worry about the syntax used to create the threads that are used. We'll explain the techniques for implementing threads a little later in this chapter.) Notice that the **Hi3People** class initiates two threads that run concurrently as our application continues on. After each thread has been created, the **start**() method of the thread is called, which tells the Java interpreter to begin processing this thread. The **main**() method is responsible for setting up each thread and determining when the threads are finished. This is necessary because our program needs to know when it is safe to execute the code starting with the line:

```
System.out.println(i + "\n");
```

Otherwise, the program will end before the threads have finished and it will hang. In this case, we have placed a **while** loop to count continuously during the execution of the threads:

```
while ((aThread.isAlive()) || (anotherThread.isAlive())) {
    i++;
}
```

If you compile and run this example, you will notice that the value stored in the variable **i** will change after each execution of the code. This variable stores the number of times the **while** loop repeats during the life of *both* threads. The fact that this value changes illustrates the control that Java can have as it executes programs that are divided up into separate processes. Running a single- or multi-threaded program is not the only task that the Java runtime system must perform. Java also has its own internal threads that it must perform to manage tasks such as garbage collection.

To thread or not to thread.

The trick to programming with threads is knowing when you need to use them. Threads have the ability to hinder as well as help the execution of programs. You should only use threads when two or more processes need to exist at the same time. For example, in a windows environment, multiple windows can be opened at once TO GIVE THE IMPRESSION that two operations are occurring at the same time. These are examples of threads being implemented into real world application. Most Java programmers implement threads for building interface components by using the AWT package, which we'll explore in Chapter 9.

Keep in mind that when an application runs, multiple processes don't actually run at the same time. It's the operating system's job to give the user the impression that everything happens at once. Even in a multithreading environment like Unix, processes do not occur at the same time. As Figure 10.1 shows, the illusion of processes running concurrently is created by carefully and quickly cycling instructions through a channel. The Java Virtual Machine handles its own type of processor management by determining what executions will occur and in what order.

When you add multiple threads to your program, you effectively set up an events manager. You must manage how the instructions from your application are handled. You determine what process receives more or less time and when to change the focus of the program. As you will see later in this chapter, you can make your application appear transparent or painfully slow just by the way you schedule your threads.

Creating A Thread

Before you can create a thread, you must set up a class to handle the thread. This is done in either of two ways: extending a class (subclassing the **Thread** class) or implementing an interface. As you'll see in the next two sections, the approach you use will depend on your own needs.

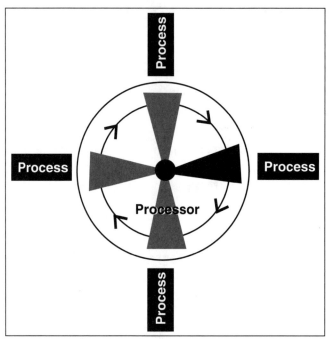

Figure 10.1   The technique of managing multiple processes.

Subclassing The Thread Class

The most obvious way to create a thread is to subclass the **Thread** class that Java provides. This approach allows you to override the methods in the **Thread** class to perform the functions you define for your program. Here is the syntax for creating a class using the **Thread** class.

```
[Modifier] class ClassName extends Thread {
    ClassBody;
}
```

Here's an example Java application that utilizes the **Thread** class as a superclass:

```
public class Hiagain extends Thread {

    public static void main(String args[]) {

        int i =0;
```

```
        Hiagain tony = new Hiagain();  // Create a new object
        Thread t1 = new Thread(tony); // Create each thread of the
                                      // object type
        Thread t2 = new Thread(tony);

        t1.start();    // Start each thread
        t2.start();

      while ((t1.isAlive()) || (t2.isAlive())) {
         i++;
      }

      System.out.println("Hello Everyone");
      t1.stop();      // End the threads
      t2.stop();
   }

   public void run() {
      System.out.println("Hi");
   }
}
```

The class **Hiagain** subclasses the **Thread** class and overrides the **run()** method defined by the **Thread** class. Because **Hiagain** is derived from **Thread**, it inherits all of the methods defined in **Thread** including **start()**, **run()**, and **stop()**. The original versions of these methods defined in **Thread** are used except in the case of the **run()** method, which has been overridden. Because this method tells the thread which operations to perform after the thread has been started, it typically needs to be overridden. The key methods that are defined in the **Thread** class will be presented later in this chapter.

Implementing The Runnable Interface

When designing class hierarchies for your Java applications or applets, situations arise where subclassing from the **Threads** class is just not possible. In such cases, you can implement the **Runnable** interface to avoid a conflict. To declare a class **Runnable**, follow the template shown here:

```
[Modifier] class ClassName extends SuperClass implements Runnable {
    ClassBody;
}
```

The advantage of this approach is that you can create a new class that is both derived from another class and uses the methods defined by the **Runnable** interface. Of course, you will then be required to go along with the implementation created by the designers of this interface. Let's take a look at a ticker tape applet because it provides a good example of an implementation of the **Runnable** interface:

```
// TickerTape Class
public class TickerTape extends Applet implements Runnable{

    ....

    // Initialize Applet
    public void init(){
    ....
    }


    ....
// Start Applet as thread
    public void start(){
        if(ttapeThread == null){
            ttapeThread = new Thread(this);
            ttapeThread.start();
        }
    }
    ...
    // Change coordinates and repaint
    public void run(){
        while(ttapeThread != null){
            try {Thread.sleep(50);} catch (InterruptedException e){}
            setcoord();
            repaint();
        }
    }
....
// Stop thread then clean up before close
    public void stop(){
        if(ttapeThread != null)
            ttapeThread.stop();
        ttapeThread = null;
    }

} // End TickerTape
```

As with all applets, you must use the **Runnable** interface to implement threads. (You are forced to subclass the **Applet** class to perform the basic operations of initializing and starting your applet.) The reason you would want to implement threads in an applet is to reduce the processor load for performing operations that occur over and over. One example would be the graphics routine in our ticker tape applet that updates the screen to make the text appear as if it floats across the screen. The **run**() method is coded to redraw the screen and then set the thread to sleep for a specified amount of time:

```
// Change coordinates and repaint
public void run() {
    while(ttapeThread != null) {
        try { Thread.sleep(50); } catch (InterruptedException e) {}
        setcoord();
        repaint();
    }
}
```

The reason for putting the thread to sleep is covered in more detail later in the chapter. The two methods responsible for moving the text are **setcoord**() and **repaint**(). They are executed as long as the thread exists.

Initializing A Thread

Before you can use a thread, you must initialize it by creating an instance of the **Thread** class. The best way to do this is to use the constructor for the **Thread** class. The simple form of this constructor is:

```
Thread Identifier = new Thread();
```

A few other variations of this constructor are also supported:

```
Thread(ObjectReference);
Thread(StringName);
Thread(ObjectReference, StringName);
```

In the first example, a parameter that references the object to be used to create the thread for is provided. We actually used this type of constructor in the **Hiagain** class example presented earlier:

```
Hiagain tony = new Hiagain();    // Create a new object
Thread t1 = new Thread(tony);    // Create a thread of the object
  type
```

The next two constructors allow you to pass a string to create references to individual threads, which can then be used as symbolic references. We'll show you how to use this feature later in this chapter to keep track of multiple threads created from the same class instance.

If you return to the ticker tape applet outlined above, you'll see that the thread is created in the **start()** method for the applet:

```
// Start Applet as thread
public void start() {
   if(ttapeThread == null) {
      ttapeThread = new Thread(this);
      ttapeThread.start();
   }
}
```

In this case, notice the **Thread()** constructor is passed the **this** parameter. Using **this** allows us to tell the constructor the name of the class that implements the **Runnable** interface. The new thread object that is created is assigned to the **variable** ttapeThread. Once the thread has been initialized, the **start()** method for the thread can be called by using the statement **ttapeThread.start()**.

Who Goes First; Who Finishes Last?

Although only one thread can be started at a time, don't expect the first one called to always be the one that finishes first. In fact, the order in which threads are called won't necessarily determine the order in which they finish. In most cases, it is impossible to determine which thread will finish first. Let's return to our simple **Hi3People** class introduced in the beginning of this chapter, to see how the execution of threads can be hard to predict:

```
public class Hi3People implements Runnable {
  public static void main(String args[]) throws InterruptedException
  {

    int i1 = 0;
    int i2 = 0;

    Hi3People person = new Hi3People();
    Thread aThread = new Thread(person, "Person 1");
    Thread anotherThread = new Thread(person, "Person 2");
    aThread.start();
```

```
anotherThread.start();
while ((aThread.isAlive()) || (anotherThread.isAlive())) {
    if (aThread.isAlive()) { ++i1;}  // Counter for the first
thread
    if (anotherThread.isAlive()) { ++i2;} // Counter for the second
thread
}

System.out.println("The time for Person1 is " + i1 + "\n");
System.out.println("The time for Person2 is " + i2 + "\n");

aThread.stop();
anotherThread.stop();
}

public void run() {
    System.out.println("Hi " + Thread.currentThread().getName());
}
}
```

First, notice the types of constructors that are used:

```
Hi3People person = new Hi3People();
Thread aThread = new Thread(person, "Person 1");
Thread anotherThread = new Thread(person, "Person 2");
```

Both the object name (**person**) and a unique string is passed to each call to **Thread**(). Since both threads are created using the same object, the string is passed to assign each thread its own unique name. In the **run**() method of the program, the **getName**() method is used to display the name of the current thread. A companion method named **setName**() is provided in the **Thread** class for setting the name of a thread.

Next, by changing a few lines of code, we converted our while loop to count the time it takes to process *each* thread instead of counting the time it takes to process the two together. You would need to run this code about 10 to 15 times before running across an instance where the first person beats the second one. This is due to the fact that Java's scheduler is still in a beta version. (Hopefully, Sun will consider implementing a method for determining the order in which threads are processed.) The scheduler is responsible for determining what threads may run and which ones must wait in the queue. This process is determined in either one of two methods: priority or first in first out (FIFO).

Priority Vs. FIFO Scheduling

When a thread is processed, it is automatically thrown into a queue. Then, the thread must wait until its turn is up. This process of waiting is called *blocking*. The implementation of the thread that is ahead of the one waiting will determine if a thread will wait until the current thread has completed. This method of waiting is referred to as *First in First Out* (*FIFO*). Like everything in this world, there are exceptions to the rules. If a thread has priority over another thread, it switches places with the thread. This process continues up the queue until a thread reaches an equal or greater priority or it is executed. The threads that were pushed aside may not continue their operation until all the higher priority threads either step aside or finish. The most common case of this is the Garbage Collector, the thread that runs in the background and has the lowest priority.

To control how the priority is set for a thread, the **Thread** class provides the following three variables:

◆ MAX_PRIORITY

◆ NORM_PRIORITY

◆ MIN_PRIORITY

Each of these variables holds integer values that specify a thread's priority level. For example, **MAX_PRIORITY** stores a number that indicates the maximum allowable value for a thread's priority. To set or retrieve the current priority setting of a thread, the **Thread** class provides the **setPriority**() and **getPriority**() methods. In setting priorities, you can use one of the three priority instance variables. For example, the following method call would set a thread's priority to the value contained in the NORM_PRIORITY variable:

```
Thread aThread = new Thread(person, "Person 1");
aThread.setPriority(aThread.NORM_PRIORITY);
```

Controlling The Life Of A Thread

A thread is like a human or plant life form; it has a beginning, middle, and an ending. During these stages, a thread will take many different paths

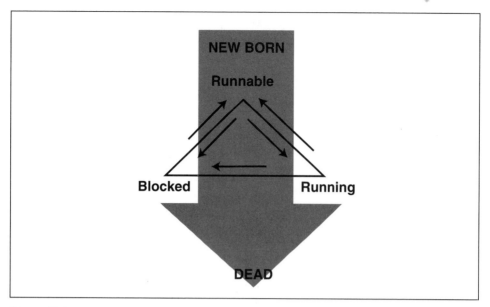

Figure 10.2 **The cycle of life pertaining to a thread.**

depending on the objective to be reached. Figure 10.2, shows the cycle of life that a thread can *possibly* take.

The stages of life of a thread are determined by a set of pre-defined methods that can be overridden to perform certain tasks.

The start() Method

This method starts the "birthing" process for a thread. By default, it sets up a few initializations and calls the **start()** method. You can override it to initialize your own variables and then call the **start()** method:

```
// Start Applet as a thread
   public void start() {
      if(ttapeThread == null) {
         ttapeThread = new Thread(this);
         ttapeThread.start();
      }
```

In this example the **start()** method checks to see if the thread **ttapeThread** exists. If it doesn't, it creates an instance of the **Thread** class and assigns the variable **ttapeThread** to it.

The run() Method

This method defines the actions to take place during the life of a thread. Here's an example:

```
// Change coordinates and repaint
   public void run() {
       while(ttapeThread != null) {
           try {Thread.sleep(50);} catch (InterruptedException e) {}
           setcoord();
           repaint();
       }
   }
```

In this example, the **run**() method makes the process sleep for 50 milliseconds while the instance of the class named **ttapeThread** is not equal to null. Then, the **setcoord**() method is called followed by the **repaint**() method.

The sleep() Method

This method releases control of a thread from the processor for a specified amount of time. The syntax for calling this method is:

```
Thread.sleep(Miliseconds);
```

In the **run**() method we just presented, the **sleep**() method is called to allow other threads to be processed while the **ttapeThread** is put on hold. This allows the browser to accept other input and not redraw the screen every instance of the thread.

The suspend() Method

This method suspends execution of a thread. As the following example shows, it requires no parameters:

```
// Handle mouse clicks
   public boolean handleEvent(Event evt) {
       if (evt.id == Event.MOUSE_DOWN) {
           if (suspended) {
               ttapeThread.resume();
           } else {
```

```
            ttapeThread.suspend();
        }
    suspended = !suspended;
    }
    return true;
}
```

This line of code states that in the event of a mouse click and the thread is running, the thread will be suspended from operation. This allows other threads in the queue to be processed; but as soon as the thread is reactivated, it will resume its place in the queue as long as a higher priority thread is not executing.

The resume() Method

This method resumes a suspended thread. Here's an example of how it is used:

```
// Handle mouse clicks
    public boolean handleEvent(Event evt) {
        if (evt.id == Event.MOUSE_DOWN) {
            if (suspended) {
                ttapeThread.resume();
            } else {
                ttapeThread.suspend();
            }
        suspended = !suspended;
        }
        return true;
    }
```

The **resume**() method is responsible for reactivating a method that is asleep. This allows for the thread to re-enter the queue.

The yield() Method

This method causes the current thread to move to the end of the queue and lets the next thread take control of the processor. Here's an example of how it can be used:

```
// Change coordinates and repaint
    public void run() {
        while(ttapeThread != null) {
```

```
        setcoord();
        repaint();
        yield();
    }
}
```

If the thread exists, the **setcoord**() method is executed followed by the **repaint**() method. Then the **yield**() method is called to permit the next thread in line to execute. Unfortunately, this is not wise if we are to depend on a scheduled **repaint**(). We could fall victim to the mercy of the threads that will be placed before the current thread that is moved to the end of the queue.

The stop() Method

This method ceases the life of a thread and performs the required cleanup operations:

```
// Stop thread then clean up before close
    public void stop(){
        if(ttapeThread != null)
            ttapeThread.stop();
        ttapeThread = null;
    }
```

In the event that the end of the process is reached, this method is called to clean up after the thread and perform any final procedures before closing out.

The destroy() Method

This method causes a thread to die without any cleanup operations being performed:

```
// Stop thread then clean up before close
    public void stop(){
        if(ttapeThread != null)
            ttapeThread.destroy();
        ttapeThread = null;
    }
```

In the event that the **stop**() method of the applet is called, the thread **ttapeThread** will be destroyed and no further lines of code for that object will be executed.

Multiple Objects Interacting With One Source

When you have multiple threads in your application running all at once, the need for limiting access to devices that write data and perform other critical tasks becomes absolutely necessary. After all, there is no way of telling when objects may try to update a storage device like a file at the same time. As a result, data may become corrupt or false information may be extracted from a device.

Synchronizing Revisited

If you recall from Chapter 7, we showed you how to declare a **synchronized** method. If you don't remember, here is the syntax.

```
synchronized ReturnType Identifier([ParameterList]) [Throws]
{
    MethodBody;
}
```

The **synchronized** modifier is used to declare a method of which only one object can execute at any one time. This is accomplished by the Java Virtual Machine setting up an object monitor for every portion of code that declares itself as synchronized. In order for the code to run, the object must attain this monitor. In the event that a thread wants to run a synchronized section of code, it is blocked until the thread ahead of it finishes executing the particular section of code. Let's look at an example of how the synchronized techniques works:

```
import java.awt.*;
import java.lang.*;

public class MyApp2 extends Frame implements Runnable {

    static TextArea t1;
    static TextArea t2;

    MyApp2() {
        // Calls the parent constructor Frame(string title)
        // Same as setTitle("Duck Duck Goose");
```

```
        super("Counting example");

        // A new panel to the south that 4 buttons and 1 choice
        t1 = new TextArea();
        t2 = new TextArea();
        add("East", t1);
        add("West", t2);

        pack();
        show();
    }

public static void main(String args[]) {

    int i = 0;

    MyApp2 game = new MyApp2();
    Thread person1 = new Thread(game, "duck");
    Thread person2= new Thread(game, "goose");

    person1.start();
    person2.start();

    while ((person1.isAlive()) || (person2.isAlive())) {
        ++i;
        t2.setText(Integer.toString(i));
    }

    t2.appendText("\n Time through the loop \n\nYour It");
    person1.stop();
    person2.stop();

}

public synchronized void run() {
    int d = 0;
    int change = 0;

    while(d < 100) {
        t1.appendText("\n   " + Thread.currentThread().getName() +
        "   " + d );
        ++d;
    }
}

public boolean handleEvent(Event evt) {

switch(evt.id) {
    case Event.WINDOW_DESTROY: {
```

```
            System.exit(0);
            return true;
      }
         default:
            return false;
      }
   }
}
```

The above code initiates two threads that cycle through the synchronized **run**() method. When you compile this program, you will see the first thread, **person1**, count up to 99, followed by the next thread, **person2**, count up to 99 and end. The thread **person2** must wait until the monitor is released by the previous thread before executing. While this process is occurring, notice that the counter timing the execution of the synchronized threading event is running alongside.

Wait() A Second... Notify() Me When...

Running a thread through a synchronized method is perfectly fine if you don't need any additional information from the outside. But let's suppose you wish to execute a thread within a synchronized method, and half way through you need to collect information from an additional thread. The first thread establishes a foundation, perhaps opening a file. Then, the following thread will enter the method and write the information and leave. Finally, the original thread will perform the cleanup necessary for closing the file. Well, this is all great, but remember we synchronized the method to permit only one thread to execute at any one time. This is easily remedied by using the **wait**() method, which causes the currently executing method to release the monitor to the next thread. The thread that released the monitor can then reacquire the monitor when the **notify**() method is called from within the same method. The thread waiting then picks up right from the point where it began waiting. Let's modify our previous example **MyApp2** to utilize the **wait**() and **notify**() methods:

```
public synchronized void run() {
    int d = 0;
    int change = 0;
```

```
while(d < 100) {
    t1.appendText("\n   " + Thread.currentThread().getName() + "   "
        + Integer.toString(d) );
    ++d;
    if( d == 50) {
        try {
            if (Thread.currentThread().getName().equals("duck"))
            {
                this.wait();
            }
        }
    catch(InterruptedException e) {
    }
  }
}
if (Thread.currentThread().getName().equals("goose")) {
    this.notify();
  }
}
```

After compiling the class again and running it, you will notice that the first thread counts to 50. The thread **person1** then releases the monitor to the next thread, **person2**. The thread then counts up to 99 and notifies the previous thread to begin executing from where it left off.

Grouping Your Threads

Once you have created your threads, they are like children who run loose in the mall. No matter how often you call them, they will go off into their own little world. Just like children, threads themselves can have parents. These parents are established by assigning them to a **ThreadGroup**. The **ThreadGroup** is actually a class just like the one the threads are derived from. You can create a **ThreadGroup** the same way you initialize any class in Java:

```
ThreadGroup parentAuthor = new ThreadGroup( " The Potts ");
```

This statement sets up a **ThreadGroup** named " The Potts " with a reference to the object **parentAuthor**. From here we can assign threads to this group by passing the name of the **ThreadGroup** with the initialization of the thread. For example, if we wish to add to threads to the **ThreadGroup** **parentAuthor**, we would enter the following:

```
Thread child1 = new Thread( parentAuthor, "Angela");
Thread child2 = new Thread( parentAuthor, "Anthony");
```

Creating hierarchies of these groups is just as easy as assigning threads to the group. For example, let's suppose that the **parentAuthor ThreadGroup** also wants to have a subgroup underneath it named **petsAuthor**. To accomplish this we would simply use the following code:

```
ThreadGroup petsAuthor = new ThreadGroup( parentAuthor, "Our Pets");
```

This allows for quick subgrouping of like threads. There are three main advantages to subgrouping threads:

◆ Controlling the states of all the threads contained within the group without having to individually set each one.

◆ Retrieving all the threads in the group easily so that you can identify a thread quickly.

◆ Setting the priority of all the threads within the group with one command to the group.

Note: Setting the priority of the ThreadGroup only affects the threads of less priority than the calling method. If a thread is currently set at a high priority, it will continue at this level until it dies.

The Java AWT

Anthony Potts

If you're wondering where to look for information on creating interface components for Java programs, you've come to the right place. The AWT provides a treasure chest of powerful interface classes.

*N*o one would use a programming language these days if it did not have built-in support for common user interface objects like windows, menus, dialogs, and buttons. Fortunately, the designers of Java did not overlook this. They created a package called the *Abstract Window Toolkit* or *AWT,* which allows Java programmers to build GUIs very easily. Although AWT is very flexible and powerful, its shear size will overwhelm you until you understand how it is organized and the basics for using it.

To help you get more out of the AWT, we'll look at how the AWT is arranged. Then we'll present each of the key AWT classes. We'll show you how to use the layout manager, and we'll present the basics for creating interface components such as menus. If we tried to cover the AWT in a lot of detail, we could easily turn this chapter into an entire book. However, since Java is still a very young language and much of the AWT is still being solidified, we will only cover enough of this library to get you started with the AWT so that you can use it effectively. You'll want to keep your browser tuned to Sun's Java site for the latest information on this powerful package.

Introducing The AWT

When you first start to work with the AWT, you may notice that it lacks many of the features that you would find in other graphical user interface (GUI) libraries. This is because Java is a cross-platform language, and the tools provided with any Java library must be designed so that they can work with all systems.

As you build more complex applets and applications, you will find it difficult to *not* use the AWT because of its extreme flexibility. If a component such as a window or menu doesn't do what you need, you can simply subclass it and add your own custom features.

To use the AWT in a Java applet or program, you must first import the AWT package by using the **import** statement as shown here:

```
import java.awt.*;   // Include the AWT
```

The asterisk (*) is used with the **import** statement to tell the Java compiler to include *all* classes in the *immediate* subdirectory. Once you include this package, you can use any of the AWT controls or packages to derive your own. With just a little bit of programming effort, you'll be amazed at the types of interface components you can create for your Java applications— everything from scrollable windows to fully functional pop-up menus.

Here's an example of a simple Java program that displays a window that contains a text message:

```
import java.awt.*;   // Include the AWT

public class testWin extends Frame {   // Use the Frame class

    public testWin(){}   // Constructor

    public static void main(String args[]) {
        testWin Test = new testWin();
        // Display a line of text
        Test.setText("This text will be displayed in the window");
        // Add a second line
        Test.appendText(" Add this text to the next line in the
          window");
```

```
    Test.show();    // Display the frame
  }
}
```

Introducing The Layout Manager

Creating applications with a visual programming language like Visual Basic and Delphi can simply involve choosing from a selection of custom components written by other programmers and then dragging a component onto a form. Visual programmers like to refer to this practice as "drop-and-drag" programming. Unfortunately, Java programming is not quite this easy (although Java development is headed in this direction). When you place controls on forms to build applications with visual languages, you usually specify absolute positions. In other words, you tell your development environment exactly where you want to place a control—right down to the pixel. The problem with this approach is that different operating systems use different methods to display graphical components. So, a form that looks good on a PC may not look right on a Mac screen.

If you have only programmed for an environment like Windows, many of these problems are not as apparent because Windows takes care of specific system and interface related details for you. To provide this type of flexibility, Java provides a development tool called the layout manager, which works in conjunction with the AWT.

Java's layout manager helps you control where items will appear on the screen. The layout manager is actually an abstract class itself that you can use to create custom layouts. There are several custom layout methods that come with the Java Development Kit. As we present the AWT in this chapter, you'll learn more about the layout manager.

What About Menus?

You can't create a good user interface without implementing some form of menus. The Macintosh and Windows environments are filled with menus. Computer users expect your applications to present them with some sort of menuing system so that they can access the available features. When creating applets, menus are not as important and can be confusing because your Web browser already has its own menu system. But when you are creating Java applications, you'll more than likely want to add menus to your programs—and that's where the AWT comes in. The AWT can help you create menus very easily. However, it's up to you to make them functional and intuitive.

The AWT Hierarchy

The AWT package consists of many classes and subclasses. Most of the controls, like buttons and text fields, are derived from the **Component** class. Since all of the AWT controls are descendants from the **Component** class, they all share some of the same key methods such as **createImage()**, **disable()**, and **hide()**. Figure 11.1 presents a tree that illustrates the class hierarchy for the controls of the AWT and Table 11.1 lists the complete set of classes.

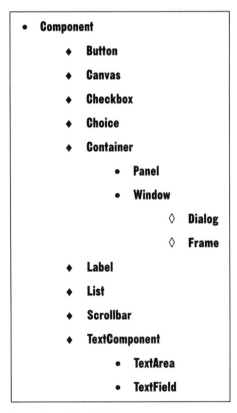

Figure 11.1   The class hierarchy of the AWT.

Table 11.1 The complete list of classes in AWT.

BorderLayout	FlowLayout	MenuComponent
Button	Font	MenuItem
Canvas	FontMetrics	Panel
CardLayout	Frame	Point
Checkbox	Graphics	Polygon
CheckboxGroup	GridBagConstraints	Rectangle
CheckboxMenuItem	GridBagLayout	Scrollbar
Choice	GridLayout	TextArea
Color	Image	TextComponent
Component	Insets	TextField
Container	Label	Toolkit
Dialog	List	Window
Dimension	MediaTracker	
Event	Menu	
FileDialog	MenuBar	

If you have done any graphics or interface programming before, some of these class names should be somewhat familiar to you. Instead of reinventing the wheel, the developers of Java used traditional user interface components—windows, dialogs, scrollbars, and so on—to build up the AWT. Of course, you'll find that the AWT heavily embraces object-oriented programming techniques.

The Component Class

Since all of the controls and GUI elements that we'll be using are subclassed from the **Component** class, let's start with it. The **Component** class is rarely (if ever) used as is. It is almost always subclassed to create new objects that inherit all its functionality. **Component** has a tremendous number of methods built into it that all of the classes that subclass it share. You will be using these methods quite often to perform tasks such as making the control visible, enabling or disabling it, or resizing it.

Key Component Class Methods

The declarations and descriptions for the **Component** class would fill up a hundred pages. Fortunately, they are available online at Sun's Java site. You can download the API reference and load up the **Component** class to examine the methods available in this class. However, there are a few methods that are important, and you will probably use them for all the controls that subclass the **Component** class. We'll introduce these methods next, and we'll examine some of the key event handling methods in Chapter 10.

BOUNDS()

This method returns the current rectangular bounds of the component.

DISABLE()

This method disables a component.

ENABLE([BOOLEAN])

This method enables a component. You can pass zero arguments, or a Boolean argument to enable or disable a control. Here's a few examples of how this method can be called:

```
myComponent.enable();
myComponent.enable(x==1);
```

GETFONTMETRICS()

This method gets the font metrics for the component. It returns null if the component is currently not on the screen.

GETGRAPHICS()

This method gets a graphics context for the component. This method returns null if the component is currently not on the screen. This method is an absolute necessity for working with graphics.

GETPARENT()

This method gets the parent of the component.

HANDLEEVENT(EVENT EVT)

This method handles all window events. It returns true if the event is handled and should not be passed to the parent of the component. The default event handler calls some helper methods to make life easier on the programmer. This method is used to handle messages from the operating system.

HIDE()

This method hides the component. It performs the opposite operation of **show**().

INSIDE(INT X, INT Y)

This method checks to see if a specified x,y location is "inside" the component. By default, x and y are inside a component if they fall within the bounding box of that component.

ISENABLED()

This method checks to see if the component is enabled. Components are initially enabled.

ISSHOWING()

This method checks to see if the component is showing on screen. This means that the component must be visible, and it must be in a container that is visible and showing.

ISVISIBLE()

This method checks to see if the component is visible. Components are initially visible (with the exception of top level components such as Frame).

LOCATE(INT X, INT Y)

This method returns the component or subcomponent that contains the x,y location. It is very useful for checking for mouse movement or mouse clicks.

LOCATION()

This method returns the current location of the component. The location will be specified in the parent's coordinate space.

MOVE(INT X, INT Y)

This method moves the component to a new location. The x and y coordinates are in the parent's coordinate space.

REPAINT([[TIME]])

This method repaints the component. This will result in a call to the **update**() method as soon as possible. You can specify a time argument so that Java knows that you want the component repainted within a specified number of milliseconds. You can also update just a certain portion of a control by sending the x and y coordinates that specify where you want to start the update and a width and height that specify how much to update. Here are some examples:

```
// Regular update
myComponent.update();

// Update within 250 milliseconds
myComponent.update(250);

// Update rectangle
myComponent.update(50, 50, 200, 200);

// Update same rectangle within 250 milliseconds
myComponent.update(250, 50, 50, 200, 200);
```

RESIZE(INT WIDTH, INT HEIGHT)

This method resizes the component to the specified width and height. You could also pass it a dimension object instead of the two integers. Here are a few examples:

```
myComponent.resize(300, 200);

myComponent.show(new dim(300, 200));
```

SETFONT(FONT)

This method sets the font of the component. The argument passed is a **Font** object. For example, this method call

```
myComponent.setFont(new Font("Helvetica", Font.PLAIN, 12);
```

would change the font of **myComponent** to a Helvetica type face with no bolding or italics or underline and a point size of 12.

SHOW([BOOLEAN])

This method "shows" the component. By calling this method you make a control visible or not. It can also be passed a conditional statement. Here are a few examples:

```
myComponent.show();
myComponent.show(x==1);
```

SIZE()

This method returns the current size of the component. The size is returned in dimensions of width and height.

The Frame Class

The **Frame** class is used to create standard application windows. It is a direct descendant of the **Window** class and is used to create windows that automatically include the menu bar, title bar, control elements, and so on. **Frame** looks like a standard window that you would expect to see running under most operating systems like Windows or Macintosh OS.

You will probably use the **Frame** class to create window interface components for the majority of your applications. However, when you need to create custom windows for special situations, you may need to use the **Window** class instead.

Hierarchy For Frame

```
java.lang.Object
  java.awt.Component
      java.awt.Container
        java.awt.Window
            java.awt.Frame
```

Declaration For Frame

To create a frame, you need to use a constructor to initialize your class. The constructor method does not even need to have any code in it; the method just needs to be provided so that you can instantiate your object. The following listing shows a complete Java application that uses a frame:

```
import java.awt.*;    // Include the AWT

public class testWin extends Frame {    // Use the Frame class

    public testWin(){}    // Constructor

    public static void main(String args[]) {
        testWin Test = new testWin();
        Test.show();    // Display a window
    }
}
```

In the **main()** method we use our class's constructor to create our object named **Test**. Then we call the object's **show()** method to make the window frame visible (frames are invisible by default). If you were running this Java program in Windows 95, you'd see a window that looks like the one shown in Figure 11.2.

As you can see, the window is quite simple. You need to use several of the **Frame** class's methods to make the frame useful. The other thing you may notice is that when you try and close the window and terminate the program, nothing happens! That's because you have not told Java to do it. You need to add an event handling method to catch windows messages. In this case, we are looking for the **WINDOW_DESTROY** call from the operating system. Here is the extended code that sets the sizes of the frame, gives it a title, and catches messages:

```
import java.awt.*;

public class winTest1 extends Frame {

    public winTest1() {}

    public synchronized boolean handleEvent(Event e) {
        if (e.id == Event.WINDOW_DESTROY) {    // Has window been
                                               // destroyed?
            System.exit(0);
            return true;
        }
        return super.handleEvent(e);
    }
```

```
   public static void main(String args[]) {
      winTest Test = new winTest();
      Test.setTitle("Test Window");
      Test.resize(300 ,200);
      Test.show();
   }
}
```

Figure 11.3 shows what the new application looks like.

We are gong to discuss event handling in more detail in the next chapter, so don't get worried if you do not understand that part of the above code.

What you should notice is the two new calls to two of the frames methods: **setTitle**() and **resize**(). These methods perform the function they are named after; they set the title of our application and resize it respectively.

Let's look at the methods that are specific to the **Frame** class.

Methods For The Frame Class

DISPOSE()

This method removes the frame. It must be called to release the resources that are used to create the frame. This method should be called when you exit a window in an applet. In an application, you would usually use the **System.exit**() method to terminate the program and release all memory used by the application. This method overrides the **dispose**() method from the **Window** class.

GETICONIMAGE()

This method returns the icon image for the frame.

GETMENUBAR()

This method gets the menu bar for the frame.

Figure 11.2   A simple windowed Java application.

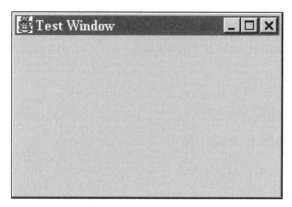

Figure 11.3   A fully functioning application using a frame.

GETTITLE()

This method gets the title of the frame.

ISRESIZABLE()

This method returns true if the user can resize the frame.

REMOVE(MENUCOMPONENT M)

This method removes the specified menu bar from the frame.

SETCURSOR(IMAGE IMG)

This method sets the current cursor image that will be used while the cursor is within the frame.

SETICONIMAGE(IMAGE IMG)

This method sets the image to display when the frame is iconized. Note that not all platforms support the concept of iconizing a window. The icon will also be displayed in the title window in Windows 95.

SETMENUBAR(MENUBAR MB)

This method sets the menu bar for the frame to the specified **MenuBar**.

SETRESIZABLE(BOOLEAN BOOL)

This method sets the resizable flag.

SETTITLE(STRING TITLE)

This method sets the title for the frame to the specified **title**.

The Panel Class

Panels are probably one of the most useful components that no one will ever see. Most of the time, panels are just used as storage containers for other components. You could also use a panel for drawing or to hold images, but panels are not usually used for these tasks.

Panels are important because they offer you a way to gain very strict control over the layout of the other interface controls in your program. Unless you have a very simple application, you will need multiple controls on the screen at once. Usually these controls will not all fit where you want them using one layout class or another. Panels provide a mechanism so that you can mix and match.

Let's look at an example. Assume you have a frame that you want to fill with a text field in the upper part of the frame, and three buttons lined up along the bottom. If you only used a single layout class for the entire form, you would not have enough control to do this. Figure 11.4 illustrates what we want the frame to look like. Figure 11.5 and 11.6 shows the best you can achieve using a single layout class. This is not bad, but if you resize the frame the layout gets pretty ugly.

What we need to be able to do is use one type of layout class for the upper part of the frame, and another for the bottom. We can do this by using a pair of panels, one for the top using a border style layout and another panel for the bottom using a flow style layout.

Now, when we add our controls, we add them to their respective panels instead of the frame, and everything is taken care of for us. The user can resize the control all they want and our controls will stay where we placed them originally. Here is the code that performs this new configuration. The output is shown in Figure 11.7.

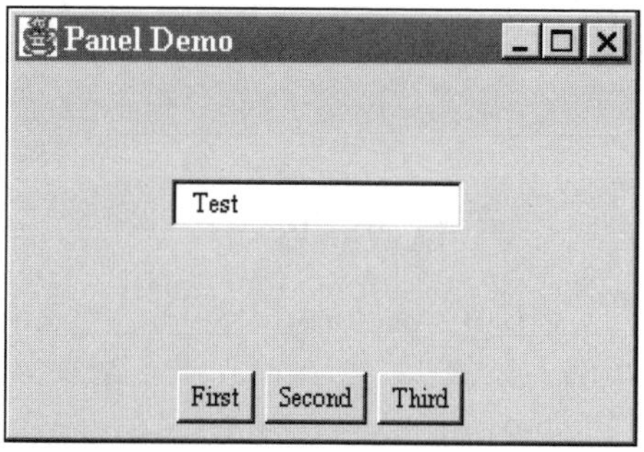

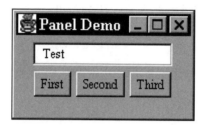

Figure 11.4 Creating a window using the Panel class.

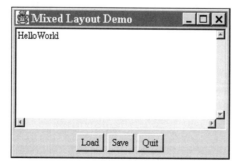

Figure 11.5 A close approximation with a single layout class.

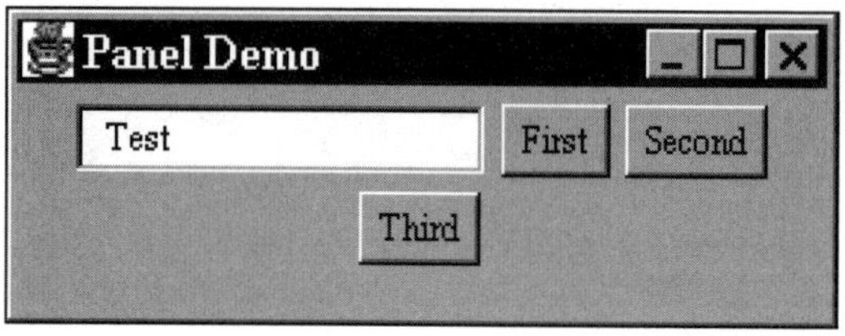

Figure 11.6 Resizing the Panel.

Figure 11.7 The new two-panel program with different layout methods.

```
import java.awt.*;

public class mixLayout extends Frame {

    public mixLayout() {
        super("Mixed Layout Demo");
        setLayout(new BorderLayout());
        Panel top = new Panel();
        Panel bottom = new Panel();
        top.setLayout(new BorderLayout());
        top.add("Center", new TextArea("HelloWorld", 15, 5));
        bottom.setLayout(new FlowLayout());
        bottom.add(new Button("Load"));
        bottom.add(new Button("Save"));
        bottom.add(new Button("Quit"));
        add("Center", top);
        add("South", bottom);
        resize(300, 200);
        show();
    }
    public static void main(String args[]) {
        mixLayout test = new mixLayout();
    }

}
```

Hierarchy For Panel

```
java.lang.Object
 java.awt.Component
      java.awt.Container
          java.awt.Panel
```

Declaration For Panel

Panels have a very straight-forward declaration because they cannot accept any arguments whatsoever.

```
Panel myPanel = new Panel();
```

Methods For Panel

Panels have very few new methods ouside of the ones inherited from the **Container** class. The key new method that is introduced is **setlayout()**.

SETLAYOUT(LAYOUTMANAGER)

As you have already seen, the **setlayout**() method is used to define which layout manager will be used to place controls on the panel. If you do not set a layout manager, the panel control defaults to **flowLayout**().

The Label Class

The **Label** class defines a very simple control that is simply used to display a text string. This text string is usually used to indicate what tasks are controlled by another user interface control. For example, if you had a group of radio buttons, a label control might be used to tell the user what the group is about.

Hierarchy For Label

```
java.lang.Object
  java.awt.Component
      java.awt.Label
```

Declaration For Label

The most common declaration for a label is to assign the text string as the control is being declared. Here's an example:

```
new Label("Fruits of the world:");
```

We can also assign the text string to an object variable like this:

```
Label fruitLabel = new Label("Fruits of the world:");
```

Table 11.2 shows the three ways you can declare a **Label** class.

Methods For Label

Labels have very little functionality of their own—they can't even process mouse clicks. They are not intended to do much more than sit there and display their string. There are, however, a few methods you should know about.

GETALIGNMENT()

This method returns the current alignment of the label.

Table 11.2   Options for declaring a label class.

Declaration	Description
Label()	This constructor will create an empty label.
Label(String)	This constructor will create a label with the given string.
Label(String, int)	This constructor will create a label with the given string as well as define the alignment of the string. The int part of the declaration is represented by setting it to Label.LEFT, Label.CENTER, or Label.RIGHT. (These labels should be pretty self-explanatory.) Remember though, that if you do not assign an alignment, the label control will default to left-justified.

GET TEXT()

This method does what it sounds like—it returns the text the label is displaying.

SET ALIGNMENT(INT)

This method changes the alignment of the label. The argument is the same as the one used with **Label.LEFT**, **Label. CENTER**, and **Label.RIGHT** (see Table 11.2 for more information).

Figure 11.8 shows a few labels with different alignments. Here is the code used to produce them:

```
add(new Label("Left")); // no need to specify alignment because it
                        // defaults to left
add(new Label("Center", Label.CENTER));
add(new Label("Right", Label.RIGHT));
```

SET TEXT(STRING)

This method sets or changes the displayed text.

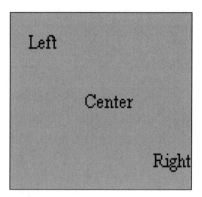

Figure 11.8   The Label component.

Button Class

The **Button** class is one of the most often used classes, for obvious reasons. How often do you see Windows or Mac programs without some sort of button somewhere?

Buttons are UI components that trigger actions when they are pressed. They have multiple states to provide feedback to the user. The neat thing about buttons (and all the UI elements for that matter) is that a button you create for a Java program will change its appearance depending on the operating system. That's one of the benefits of cross-platform. A button on your application or applet will look like a standard Windows button on a PC. Or, it will look like a standard Mac button on a Mac. The disadvantage here is that if you create other elements that are dependent on the size and/or shape of the graphics for your button, then you will run into trouble.

Figure 11.9 illustrates a few different buttons. Notice that the size of the buttons depends on the length of the caption.

Hierarchy For Button

```
java.lang.Object
  java.awt.Component
      java.awt.Button
```

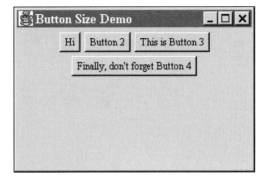

Figure 11.9   A few Button components.

Declaration For Button

Buttons have two different constructor options. The first one simply creates a blank button. The second option creates a button that you assign a string to display.

```
new Button(); // Empty button
new Button(String); // Button with "String" as the caption
```

Methods For Button

There are only two methods specific to the button component.

GETLABEL()

This method returns the current caption of the button.

SETLABEL()

This method changes the caption of the button.

The real power behind buttons is realized when you handle the events a button triggers. This is usually handled in the **handleEvent()** method that we will be showing you how to use in the next chapter.

The Canvas Class

The **Canvas** class is a very simple component. It is designed to be subclassed and used as a container for graphics methods, much like an artist's canvas.

Hierarchy For Canvas

```
java.lang.Object
 java.awt.Component
       java.awt.Canvas
```

Declaration For Canvas

The **Canvas** component has only a single constructor:

```
new Canvas();
```

Methods For Canvas

The only method that is used with the **Canvas** component is the **paint**() method which is called to update the contents. If you do not override this method, the **Canvas** component is pretty much worthless because it has very little functionality of its own.

When you subclass a **Canvas** component, you can really have some fun. Override the **paint**() method and add in calls to painting and geometric methods. Or, you can create a Canvas object and make up your own calls to it that react to button clicks, mouse movements, and so on.

The Checkbox Class

The **Checkbox** class is actually two controls in one. Along with checkboxes you also can implement the functionality of radio buttons by grouping multiple checkbox controls. Checkboxes are great for giving yes/no options. Radio buttons are good for multiple choice questions.

Figure 11.10 shows a couple of individual checkboxes on the left and a single group of checkboxes on the right. Here is the code that produced them:

```
import java.awt.*;

public class testMe extends Frame {

    public testMe() {
        super("Checkbox Demo");
        Panel P1 = new Panel();
        Panel P2 = new Panel();
```

```
        CheckboxGroup G1 = new CheckboxGroup();
        setLayout(new GridLayout(1,2));
        add(P1);
        add(P2);
        P1.setLayout(new FlowLayout());
        P1.add(new Checkbox("E-Mail Tom"));
        P1.add(new Checkbox("E-Mail Jack"));
        P2.setLayout(new FlowLayout());
        P2.add(new Checkbox("Me", G1, true));
        P2.add(new Checkbox("You", G1, false));
        P2.add(new Checkbox("Them", G1, false));
        resize(300, 200);
        show();
    }

    public static void main(String args[]) {
        testMe test = new testMe();
    }
}
```

Hierarchy For Checkbox

```
java.lang.Object
 java.awt.Component
     java.awt.Checkbox
```

Declaration For Checkbox

A number of options are available for calling a **Checkbox** constructor. Here is each option with a summary description:

```
new Checkbox();
```

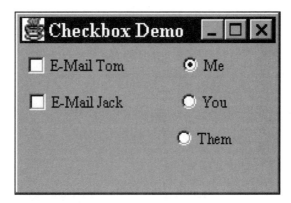

Figure 11.10   A few iterations of the Checkbox component.

Constructs a checkbox with no label, no checkbox group, and initializes it to a false state.

```
new Checkbox(String);
```

Constructs a checkbox with the specified label, no checkbox group, and initializes it to a false state.

```
new Checkbox(String, boolean);
```

Constructs a checkbox with the specified label, no checkbox group, and initializes it to a specified boolean state.

```
new Checkbox(String, CheckboxGroup, boolean);
```

Constructs a checkbox with the specified label, specified checkbox group, and initializes it to a specified boolean state.

Methods For Checkbox

Although checkboxes are simple UI components, they offer us a lot of options and therefore provide a few custom methods we can use to control them.

getCheckboxGroup()

This method returns the checkbox group that this checkbox belongs to.

getLabel()

This method gets the label of the button.

getState()

This method returns the boolean state of the checkbox.

setCheckboxGroup(CheckboxGroup)

This method sets the **CheckboxGroup** of the check box.

setLabel(String)

This method changes the label of the checkbox.

SET*S*TATE(BOOLEAN)

This method sets the checkbox to the specified boolean state.

The Choice Class

The **Choice** class implements a pop-up menu that shows the currently chosen option normally; but when it has the focus, it opens up and displays all the options a user can select from. Figure 11.11 shows a **Choice** component at rest and Figure 11.12 shows the same component in action..

Here is the code that creates the **Choice** component shown in Figures 11.11 and 11.12:

```java
import java.awt.*;

public class testMe extends Frame {

    public testMe() {
        super("Choice Demo");
        Choice C1 = new Choice();
        setLayout(new FlowLayout());
        add(C1);
        C1.addItem("You");
        C1.addItem("Me");
        C1.addItem("Them");
        C1.addItem("Us");
        C1.addItem("Everyone");
        resize(300, 200);
        show();
    }

    public static void main(String args[]) {
        testMe test = new testMe();
    }
}
```

Hierarchy For Choice

```
java.lang.Object
 java.awt.Component
      java.awt.Choice
```

Figure 11.11   The Choice component without the focus.

Figure 11.12   The Choice component with the focus.

Declaration For Choice

When you are creating a **Choice** component, you cannot set any options. All the options must be set after the object is created. The call for initializing **Choice** is simply:

```
new Choice();
```

Methods For Choice

The set of special methods available for the **Choice** class include:

ADDITEM(STRING)

This method adds an item to the list of choices.

COUNTITEMS()

This method returns the number of items.

GETITEM(INT)

This method returns the item at the specified index.

GETSELECTEDINDEX()

This method returns the index of the currently selected item.

GETSELECTEDITEM()

This method returns a string representation of the current choice.

SELECT(INT)

This method selects the item with the specified index position.

SELECT(STRING)

This method selects the item with the specified **String** if present.

The List Class

The **List** class is actually very similar to **Choice** except that it allows you to display multiple items and scroll through the ones not displayed. It also gives you the ability to select multiple items.

Figure 11.13 shows a form that contains a simple list with multiple elements. Here is the code that created these lists:

```
import java.awt.*;

public class testMe extends Frame {

    public testMe() {
        super("List Demo");
        List L1 = new List();
        setLayout(new FlowLayout());
        add(L1);
        L1.addItem("You");
        L1.addItem("Me");
        L1.addItem("Them");
        L1.addItem("Us");
        L1.addItem("Everyone");
```

```
        resize(300, 200);
        show();
    }

    public static void main(String args[]) {
        testMe test = new testMe();
    }
}
```

Hierarchy For List

```
java.lang.Object
 java.awt.Component
      java.awt.List
```

Declaration For List

Here are the two constructors you can call to initialize a **List** class:

```
new List();
```

Creates a scrolling list initialized with no visible lines and multiple selections disabled.

```
new List(int, boolean);
```

Creates a new scrolling list initialized with the specified number of visible lines and a boolean stating if multiple selections are allowed or not.

Methods For List

You'll find a number of methods for this class because of all the different options it offers.

Figure 11.13   Create lists with the List class.

ADDITEM(STRING)

This method adds the specified item to the end of list.

ALLOWSMULTIPLESELECTIONS()

This method returns true if the list allows multiple selections.

CLEAR()

This method clears the list.

COUNTITEMS()

This method returns the number of items in the list.

DELITEM(INT)

This method deletes an item from the list at the specified index.

DELITEMS(INT, INT)

This method deletes multiple items from the list. Items are deleted from the index position specified by the first parameter to the index position specified by the second parameter.

DESELECT(INT)

This method deselects the item at the specified index.

GETITEM(INT)

This method gets the item associated with the specified index.

GETROWS()

This method returns the number of visible lines in the list.

GETSELECTEDINDEX()

This method returns the selected item in the list or -1 if no item is selected.

GETSELECTEDINDEXES()

This method returns the selected indexes in the list in the form of an array.

GETSELECTEDITEM()

This method returns the selected item in the list or null if no item is selected, or it returns the first selected item if multiple items are selected.

GETSELECTEDITEMS()

This method returns the selected items in the list into an array of strings.

GETVISIBLEINDEX()

This method gets the index of the item that was last made visible by the method **makeVisible**().

ISSELECTED(INT)

This method returns true if the item at the specified index has been selected; false otherwise.

MAKEVISIBLE(INT)

This method forces the item at the specified index to be visible. The method automatically scrolls the list to display the specified index.

MINIMUMSIZE()

This method returns the minimum dimensions needed for the list.

MINIMUMSIZE(INT)

This method returns the minimum dimensions needed for the number of rows in the list.

PREFERREDSIZE()

This method returns the preferred dimensions needed for the list.

PREFERREDSIZE(INT)

This method returns the preferred dimensions needed for the list with the specified amount of rows.

SELECT(INT)

This method selects the item at the specified index.

SETMULTIPLESELECTIONS(BOOLEAN)

This method sets up a list to allow for multiple selections or not.

TextField And TextArea Classes

The **TextField** and **TextArea** classes implement other controls that you will use often. They are often accompanied with **Label** controls that tell the user what a text entry box is used for. Text fields can only have a single line of text, while text areas can have multiple lines like a word processor. One of the nice things about the **TextField** and **TextArea** components is that they interact with both the keyboard and the mouse. You can enter text by typing it on the keyboard. Then, you can use the mouse to place the cursor within that text. If you are a Windows 95 user, the components even support the right mouse button. If you right-click within a text field or text area, a pop-up menu will be displayed like the one shown in Figure 11.14.-

Hierarchy For TextField And TextArea

```
java.lang.Object
  java.awt.Component
      java.awt.TextComponent
        java.awt.TextField
        java.awt.TextArea
```

Declaration For TextField And TextArea

A number of constructors are available for initializing **TextField** and **TextArea** classes:

```
new TextField();
```

Constructs a new **TextField**.

Figure 11.14   Right-clicking on a TextField component to display a pop-up menu.

```
new TextField(int);
```

Creates a new **TextField** initialized with the specified number of columns (1 column = 1 character).

```
TextField(String)
```

Creates a new **TextField** initialized with the specified text.

```
new TextField(String, int);
```

Creates a new **TextField** initialized with the specified text and number of columns.

```
new TextArea();
```

Creates a new **TextArea**.

```
new TextArea(int, int);
```

Creates a new **TextArea** with the specified number of rows and columns.

```
new TextArea(String);
```

Constructs a new **TextArea** with the specified text displayed.

```
new TextArea(String, int, int);
```

Creates a new **TextArea** with the specified text and the specified number of rows and columns.

Methods For TextField And TextArea

Many of the methods used with these two classes are actually methods of the **TextComponent** class which both of these classes subclass. Let's look at these methods first.

GETSELECTIONEND()

This method returns the selected text's end position.

GETSELECTEDTEXT()

This method returns the selected text contained in the text component.

GETSELECTIONSTART()

This method returns the start position of the selected text. If no text is selected, the method returns -1.

GETTEXT()

This method returns the text contained in the text component.

ISEDITABLE()

This method returns a boolean value that tells us if the text component is editable or not. Text components are editable by default.

SELECT(INT, INT)

This method selects the text found between the specified start and end locations.

SELECTALL()

This method causes all of the text in the text component to be selected.

SETEDITABLE(BOOLEAN)

This method sets whether or not this text component can be edited.

SETTEXT(STRING)

This method changes the text of the text component to the specified text.

Now, let's look at a few methods that are specific to the **TextField** component:

ECHOCHARISSET()

This method returns true if the **TextField** has a character set for echoing. Echoing is used for situations where you do not want the text people are typing to be displayed.

GETCOLUMNS()

This method returns the number of columns in the **TextField**.

GETECHOCHAR()

This method returns the character to be used for echoing. The character is not returned in a **String** format, just a simple **char**.

MINIMUMSIZE()

This method returns the minimum size dimensions needed for the **TextField** in columns.

MINIMUMSIZE(INT)

This method is used to request a minimum size for the text box. The parameter specifies the number of columns for the text box. The method returns the minimum size dimensions needed for the **TextField** with the specified amount of columns.

PREFERREDSIZE()

This method returns the preferred size dimensions needed for the **TextField** class.

PREFERREDSIZE(INT)

This method returns the preferred size dimensions needed for the **TextField** with the specified amount of columns being passed to it.

SETECHOCHARACTER(CHAR)

This method sets the echo character for the **TextField**. Most often you'll want to set this character to the asterisk symbol, especially if you are working with password boxes.

Now, we need to look at the methods specific to the **TextArea** class:

GETCOLUMNS()

This method returns the number of columns in the **TextArea**.

GETROWS()

This method returns the number of rows in the **TextArea**.

INSERTTEXT(STRING, INT)

This method inserts the specified text at the specified position. The position tells Java the number of characters it needs to move over before it inserts the string.

PREFERREDSIZE()

This method returns the preferred size dimensions of the **TextArea**.

PREFERREDSIZE(INT, INT)

This method returns the row and column dimensions of the **TextArea**.

MINIMUMSIZE()

This method returns the minimum size dimensions of the **TextArea**.

MINIMUMSIZE(INT, INT)

This method returns the specified minimum size dimensions of the **TextArea**.

REPLACETEXT(STRING, INT, INT)

This method replaces text from the indicated start to end positions with the specified new text.

The Scrollbar Class

Several of the Java components we've been discussing in this chapter automatically use scrollbars when needed. For example, the **TextArea** control we just described will automatically create scrollbars when the text runs off the edge or the bottom. Scrollbars can also be created as standalone components. Scrollbars are useful when you need a user to pick a value. They offer a graphical interface rather than a simple text box where a user would usually have to type in a value.

Scrollbars are implemented using the concepts of a minimum, maximum, and current value. A scrollbar can be moved in three ways: small increments, large increments, or to an absolute position. The small increment occurs when the user clicks on the arrows at the top or bottom of the scrollbar. The large changes occur when the user clicks on the space between the current position and either arrow. Finally, the absolute change occurs when the user drags the current location indicator (sometimes called an *elevator*) and drags it to a specific spot within the scrollbar. Figure 11.15 shows a standard scrollbar and labels each part.

Let's consider a very typical use of a scrollbar. In this case, we have two components, a **Textfield** control and a **Scrollbar** control. We want to display the current value of the **Scrollbar** in the text box. Also, when the user changes the value in the text box, the scrollbar should match the change. Figure 11.16 shows what this simple application looks like.

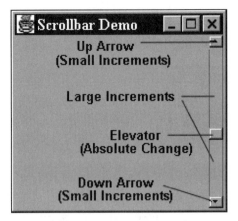

Figure 11.15   A typical Java scrollbar.

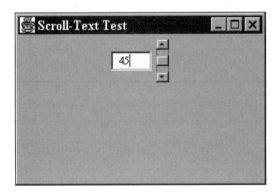

Figure 11.16   A Scrollbar control and a Textfield control with linked values.

And, here is the code for the entire application. Type it in and give it a try:

```
import java.awt.*;

public class ScrollTest extends Frame {
    TextField text;
    Scrollbar scroll;
    public ScrollTest() {
        super("Scroll-Text Test");
        text = new TextField(5);
        scroll = new Scrollbar(Scrollbar.VERTICAL, 0, 10, 0, 100);
        setLayout(new FlowLayout());
        add(text);
        add(scroll);
        resize(300, 200);
        show();
```

```
        }
    public boolean handleEvent(Event evt) {
        if (evt.target.equals(scroll)) {
            text.setText("" + scroll.getValue());
        } else if (evt.target.equals(text))
            {scroll.setValue(Integer.parseInt(text.getText()));
        } else if (evt.id == Event.WINDOW_DESTROY) {
            System.exit(0);
            return true;
        }
        return super.handleEvent(evt);
    }
    public static void main(String args[]) {
        ScrollTest test = new ScrollTest();
    }
}
```

Keep in mind that the scrollbar, like all the other controls, will change its appearance to match the operating system. Obviously, you would not want Windows 95 style scrollbars being displayed on a Macintosh. That would sure cause a commotion!

Hierarchy For Scrollbar

```
java.lang.Object
  java.awt.Component
      java.awt.Scrollbar
```

Declaration For Scrollbar

The three constructors provided for initializing scrollbars include:

```
new Scrollbar();
```

Constructs a new vertical **Scrollbar**.

```
new Scrollbar(int);
```

Constructs a new **Scrollbar** with the specified orientation. You can specify **Scrollbar.HORIZONTAL** or **Scrollbar.VERTICAL**. Scrollbars are vertical by default.

```
new Scrollbar(int, int, int, int, int);
```

creates a new **Scrollbar** with the specified orientation, current value, large change size, minimum value, and maximum value.

Methods For Scrollbar

Here are the set of specialized methods for the **Scrollbar** class:

GETMAXIMUM()

This method returns an integer representing the maximum value of the scrollbar.

GETMINIMUM()

This method returns an integer representing the minimum value of the scrollbar.

GETORIENTATION()

This method returns an integer that gives us the orientation for the scrollbar. You can check the returned integer against **Scrollbar.HORIZONTAL** and **Scrollbar.VERTICAL** to determine the scrollbar's orientation.

GETVALUE()

This method returns an integer representing the current value of the scrollbar.

GETVISIBLE()

This method returns the visible amount of the scrollbar.

SETVALUE(INT)

This method sets the value of the scrollbar to the specified value. If you try to set the current value to a number that is greater than the maximum or less than the minimum, the number becomes the new maximum or minimum, respectively.

SETVALUES(INT, INT, INT, INT)

This method changes the values for the scrollbar. The arguments in order of appearance include:

◆ value—the position in the current window

◆ large change—the value that will be moved each time the user clicks in the area between the elevator and the arrows. This value is also called the *amount visible per page*.

◆ minimum—the minimum value of the scrollbar

◆ maximum—the maximum value of the scrollbar

Building Menus

Menus in Java are as easy to build and manage as the other visual components. Every part of a menu, from the menu bar to individual items is represented as a separate class, each having specialized properties and methods. Let's start our investigation of menus with the main component— the menu bar. Then, we'll work our way down into the other more specialized components, such as a menu itself and menu items.

The MenuBar Class

Each window or frame you create in a Java application or applet can have its own menu bar. The standard menu bar is always displayed along the top of the window. You are not allowed to have multiple menu bars within a single window unless you create the entire system yourself (but why would you want to!).

The **MenuBar** class itself provides little functionality. By itself it looks like a blank bar across the top of your window. To give your menuing system functionality, you need to add **Menu** and **MenuItem** components, which we will discuss later.

Hierarchy For MenuBar

```
java.lang.Object
  java.awt.MenuComponent
      java.awt.MenuBar
```

Declaration For MenuBar

Only a single constructor is provided for initializing a **MenuBar** class. This constructor creates a menu object but does not display it. You must first assign the **MenuBar** to a frame for it to be displayed:

```
new MenuBar();
```

Methods For MenuBar

ADD(MENU)

This method adds the specified menu to the menu bar.

countMENUS()

This menu returns an integer representing the number of menus on the menu bar.

getHELPMENU()

This method returns the name of the menu component on the current menu bar that has been designated as the "Help" menu. Help menus are discussed in the next section in more detail.

getMENU(INT)

This menu gets the specified menu. Input is an integer representing the index position of a menu and it returns a **Menu** object.

REMOVE(INT)

This method removes the menu located at the specified index from the menu bar.

REMOVE(MENU)

This method removes the specified menu from the menu bar.

setHELPMENU(MENU)

This method sets the current help menu to the specified menu on the menu bar.

The Menu Class

The **Menu** class is used to implement the selections for the section headings for each type of menu. Typical **Menu** components will be labeled "File," "Options," and "Help." Figure 11.17 shows a few menus.

Menu classes are always children of a single **MenuBar** class. They usually have **MenuItem** classes as children. However, a **Menu** class does not *need*

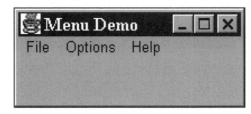

Figure 11.17   Examples of menus created with the Menu class.

to have menu items under it; it can react to events on its own. In Figure 11.17, you could click on the **Menu** component labeled "File" to expose its **MenuItem** children. However, if you were to click on the "Help" **Menu** item, it would not display any child **MenuItem** components because it does not have any. It acts on its own.

Hierarchy For Menu

```
java.lang.Object
  java.awt.MenuComponent
        java.awt.MenuItem
          java.awt.Menu
```

Declaration For Menu

Here are the two constructors provided for the **Menu** class:

```
new Menu(String);
```

Constructs a new **Menu** with the specified string as the label. This menu will not be able to be "torn off." Tear-off menus are menus that will still appear on the screen after the mouse button has been released.

```
new Menu(String, boolean);
```

Constructs a new **Menu** with the specified label. The menu will be able to be torn off if the boolean value is set to true.

Methods For Menu

The specialized methods for the **Menu** class include:

ADD(MENUITEM)

This method adds the specified item to the menu.

ADD(STRING)

This method adds an item with the specified label to the menu.

ADDSEPARATOR()

This method adds a separator line to the menu at the current position.

COUNTITEMS()

This method returns the number of elements in the menu as an integer.

GETITEM(INT)

This method returns the menu item located at the specified index of the menu.

ISTEAROFF()

This method returns true if the menu is a tear-off menu.

REMOVE(INT)

This method deletes the item at the specified index from the menu.

REMOVE(MENUITEM)

This method deletes the specified item from the menu.

The MenuItem Class

The **MenuItem** class is the last in the line of children of the three menu classes. We should mention, however, that **Menu** classes can have other **Menu** classes as children. These child **Menu** components look like menu items, but another menu would be under each menu to display more menu items. This is technique is used to create cascading menus as shown in Figure 11.18.

Here is the Java code that implements the menu system shown in Figure 11.18:

```
import java.awt.*;

public class testMe extends Frame {
    public testMe() {
```

```
        super("Menu Demo");
        MenuBar MB = new MenuBar();
        Menu M1 = new Menu("File");
        Menu M2 = new Menu("Options");
        Menu M3 = new Menu("More");
        MB.add(M1);
        MB.add(M2);
        MB.add(new Menu("Help"));
        M1.add(new MenuItem("Open"));
        M1.add(new MenuItem("Close"));
        M1.add(new MenuItem("Save"));
        M2.add(new MenuItem("General"));
        M2.add(M3);
        M3.add(new MenuItem("Screen"));
        M3.add(new MenuItem("Font"));
        setMenuBar(MB);
        resize(300, 200);
        show();
    }
    public static void main(String args[]) {
        testMe test = new testMe();
    }
}
```

The AWT also provides a subclass of the **MenuItem** class called **CheckboxMenuItem**. This class is identical to the standard **MenuItem** class except that it provides the ability to be "checked" or "unchecked" when the user clicks on a menu item. Figure 11.19 shows an example of this component.

Hierarchy For MenuItem

```
java.lang.Object
 java.awt.MenuComponent
        java.awt.MenuItem
```

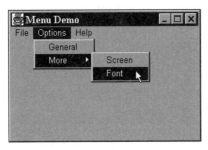

Figure 11.18   Creating cascading menus using Menus as subclasses.

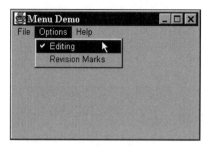

Figure 11.19   Using the CheckboxMenuItem to check and uncheck menu items.

Declaration For MenuItem

The **MenuItem** class provides a single constructor that takes one argument:

```
new MenuItem(String);
```

This class constructs a new **MenuItem** with the specified **String** displayed as the menu component's label. Note that the hyphen symbol (-) is reserved to mean a separator between menu items. Separators should do nothing except delineate different sections of a menu.

Methods For MenuItem

The specialized methods for the **MenuItem** class include:

DISABLE()

This method makes the menu item "unselectable" by the user and grays it out.

ENABLE()

This method makes the menu item "selectable" by the user. The user is given a visual cue when the menu is disabled because it is grayed out.

ENABLE(BOOLEAN)

This method conditionally enables a component.

GETLABEL()

This method gets the label for the menu item. The value is returned as a string.

ISENABLED()

This method checks to see if the menu item is enabled. The return value is a boolean value.

SETLABEL()

This method sets the label to be the specified string.

The following two methods are used only with the **CheckboxMenuItem** component.

GETSTATE()

This method returns a boolean value that represents the state of the menu item.

SETSTATE(BOOLEAN)

This method sets the state of the menu item.

Creating A Sample Menu Application

Now that we've introduced you to each of the three key classes for creating menus (**MenuBar**, **Menu**, and **MenuItem**), you're probably anxious to write a Java program that puts them to work. Let's build a sample application that incorporates all of them to create a practical menuing system. The application will not respond to any of the menu items being chosen, but it will show you the basic techniques for constructing a menuing system.

We need to start by planning our menu. Let's use three **Menu** components with the labels "File," "Options," and "Help." Under the File menu we will have seven **MenuItems** including two separators. The "Options" **Menu** component will have two **CheckboxMenuItem** components, and the "Help" menu will not have any menu items associated with it.

Figures 11.20 through 11.22 show several different views of our test program with different menu options being chosen. The code that creates this menuing system is as follows:

```
import java.awt.*;

class TestFrame extends Frame {
```

```
TestFrame() {
    super("Menu Test");
    MenuBar mb = new MenuBar();
    Menu fileMenu = new Menu("File");
    Menu optionMenu = new Menu("Option");
    Menu helpMenu = new Menu("Help");
    fileMenu.add(new MenuItem("New"));
    fileMenu.add(new MenuItem("-"));
    fileMenu.add(new MenuItem("Open"));
    fileMenu.add(new MenuItem("Close"));
    fileMenu.add(new MenuItem("Save"));
    fileMenu.addSeparator();
    fileMenu.add(new MenuItem("Exit"));
    optionMenu.add(new CheckboxMenuItem("Large Fonts"));
    optionMenu.add(new CheckboxMenuItem("Save Settings on Exit"));
    mb.setHelpMenu(helpMenu);
    mb.add(fileMenu);
    mb.add(optionMenu);
    mb.add(helpMenu);
    setMenuBar(mb);
    resize(300,200);
    show();
}

public boolean action(Event evt, Object obj) {
    String label = (String)obj;
    if (evt.target instanceof MenuItem) {
        if (label.equals("Exit")) {
            System.exit(0);
            return true;
            }
    }
    return true;
}

public boolean handleEvent(Event evt) {
    if (evt.id == Event.WINDOW_DESTROY) {
        System.exit(0);
        return true;
    }
    return super.handleEvent(evt);
}
public static void main(String args[]) {
    TestFrame tf = new TestFrame();
}
}
```

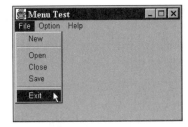

Figure 11.20   Menu test app view #1.

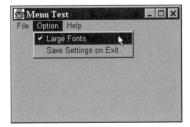

Figure 11.21   Menu test app view #2.

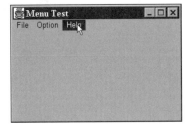

Figure 11.22   Menu test app view #3.

You my notice that we used two different methods for creating the two separators in the "File" menu. The **addSeparator**() method is probably easier. However, if using the standard **add**() method with the hyphen character, you can create a full-fledged menu item that you can then change options for and set up so that it can respond to mouse clicks. Now that you've seen the basics for creating menus and GUI objects, you'll need a way to position them within the frames you build. And that's where the layout manager comes in.

Working With The Layout Manager

To most programmers, the layout manager is a pretty strange concept. Instead of telling Java exactly where you want components to be located within a window, you use the layout manager to actively place interface components depending on the container size, shape, and on a few variables you set.

All controls you create for a Java application must *always* use the layout manager. Even if you do not implicitly tell Java what to do, it defaults to using a particular version of the layout manager. The layout manager comes in different "flavors" for different situations. At this point in the evolution of Java, five different layout managers are provided:

◆ FlowLayout

◆ BorderLayout

◆ GridLayout

◆ GridBagLayout

◆ CardLayout

The layout manager is actually just an Interface. You then create classes that implement the **LayoutManager** interface. These classes are used by the AWT and your program to get the look and feel you want for the user. Let's look at each of the layout manager classes in detail.

Any component that is a container in Java can use a different layout. So, you could have a **Frame** that uses one class to lay out two panels which each have their own layouts, and so on.

The FlowLayout Class

The **FlowLayout** class is the default layout for all containers in Java. This class tries to lay out components in a very orderly fashion that is much like a word processor that wraps your words and centers them. The order in which you add components to a container using **FlowLayout** is vital. The first component you add is the first in line and the last will be placed at the end. It is possible to go back and insert and remove components, but it is much easier to do it all correctly at the beginning.

Figure 11.23 shows several buttons on a panel. As you can see, they are centered as a group within the panel. If we resize the panel, the buttons automatically align themselves again to be centered. If we continue to shrink the panel so that all the buttons no longer fit across the panel, the last button will be "wrapped" to the next row as shown in Figure 11.24.

Declaration For FlowLayout

To set the layout for a container, you use the **setLayout**() method. This method has a single argument which is an instance of one of the layout classes. Let's look at an example. The code shown here is used to create the arrangements shown in Figures 11.23 and 11.24:

```
import java.awt.*;

class LayoutFrame extends Frame {

    LayoutFrame() {
        super("Layout Test");
        setLayout(new FlowLayout());
        add(new Button("Button 1"));
        add(new Button("Button 2"));
        add(new Button("Button 3"));
        add(new Button("Button 4"));
        add(new Button("Button 5"));
        resize(300,200);
        show();
    }

    public static void main(String args[]) {
        LayoutFrame lf = new LayoutFrame();
    }
}
```

Here we call the **setLayout**() method of the **Frame** we have extended, sending it a new instance of the **FlowLayout** class. The frame will then query the **FlowLayout** object where to position each component. This query happens whenever the window needs to be refreshed, such as when it is resized or uncovered.

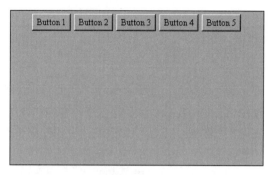

Figure 11.23   Using the FlowLayout class to lay out some buttons.

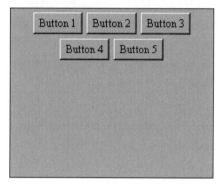

Figure 11.24   The same panel resized so that the buttons wrap to the next row.

Methods For FlowLayout

The specialized methods for **FlowLayout** include:

*LAYOUT*CONTAINER*(CONTAINER)*

This method lays out the container. It will actually reshape the components in the target container to satisfy the constraints of the **FlowLayout** object.

*MINIMUM*LAYOUT*SIZE (CONTAINER)*

This method returns the minimum dimensions needed to lay out the components contained in the specified target container. These dimensions are extremely useful because they can help you ensure that the user will not shrink the container to such a small size that it forces some of the UI components to slip off the visible screen.

PREFERRED*L*AYOUT*S*IZE(*C*ONTAINER)

This method returns the preferred dimensions for this layout given the components in the specified target container. The return value is a **Dimension** variable consisting of two values representing the width and height of the layout.

TO*S*TRING()

This method returns a string representation of this **FlowLayout**'s values, including: (in this order) X position, Y position, container dimensions, layout class being used, whether or not the container can be resized, and the title of the container.

The BorderLayout Class

The **BorderLayout** class creates a unique layout scheme that is useful for working with components that need to maintain their position relative to an edge of your container. Border layouts use a compass analogy to allow you to specify which side of the container to attach your control to.

The controls you use for border layouts are automatically sized to take up as much space as possible. Figure 11.25 shows a sample container with five panels, one in each area of the container that the border layout allows.

To create this sample, we used the same code from the previous figure and made a few very minor changes. In fact, all the changes take place in the constructor for the class, so we will only show you that:

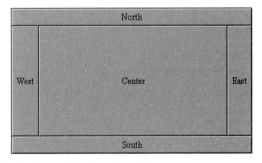

Figure 11.25   The BorderLayout() class in action.

```
LayoutFrame() {
     super("Layout Test");
     setLayout(new BorderLayout());
     add("North", new Button("North"));
     add("East", new Button("East"));
     add("South", new Button("South"));
     add("West", new Button("West"));
     add("Center", new Button("Center"));
     resize(300,200);
     show();
  }
```

The first change is obviously the switch to specifying the **BordeLayout**()
class as our layout scheme. The other changes occur in the **add**() method.
What are those extra strings doing there? They specify which side of the
container to place the new control. In this case, we are using buttons with
labels that match the position names (North, East, South, West, and Center).
We used buttons here for clarity sake, but you would probably not use
them for any real projects. Panel components are probably the best for this
type of layout. You would specify a few panels using a border style layout
and then use a different layout scheme for the individual panels. Since
panels are for design purposes mostly—they do not show up since they
default to the same color as the background of the frame—they blend in
perfectly and bring the whole thing together.

Declaration For BorderLayout

There are two ways to declare a border layout. You can use the simple
constructor we used in the sample application or you can also specify a
vertical and horizontal space.

```
new BorderLayout();
```

The simple way. Constructs a new **BorderLayout**.

```
new BorderLayout(int, int);
```

Constructs a **BorderLayout** with the specified gaps. The first integer
represents the horizontal gap to be placed between components and the
second integer represents the vertical gap to be used.

Methods For BorderLayout

The specialized methods for **BorderLayout** include:

ADDLAYOUTCOMPONENT(STRING, COMPONENT)

This method adds the specified named component to the layout. The **String** argument gives us a name to refer to the component within the layout. The component can be any type of interface component we want to add.

LAYOUTCONTAINER(CONTAINER)

This method lays out the specified container. It will actually reshape the components in the specified target container to satisfy the constraints of the **BorderLayout** object.

MINIMUMLAYOUTSIZE(CONTAINER)

This method returns the minimum dimensions needed to lay out the components contained in the specified target container. The return value is a dimension variable.

PREFERREDLAYOUTSIZE(CONTAINER)

This method returns the preferred dimensions for the layout given the components in the specified target container. The method also returns a dimension style variable.

REMOVELAYOUTCOMPONENT(COMPONENT)

This method removes the specified component from the layout.

TOSTRING()

This method returns the string representation of the **BorderLayout**'s values. At this point in the development of Java, this method only returns the size of the horizontal and vertical gaps.

The GridLayout Class

The grid style layout works just like it sounds; it creates a grid pattern for laying out components. You can control the number of rows and columns as well as the space between the components and the space between the

Figure 11.26   Using the GridLayout() class to create a sample frame.

components and the edge of the container. Figure 11.26 shows a sample frame using a grid layout.

Declaration For GridLayout

Like the **BorderLayout** class, **GridLayout** gives you a few constructor options. If the number of rows or columns is invalid, you will get an error (i.e., no negative numbers). Also, if you specify more columns than you need, the columns will not be used and your grid will appear as if you've specified fewer columns. However, if you specify more rows than you need, they will show up as blank space with enough space that matches the amount of space taken up by a component in this layout. We think this is a bug in Java, so you should experiment with this phenomenon if you plan on using this layout style.

```
new GridLayout(int, int);
```

Creates a grid layout with the specified rows and columns.

```
new GridLayout (int, int, int ,int);
```

Creates a grid layout with the specified rows, columns, horizontal gap, and vertical gap.

Methods For GridLayout

The specialized methods for **GridLayout** include:

addLayoutComponent(String, Component)

This method adds the specified named component to the layout. The **String** argument gives us a name to refer to the component within terms of the layout. The component can be any interface component you want to add.

layoutContainer(Container)

This method lays out the specified container. It will actually reshape the components in the specified target container to satisfy the constraints of the **GridLayout** object.

minimumLayoutSize(Container)

This method returns the minimum dimensions needed to lay out the components contained in the specified target container. The return value is a dimension variable.

preferredLayoutSize(Container)

This method returns the preferred dimensions for this layout given the components in the specified target container. It also returns a dimension style variable.

removeLayoutComponent(component)

This method removes the specified component from the layout.

toString()

This method returns the string representation of the **GridLayout**'s values. At this point in the development of Java, this method only returns the size of the horizontal and vertical gaps.

The GridBagLayout Class

The **GridBagLayout** class is one of the most versatile of all the layout classes. It allows you to create a grid of an arbitrary size and use it to create components within the grid that are of variable size.

You use this layout method to align components vertically and horizontally, without requiring that the components be the same size or without them being sized for you in ways you may not want. Each

GridBagLayout uses a rectangular grid of cells, with each component occupying one or more cells.

Each component that resides in a container that is using a **GridBagLayout** has an associated **GridBagConstraints** instance that specifies how the component is laid out within the grid. How a **GridBagLayout** places a set of components depends on each component's **GridBagConstraints**, minimum size, and preferred size.

To use a **GridBagLayout** effectively, you must customize one or more of its component's **GridBagConstraints**. Here are some of the variables you need to customize to create a layout:

◆ **gridx**, **gridy** Specifies the cell in the grid at the upper left of the component. The upper-left-most cell of a container has address gridx=0, gridy=0.

◆ **gridwidth**, **gridheight** Specifies the width and height of our component in grid space terms. You can set either of these to **GridBagConstraints.REMAINDER** to make the component be the last one in its row or column.

◆ **fill** Used when the component's display area is larger than the component's requested size to determine whether (and how) to resize the component.

◆ **ipadx**, **ipady** Specifies the internal padding. Padding represents the amount of space to add to the minimum size of the component. The width of the component will be at least its minimum width plus **ipadx*2** pixels (since the padding applies to both sides of the component). Similarly, the height of the component will be at least the minimum height plus **ipady*2** pixels.

◆ **insets** Sets the external padding of the component—the minimum amount of space between the component and the edges of its display area.

◆ **anchor** Used when the component is smaller than its display area to determine where to place the component. Valid values are:

```
GridBagConstraints.CENTER (the default)
GridBagConstraints.NORTH
```

```
GridBagConstraints.NORTHEAST
GridBagConstraints.EAST
GridBagConstraints.SOUTHEAST
GridBagConstraints.SOUTH
GridBagConstraints.SOUTHWEST
GridBagConstraints.WEST
GridBagConstraints.NORTHWEST
```

◆ **weightx, weighty** Used to determine how to distribute space; this is important for specifying resizing behavior. Unless you specify a weight for at least one component in a row and column, all the components clump together in the center of their container. This is because when the weight is zero (the default), the GridBagLayout puts any extra space between its grid of cells and the edges of the container.

It is probably easiest to give you an example. Figure 11.27 shows the layout we wish to end up with. Following it is the code that we used to create it:

```
import java.awt.*;
import java.util.*;

public class GridBagTest extends Frame {

    GridBagTest() {
        super("GridBag Test");
        GridBagLayout gridbag = new GridBagLayout();
        GridBagConstraints c = new GridBagConstraints();
        setFont(new Font("Helvetica", Font.PLAIN, 14));
        setLayout(gridbag);
        c.fill = GridBagConstraints.BOTH;
        c.weightx = 1.0;
        makebutton("Button1", gridbag, c);
        makebutton("Button2", gridbag, c);
        makebutton("Button3", gridbag, c);
        c.gridwidth = GridBagConstraints.REMAINDER; //end row
        makebutton("Button4", gridbag, c);
        c.weightx = 0.0;                    //reset to the default
        makebutton("Button5", gridbag, c); //another row
        c.gridwidth = GridBagConstraints.RELATIVE; //next-to-last in row
        makebutton("Button6", gridbag, c);
        c.gridwidth = GridBagConstraints.REMAINDER; //end row
        makebutton("Button7", gridbag, c);
        c.gridwidth = 1;                    //reset to the default
        c.gridheight = 2;
        c.weighty = 1.0;
```

```
    makebutton("Button8", gridbag, c);
    c.weighty = 0.0;                          //reset to the default
    c.gridwidth = GridBagConstraints.REMAINDER; //end row
    c.gridheight = 1;                         //reset to the default
    makebutton("Button9", gridbag, c);
    makebutton("Button10", gridbag, c);
    resize(300, 100);
    show();
}

protected void makebutton(String name, GridBagLayout gridbag,
                          GridBagConstraints c) {
    Button button = new Button(name);
    gridbag.setConstraints(button, c);
    add(button);
}

public static void main(String args[]) {
    GridBagTest test = new GridBagTest();
}
}
```

Declaration For GridBagLayout

Since most of the work of setting up a **GridBagLayout** is achieved using a **GridBagConstraints** class, the constructor for **GridBagLayout** is very simple, in fact, it requires no arguments at all:

```
new GridBagLayout();
```

Methods For GridBagLayout

The specialized methods for **GridBagLayout** include:

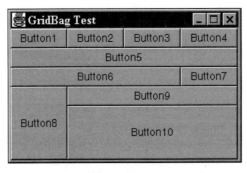

Figure 11.27   Sample program using the GridBagLayout class.

DumpConstraints(GridBagConstraints)

This method prints the layout constraints to the **System** object. It is useful for debugging.

getConstraints(Component)

This method returns a copy of the **GridBagConstraints** object for the specified component.

layoutContainer(Container)

This method lays out the specified container. This method will actually reshape the components in the specified target container to satisfy the constraints of the **GridBagLayout** object.

lookupConstraints(Component)

This method retrieves the constraints for the specified component. The return value is not a copy, but is the actual constraints class used by the layout mechanism. The object returned by this method can then be altered to affect the looks of the component.

minimumLayoutSize(Container)

This method returns the minimum dimensions needed to lay out the components contained in the specified target container. The return value is a dimension variable.

preferredLayoutSize(Container)

This method returns the preferred dimensions for this layout given the components in the specified target container. It also returns a dimension style variable.

setConstraints(Component, GridBagConstraints)

This method sets the constraints for the specified component.

toString()

This method returns the string representation of the **GridBagLayout**'s values. At this point in the development of Java, this method only returns the size of the horizontal and vertical gaps.

The CardLayout Class

The card layout style is much different than the previous four. Instead of using this class to lay out your controls, you use it like a layering system to specify which layer certain controls appear on. The most common use for this class is to simulate tabbed dialogs. You can create a card layout containing several panels that each use their own layout method and controls. Then, you can make a call to the class to specify which card to display and therefore which panel and respective components to show.

Declaration For CardLayout

Two versions of the **CardLayout()** constructor are available—one requires no parameters. To add extra cards, you simply use the **add()** method and the layout manager automatically handles the extra cards. Optionally, you can specify the horizontal and vertical gaps that surround your cards.

```
new CardLayout();
// Creates a new card layout.
new CardLayout(int, int);
```

Creates a card layout with the specified horizontal and vertical gaps.

Methods For CardLayout

The specialized methods for **CardLayout** include:

addLayoutComponent(String, component)

This method adds the specified named component to the layout. The **String** argument gives us a name to refer to the component within terms of the layout. The component can be any interface component you want to add.

first(Container)

This method flips to the first card. The argument is the parent container that you assigned the layout style to.

last (Container)

This method flips to the last card of the specified container.

LAYOUTCONTAINER(CONTAINER)

This method lays out the specified container. This method will actually reshape the components in the specified target container to satisfy the constraints of the **CardLayout** object.

MINIMUMLAYOUTSIZE(CONTAINER)

This method returns the minimum dimensions needed to layout the components contained in the specified target container. The return value is a dimension variable.

NEXT(CONTAINER)

This method flips to the next card in the stack.

PREFERREDLAYOUTSIZE(CONTAINER)

This method returns the preferred dimensions for the layout given the components in the specified target container. This also returns a dimension style variable.

PREVIOUS(CONTAINER)

This method flips to the previous card.

REMOVELAYOUTCOMPONENT(COMPONENT)

This method removes the specified component from the layout.

SHOW(CONTAINER, STRING)

This method flips to the specified component name in the specified container. This method is best used when you cannot use any of the previous four methods and/or you want to switch directly to a specified card. The **Container** argument specifies the owner of the card layout and the string is the name of the component you wish to switch to.

TOSTRING()

This method returns the string representation of the **CardLayout**'s values. At this point in the development of Java, this method only returns the size of the horizontal and vertical gaps.

Programming Java Applets 12

Anthony Potts

Once you master the basics of using the Java language, you'll want to learn as much as you can about writing powerful applets.

*T*he Java language offers a unique option—to be able to create programs that run as a "stand-alone" applications or as applets that are dependent on a controlling program such as a Web browser. The big difference between applications and applets is that applications contain enough code to work on their own and applets need a controlling program to tell the applet when to do what.

By itself, an applet has no means of starting execution because it does not have a **main**() method. In an application, the **main**() method is the place where execution starts. Any classes that are not accessed directly or indirectly through the **main**() method of an application are ignored.

If you have programmed in a visual environment before, the concept of an applet should be easy to understand. You can think of an applet as you would a type of custom control. When a custom control is used, you don't have to create code to make it go; that is handled for you. All you have to do is respond to events. With applets, you do not have to create the code that makes it go; you only need to write code to respond to events that the parent program calls—usually the browser.

Applet Basics

Let's look closely at some of the key areas you need to be aware of when creating applets. To start, you need to subclass the **Applet** class. By doing this, you inherit quite a bit of applet functionality that is built-in to the **Applet** class.

Listing 12.1 shows the hierarchy of the Applet class and Table 12.1 provides a detailed look at the components of the **Applet** class that are inherited when you implement it.

Table 12.1   Methods available in the Applet class.

Method	Description
destroy()	Cleans up whatever resources are being held. If the applet is active, it is first stopped.
getAppletContext()	Returns a handle to the applet context. The applet context is the parent object—either a browser or applet viewer. By knowing this handle, you can control the environment and perform operations like telling a browser to download a file or jump to another Web page.
getAppletInfo()	Returns a string containing information about the author, version, and copyright of the applet.
getAudioClip(URL)	Returns the data of an audio clip that is located at the given URL. The sound is not played until the play() method is called.
getAudioClip(URL, String)	Returns the data of an audio clip that is located at the given location relative to the document's URL. The sound is not played until the play() method is called.
getCodeBase()	Returns the URL of the applet itself.
getDocumentBase ()	Gets the URL of the document that the applet is embedded in. If the applet stays active as the browser goes from page to page, this method will still return the URL of the original document the applet was called from.

Continued

Table 12.1   Methods available in the Applet class (Continued).

Method	Description
getImage(URL)	Gets an image at the given URL. This method always returns an image object immediately even if the image does not exist. The actual image details are loaded when the image is first needed and not at the time it is loaded. If no image exists, an exception is thrown.
getImage(URL, String)	Gets an image at a URL relative to the document's URL. This method always returns an image object immediately even if the image does not exist. The actual image details are loaded when the image is first needed and not at the time it is loaded. If no image exists, an exception is thrown.
getParameter(String)	Returns a parameter that matches the value of the argument string.
getParameterInfo()	Returns an array of strings describing the parameters that are understood by this applet. The array consists of sets of three strings: name, type, and description. Often, the description string will be empty.
init()	Initializes the applet. You never need to call this method directly; it is called automatically by the system once the applet is created. The init() method is empty so you need to override it if you need anything initialized at the time your applet is loaded.
isActive()	Returns true if the applet is active. An applet is marked active just before the start() method is called.
play(URL)	This method plays an audio clip that can be found at the given URL. Nothing happens if the audio clip cannot be found.
play(URL, String)	This method plays an audio clip that resides at a location relative to the current URL. Nothing happens if the audio clip is not found.

Continued

Table 12.1   Methods available in the Applet class (Continued).

Method	Description
resize(int, int)	Requests that an applet be resized. The first integer is height and the second is width. This method overrides the resize() method of the Component class that is part of the Applet class's hierarchy.
showStatus(String)	Shows a status message in the Applet's context. This method allows you to display a message in the applet context's status bar, usually a browser. This is very useful for displaying URL's when an action the user is about to do will result in a jump to a new Web page.
start()	Starts the applet. You never need to call this method directly; it is called when the applet's document is visited. Once again, this method is empty and you need to override it to make it useful. This is usually where you would put the guts of your code. However, be aware that this method is called every time the page that embeds the applet is called. So make sure that the applet is being destroyed if necessary.
stop()	This method is called when the browser leaves the page the applet is embedded in. It is up to you to take this opportunity to use the destroy() method to terminate your applet. There may be times, however, when you do not want to destroy it here and instead wait until a "Quit" button is pressed, or until the browser itself closes (then everything is dumped rather ungraciously). stop() is guaranteed to be called before the destroy() method is called. You never need to call this method directly because the browser will call it for you.

LISTING 12.1   HIERERACHY OF THE APPLET CLASS

```
java.lang.Object
    java.awt.Component
        java.awt.Container
            java.awt.Panel
                java.applet.Applet
```

As illustrated above, the listing illustrates, the **Applet** class is a descendant of the **Container** class; thus, it can hold other objects. You do not need to create a panel first to place objects on because the **Applet** class extends the **Panel** class. Finally, because the **Container** class is derived from the **Component** class, we have the ability to respond to events, grab and display images, and display text among many other things. Table 12.2 presents some of the key methods you have access to because of all the classes that have been extended to get to the **Applet** class.

Applet Drawbacks

Applets can really eat up system resources. If you do not use threads and you create loops in an applet, you may run into serious performance

---

Table 12.2   Key methods that the Applet class can use.

Derived from the Component class:

Method	Description
getBackground()	Gets the background color. If the component does not have a background color, the background color of its parent is returned.
getFont()	Gets the font of the component. If the component does not have a font, the font of its parent is returned.
getFontMetrics(Font)	Gets the font metrics for this component. It will return null if the component is currently not on the screen. Font metrics tell you things like the height and width of a string using the given font on the current component.

Continued

Table 12.2   Key methods that the Applet class can use (Continued).

Derived from the Component class:

Method	Description
getForeground()	Gets the foreground color. If the component does not have a foreground color, the foreground color of its parent is returned.
getGraphics()	Gets a Graphics context for this component. This method will return null if the component is currently not visible on the screen.
handleEvent(Event)	Handles all events. Returns true if the event is handled and should not be passed to the parent of this component. The default event handler calls some helper methods to make life easier on the programmer.
hide()	Hides the component.
inside(int, int)	Checks if a specified x,y location is inside this component.
locate(int, int)	Returns the component or subcomponent that contains the x,y location.
location()	Returns the current location of this component. The location will be in the parent's coordinate space. The return value is a point object which is simply an x and y integer value.
move(int, int)	Moves the component to a new location. The integers are the x and y coordinates and are in the parent's coordinate space.
repaint()	Repaints the component. This will result in a call to update as soon as possible. The screen will also be cleared resulting in a brief flicker.
repaint(long)	Repaints the component. However, the extra argument is a long value that instructs Java that it must perform the update within that value in milliseconds.

Continued

Table 12.2   Key methods that the Applet class can use (Continued).

Derived from the Component class:

Method	Description
reshape(int, int, int, int)	Reshapes the component to the specified bounding box. The first two integers represent the new x an y coordinates the component should be moved to, and the second set of integers represent the new width and height.
resize(int, int)	Resizes the component to the specified width and height.
setBackground(Color)	Sets the background color.
setFont(Font)	Sets the font of the component.
setForeground(Color)	Sets the foreground color.
show()	Shows the component.
size()	Returns the current size of the component. The return value is a dimension object that has two integer values representing the width and height.
update(graphics)	Updates the component. This method is called in response to a call to repaint(). If you override this method and call it instead of the paint() method, the screen will not be cleared first.

Derived from the Container class:

add(Component)	Adds the specified component to this container.
countComponents()	Returns the number of components in this panel.
getComponents()	Gets all the components in this container. The return value is actually an array of Component objects.
getLayout()	Returns the layout manager for the container.
remove(Component)	Removes the specified component from the container.
removeAll()	Removes all the components from the container. It is dangerous to use if you are not careful.
setLayout(LayoutManager)	Sets the layout manager for the container.

problems with your browser. The browser can get so busy working with the applet that it does not have time to respond to Web page events such as refreshes, scrolls, and mouse clicks.

When some developers first heard about applets and their ability to run on many types of machines, there first response was, "That's dangerous!" Many were concerned that applets would be used for mischievous causes. To prevent applets from causing problems on machines, there are several built-in security measures you can take advantage of.

LIMITED FILE ACCESS

Applets cannot read from or write to files on an end user's hard drive. They can only read files that reside on the machine the applet was called from. Eventually, a user will be able to set up specific directories that an applet can have access to, but that functionality is not very robust yet and may not be implemented on all browsers, so don't count on it.

NATIVE METHODS

The other option or loop-hole (depending on how you look at it) is the use of *native methods*. You can create methods in C++ that can be called directly from Java. This is a very powerful option, especially if you are creating platform-specific programs that need the extra speed that you can get from natively compiled code. However, it can also be a potential gateway for mischievous programs. This feature may or may not be disabled, depending on the browser, so be cautious of how you use it.

FILE EXECUTION

Java applets are not allowed to execute programs on a user's system. So, you can't just run the **Format** program and wipe a hard drive.

NETWORK COMMUNICATION

Applets are only allowed to communicate with the server from which they were downloaded. This is another one of the security features that may or not be in effect depending on the browser. So, once again, do not program for it. This is actually one security option we would like to see go away or at least be able to have the user override it. The ability to talk with multiple servers could be incredibly powerful if implemented well. Just think of a large company with servers all over the world. You could create a little applet that could converse with them all and gather information for the end users.

A DISCLAIMER

Just because Java provides a few security features does not mean that it is completely secure. Java is a language that is still very much in its infancy and someone, somewhere will find a way to hack the system. However, since Java was produced to be an Internet friendly language (one of the first), it is much more secure than other languages. The problem is that it is also getting much more attention than all the others combined. Attention from users, programmers, and *hackers*!

Let's Play

Now that you have seen all the methods that you can use and learned a little about applet security, let's create an applet that uses some of these features.

The applet we'll create is a simple navigation applet that will offer the user several buttons with URLs as labels. When the user clicks on a button, the browser will be instructed to go to a particular site. We have also included some sound support just for the fun of it. Lets see the code first:

```
import java.applet.*;
import java.awt.*;
import java.net.*;

// testNav Class
public class testNav extends Applet {
    AudioClip startClip;
    AudioClip linkClip;
    AudioClip stopClip;
```

```
public testNav() {
    setLayout(new GridLayout(4, 1));
    add(new Button("http://www.coriolis.com"));
    add(new Button("http://www.javasoft.com"));
    add(new Button("http://www.gamelan.com"));
    add(new Button("http://www.microsoft.com"));
}

public boolean action(Event evt, Object arg) {
    if (evt.target instanceof Button) {
        linkClip.play();
        fetchLink((String)arg);
        return true;
    }
    return super.handleEvent(evt);

    void fetchLink(String s) {
    URL tempURL = null;
    try { tempURL  = new URL(s); }
    catch(MalformedURLException e) {
        showStatus("Malformed URL Exception has been thrown!");
    }
    getAppletContext().showDocument(tempURL);
}

public void init(){
    startClip = getAudioClip(getCodeBase(),  "start.au");
    linkClip = getAudioClip(getCodeBase(), "link.au");
    stopClip = getAudioClip(getCodeBase(), "stop.au");
}

public void start(){
    testNav TN = new testNav();
    startClip.play();
}

public void stop(){
    stopClip.play();
}

} // End testNav
```

Figure 12.1 shows the testNav applet running in the Netscape browser.

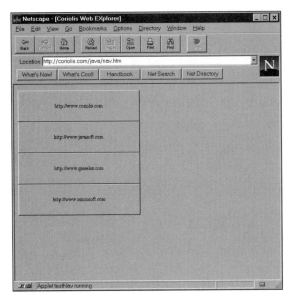

Figure 12.1   Running the testNav applet.

Interacting With The Browser

Quite often, you may want your applet to interact with the host browser. That interaction will usually come in the form of asking the browser to go to another Web site, or changing the text displayed in the status bar at the bottom of the browser. Let's look at how to switch Web pages now, then we'll show you how to control the status bar.

For our little demo program, we need the browser to change pages whenever a button is pushed. To accomplish this, we need to use an event handling method. The **action()** method is the best place to do this, so let's look at that method in more detail:

```
public boolean action(Event evt, Object arg) {
    if (evt.target instanceof Button) {
        linkClip.play();
        fetchLink((String)arg);
        return true;
    }
    return super.handleEvent(evt);
}
```

This method handles mouse and keyboard actions for us. The first thing it does is check to see if the **target** of the action is a **Button** or not. If it is, we play a sound file and call the **fetchLink()** method that we created to actually go to other sites. We will cover the sound stuff in a minute. Right now, let's look at the **fetchLink()** method and see how we instruct the browser to grab other pages:

```
void fetchLink(String s) {
    URL tempURL = null;
    try { tempURL  = new URL(s); }
    catch(MalformedURLException e) {
        showStatus("Malformed URL Exception has been thrown!");
    }
    getAppletContext().showDocument(tempURL);
}
```

This method accepts a string representation of a URL, changes it into a URL object, then calls the **showDocument()** method that really does the work. We are forced to use a **try...catch** operation when we are creating a URL because it throws exceptions. In particular, it throws the **MalformedURLException**. Basically, if the URL string you are trying to turn into a URL object is poorly constructed, you will get an error. For example, if you leave off the "http://" part, you will get this error.

Once the URL is properly created, we call the **showDocument()** method that actually belongs to the browser. This is not an applet method. You can figure this out because we are calling the **getAppletContext()** method at the beginning of the line. This method returns the object representation of the browser which has its own methods, variables, and so on.

Changing The Status Bar

If you look at the **action()** method again, you will notice that we make an interesting method call whenever there is an error. Here is that line:

```
showStatus("Malformed URL Exception has been thrown!");
```

You can also code this operation like this:

```
getAppletContext().showStatus("Malformed URL Exception has been
 thrown!");
```

To some people, this is easier to read because it becomes immediately apparent which object is accepting the **showStatus()** method.

Changing this text at key times is a great way to interact with the user because the status bar is a consistent object across many applications so they expect it to be there and they expect useful information from it. For a little test, try and make the status bar display the link for any button that the mouse pointer is moving over.

Playing Sounds

For loading and playing sounds from within an applet we have two options. First, we can use the **play()** method of the applet that loads and plays the given sound right away. Second, we can load an applet into an **AudioClip** object using the **getAudioClip()** method and play the sound whenever we want. It's up to you to decide if the sounds should be loaded before they are played, or loaded and played at the same time.

To use the **play()** method, you invoke the method, sending the URL of the sound file you want as an argument. Or, you can split the URL into two pieces. The first piece would be a URL representing the code base, and the second argument would be the file name and directory relative to the code base. Here are the declarations for these methods:

```
play(URL);  // This is the full URL of the sound file you want to
            // play
play(URL, String);  // This is the call that uses a base URL and a
                    // string representing the file name
```

The other option we have for playing sounds is to load them into an object first. To do this we will create an **AudioClip** object and use the **getAudioClip()** method to load the sound file into the audio object. Once the sound file is loaded, we call the **play()** method of the **AudioClip** object to hear the sound. Here are the declarations and calls to handle sounds in this manner:

```
getAudioClip(URL); // This requires a fully-qualified URL that points
                   // to a sound file
```

```
getAudioClip(URL, String); // This is the call that uses a base URL
                           // and a string representing the file
                           // name
```

To declare an **AudioClip** object, just follow this code:

```
AudioClip myClip;
```

Then, to load in the image do this:

```
myClip = getAudioClip(soundURL);
```

Finally, here's the call needed to play the file:

```
myClip.play();
```

You can also stop or loop the sound clip with these methods:

```
myClip.stop();
myClip.loop();
```

If a sound file being requested cannot be found, the **AudioClip** object will be set to null. No exception will be raised, but if you then try to play, stop, or loop the file, an exception will be thrown.

Displaying Images

One other key area we need to cover is the quick and painless use of images within applets. Images are just as easy to download as sounds. Here is a little sample applet that downloads an image and blasts it onto the screen:

```
import java.awt.*;
import java.applet.*;

public class testImg extends Applet {
   Image testImage;

   public void paint(Graphics g) {
      g.drawImage(testImage, 0, 0, this);
   }

   public void init() {
      testImage = getImage(getDocumentBase(), "sample.gif");
   }
}
```

This is an extremely simple program but it illustrates how easy downloading images is. The syntax for downloading images is almost identical to what we used for downloading sounds.

The syntax for declaring an image object is :

```
Image myImage;
```

And the syntax for the **getImage()** method is:

```
getImage(URL); // Downloads the image that resides at the given
               // fully-qualified URL
getImage(URL, String); // The URL is the code or document base,
                        // and the string is the directory and file
                        // name for the image relative to the code
                        // base
```

These image methods will support whatever format the browser supports.

Event Handling

Anthony Potts

Whether you use Java to write applications or applets, you'll need to master the art of handling events.

*E*very time you perform an action while running a Java application, such as clicking a mouse button or dragging a window, an event occurs. But, of course, events can also be triggered by internal actions that occur within a program. Many of the common events that occur in Java programs are handled by classes in the AWT package we discussed in Chapter 11. However, we decided to give events a chapter of their own because of their importance. This way, we can focus on events without being sidetracked by GUI creation issues.

We'll start by introducing the basics of how events are handled in Java. Then we'll present the **Events** class, which is used to derive objects for handling events in Java programs. As you'll see, this class defines a number of instance variables and methods to help process the different types of events that can occur in a Java program. After we cover the essentials of the **Events** class, we'll dig in and look at some of the specific methods that are triggered when events occur. As we explore different types of events, we'll present a number of programming examples to illustrate different techniques available for processing events.

Introducing Events

In the following applet, the program scrolls a line of text across the applet space. If you click the mouse button on top of the applet while it is running, the scrolling text will stop and then start when the mouse is clicked again. These mouse clicks cause events to occur. In our applet, the event is caused by pressing down the mouse button.

```
// TickerTape Applet

import java.applet.*;
import java.awt.*;

// TickerTape Class
public class TickerTape extends Applet implements Runnable {
    // Declare Variables
    String inputText;
    String animSpeedString;
    Color color = new Color(255, 255, 255);
    int xpos;
    int fontLength;
    int fontHeight;
    int animSpeed;
    Font font;
    Thread ttapeThread = null;
    Image im;
    Graphics osGraphics;
    boolean suspended = false;

    // Initialize Applet
    public void init(){
        inputText = getParameter("TEXT");
        animSpeedString = getParameter("SPEED");
        animSpeed = Integer.parseInt(animSpeedString);
        im=createImage(size().width, size().height);
        osGraphics = im.getGraphics();
        xpos = size().width;
        fontHeight = 4 * size().height / 5;
        font = new Font("Helvetica", 1, fontHeight);
    }

    // Override Applet Class' paint method
    public void paint(Graphics g){
        paintText(osGraphics);
        g.drawImage(im, 0, 0, null);
    }

    // Draw background and text on buffer image
    public void paintText(Graphics g){
        g.setColor(Color.black);
        g.fillRect(0, 0, size().width, size().height);
        g.clipRect(0, 0, size().width, size().height);
```

```
      g.setFont(font);
      g.setColor(color);
      FontMetrics fmetrics = g.getFontMetrics();
      fontLength = fmetrics.stringWidth(inputText);
      fontHeight = fmetrics.getHeight();
      g.drawString(inputText, xpos, size().height - fontHeight / 4);
   }

   // Start Applet as thread
   public void start(){
      if(ttapeThread == null){
         ttapeThread = new Thread(this);
         ttapeThread.start();
      }
   }

   // Animate coordinates for drawing text
   public void setcoord(){
      xpos = xpos - animSpeed;
      if(xpos <- fontLength){
         xpos = size().width;
      }
   }

   // Change coordinates and repaint
   public void run(){
      while(ttapeThread != null){
         try {Thread.sleep(50);} catch (InterruptedException e){}
         setcoord();
         repaint();
      }
   }

   // Re-paint when buffer is updated
   public void update(Graphics g) {
      paint(g);
   }

   // Handle mouse clicks
   public boolean handleEvent(Event evt) {
      if (evt.id == Event.MOUSE_DOWN) {
         if (suspended) {
            ttapeThread.resume();
         } else {
            ttapeThread.suspend();
         }
         suspended = !suspended;
      }
      return true;
   }
```

```
// Stop thread then clean up before close
public void stop(){
   if(ttapeThread != null)
      ttapeThread.stop();
   ttapeThread = null;
}

} // End TickerTape
```

Here is the portion of code responsible for halting the scrolling text:

```
// Handle mouse clicks
   public boolean handleEvent(Event evt) {
      if (evt.id == Event.MOUSE_DOWN) {
         if (suspended) {
            ttapeThread.resume();
         } else {
            ttapeThread.suspend();
         }
      suspended = !suspended;
      }
      return true;
   }
```

The key to the inner workings of this error handler method (**handleEvent()**) is the argument **evt**. It is declared as an object of the **Event** class, a special class that Java provides for processing events. In our code, we simply check the **id** instance variable to make sure a **MOUSE_DOWN** event has occurred. If so, we either resume or suspend the applet.

Event Types

Events in Java can be split into three main groups: *mouse, keyboard,* and *system events.* All of these events can be handled very similarly. Java events are actually objects derived from their own classes, as we saw in the applet example we just discussed. This method of handling events makes perfect sense when you realize the power you gain from being able to manipulate an event as an object. In other programming languages, events only trigger certain methods, which limits you to receiving very little information about the current state of the system.

The Event Class

Let's take a close look at the **Event** class so we can use it throughout this chapter. This class has many variables and methods that can be used for finding out information about an event that has occurred, such as where and when the event has happened, and who it has happened to. Many of the variables give us status information, such as if the Shift or Page Up key was pressed when the event has occurred.

Table 13.1 presents the variables defined in the **Event** class and Table 13.2 presents the methods. Later in this chapter you'll learn more about how to apply them. The variables that are listed in all capital letters represent static values that correspond to certain events and conditions. We will use these values to compare events that occur in our applications so that we can tell what event has occurred.

Table 13.1   Variables defined in the events class.

Variable	Description
SHIFT_MASK	The shift modifier constant. This is an integer that indicates if the Shift key was down when the event occurred. This variable is used to process keyboard events.
CTRL_MASK	The control modifier constant. This is an integer that indicates if the Ctrl key was down when the event occurred. This variable is used to process keyboard events.
ALT_MASK	The alt modifier constant. This is an integer that indicates if the Alt key was down when the event occurred. This variable is used to process keyboard events.
HOME	Represents the Home key.
END	Represents the End key.
PGUP	Represents the Page Up key.
PGDN	Represents the Page Down key.
UP	Represents the Up arrow key.
DOWN	Represents the Down arrow key.

Continued

Table 13.1   Variables defined in the events class (Continued).

Variable	Description
LEFT	Represents the left arrow key.
RIGHT	Represents the right arrow key.
F1 ... F12	Represents one of the function keys.
ESC	Represents the escape key.
WINDOW_DESTROY	Represents the event that occurs when a user tries to close a frame or window.
WINDOW_EXPOSE	Represents the event that occurs when part of your application has been covered by another application and the second app is removed.
WINDOW_ICONIFY	Represents the event that occurs when a window is minimized.
WINDOW_DEICONIFY	Represents the event that occurs when a window is restored from a minimized state.
WINDOW_MOVED	Represents the event that occurs when the window is moved.
KEY_PRESS	Represents the event that occurs when any key on the keyboard is pressed down.
KEY_RELEASE	Represents the event that occurs when any key on the keyboard is released.
MOUSE_DOWN	Represents the event that occurs when a mouse button is pressed down.
MOUSE_UP	Represents the event that occurs when a mouse button is released.
MOUSE_MOVE	Represents the event that occurs when a mouse button is moved across a part of the application or applet.
MOUSE_ENTER	Represents the event that occurs when a mouse enters a component.
MOUSE_EXIT	Represents the event that occurs when a mouse exits a component.
MOUSE_DRAG	Represents the event that occurs when the mouse button is down and the mouse is moved.

Continued

Table 13.1   Variables defined in the events class (Continued).

Variable	Description
LIST_SELECT	Represents the event that occurs when an option is selected from within a list object.
LIST_DESELECT	Represents the event that occurs when an option is de-selected from within a list object.
GOT_FOCUS	Represents the event that occurs when a component gains the focus.
LOST_FOCUS	Represents the event that occurs when a component loses the focus.
Target	Holds an object that was the "target" of an event.
When	Indicates the precise time when an event occurred.
Id	Indicates the type of event.
X	The x coordinate of the event.
Y	The y coordinate of the event.
Key	The key that was pressed in a keyboard event.
Arg	An arbitrary argument.

Table 13.2   Methods defined in the events class.

Method	Description
translate(int, int)	Translates an event relative to the given component. This involves translating the coordinates so they make sense within the given component.
shiftDown()	Checks to see if the Shift key is pressed; returns true if it is pressed.
controlDown()	Checks to see if the Control key is pressed; returns true if it is pressed.
ToString()	Returns the string representation of the event's values.

Continued

Table 13.2   Methods defined in the events class (Continued).

metaDown()	Checks to see if the meta key is pressed. Returns true if it is pressed. The meta key is different for each operating system. On a PC, the meta key is the Alt key and on a Mac, the meta key is the Apple key.

Mouse Events

Now that you are familiar with the **Event** class, let's look at some of the methods that are triggered when an event happens. The first ones we'll discuss are the mouse events. These events are probably the most common ones that you will need to check for. The methods for processing these events can be placed in several different places in your program. At the highest level, you can override the events of the GUI elements themselves. For example, you can create your own button class by extending the **Button** class. Then, you can override the default mouse events with your own code. The next option is to place a button or multiple buttons on a panel and override a button's mouse events. With this scenario, you must use **if** or **switch** statements to detect which button is pressed.

The final option is to override the mouse events of the applet or frame you are using for the entire program. This method gets difficult when you have complex UI environments. Let's take a close look at each of the mouse events in detail.

MOUSEDOWN()

Clicking on a mouse button creates two distinct events, **mouseDown** and **mouseUp**. The **mouseDown** event occurs when a button is initially pressed and the **mouseUp** event occurs when a button is released. Why are two events required? Often, you will want to perform different tasks when a button is pressed and when it is released. For example, consider a standard screen button. If you press a mouse button while you are over the screen button, the button should look like it has been depressed. The button would remain in this "down" state until the mouse button is released.

The **mouseDown**() method accepts three arguments:

```
public boolean mouseDown(Event, int, int) {}
```

The first argument is an **Event** object that holds all the information about the event that has occurred. The second and third arguments are the x and y coordinates representing where the event took place. The values stored in these arguments are the same as the values stored in the **x** and **y** variables found in the **Events** class.

Here is an example that uses the **mouseDown**() method. It illustrates that the x,y coordinate values set by this method are the same as the values stored in the x,y instance variables contained in the **Events** class:

```
import java.awt.*;

class testEvents extends Frame {
   Panel P1;

   testEvents() {
      super("Test Events");
      P1 = new Panel();
      setLayout(new FlowLayout());
      P1.setBackground(new Color(255,255,255));
      add(P1);
      resize(300,200);
      show();
   }

   public boolean mouseDown(Event evt, int x, int y) {
      System.out.println("X, Y = " + x + ", " + y);
      System.out.println("Event X, Y = " + evt.x + ", " + evt.y);
      return true;
   }

   public static void main(String args[]) {
      testEvents TE = new testEvents();
   }
}
```

MOUSEUP()

The **mouseUp**() event method is implemented in the exact same way as the **mouseDown**() event method. When you are creating routines that respond to simple mouse clicks this is usually the place to put the code.

Why here instead of in a **mouseDown** event method? Well, think about how people use an interface. Is it more natural for a mouse click event to occur the instant the button is pressed, or when it is released? If you look at how other programs work, you will notice that most, if not all, don't respond until the mouse button is released.

You should follow this paradigm for two reasons. First, it represents the standard way of processing mouse clicks and you do not want to create an interface that seems inconsistent to the user. Second, it gives the user an opportunity to change his or her mind. After all, how many times have you started to press a button in a program only to change your mind, move the mouse off the button, and *then* let go?

Here is the declaration for the **mouseUp**() method:

```
public boolean mouseUp(Event, int, int) {}
```

Once again, we are given three arguments—an **Event** object, and two integers that give us the x and y coordinates of the event.

MOUSEMOVE() AND MOUSEDRAG()

The **mouseMove**() event method is used to constantly give feedback when the mouse pointer is over a component. The **mouseDrag**() event method tells us the same thing, but only while one of the mouse buttons is pressed. Whenever the mouse is being moved over your component, one of these methods will constantly be called. Be careful not to put code in these methods that takes too long to execute. If you do, you may see some performance degradation in your program.

Here are the declarations for the **mouseMove**() and **mouseDrag**() event methods:

```
public boolean mouseMove(Event, int, int) {}
public boolean mouseDrag(Event, int, int) {}
```

Again, three arguments are used; an **Event** object, and two integers that represent the x and y coordinates where the event occurs.

Here is a very simple program that responds to mouse movement and dragging by displaying the location of the event in the title bar:

```java
import java.awt.*;

class testEvents extends Frame {

    testEvents() {
        super("Test Events");
        resize(300,200);
        show();
    }

    public boolean mouseMove(Event evt, int x, int y) {
        setTitle("mouseMove at: " + x + ", " + y);
        return true;
    }

    public boolean mouseDrag(Event evt, int x, int y) {
        setTitle("mouseDrag at: " + x + ", " + y);
        return true;
    }

    public static void main(String args[]) {
        testEvents TE = new testEvents();
    }
}
```

As you can see, it is extremely easy to respond to mouse events. You may notice that in this example and in the previous one, you cannot exit out of the program. Basically, what you need to do is check for another event, a system event that tells you that the user is trying to close the window. This is a very easy thing to look for, but we did not want to confuse the code with extra methods. Later in this chapter we'll show you how to check for system events.

MOUSEENTER() AND MOUSEEXIT()

These two events come in handy for certain situations. For example, if you want to provide feedback to the user when he or she moves the mouse pointer into or out of your components, you may want to display a message in a status bar. You can get basically the same effect by checking for the **mouseMove**() method, but this method gets called many times while the mouse is over a component and the **mouseEnter()** and **mouseExit()** methods get called only once. The declarations for these event methods are:

```
public boolean mouseEnter(Event, int, int) {}
public boolean mouseExit(Event, int, int) {}
```

These methods are also useful for keeping track of how long a person keeps their mouse over a certain component. For example, assume you were creating a game and you wanted to cause an event to occur if the player keeps the pointer over the "fire" button for too long. You could then respond with a sound or message. Here is an example that checks the time at which the user moves the mouse onto the applet and if the user stays for more than two seconds, the status bar displays an error message. When the user leaves the applet space and returns, the message returns to normal.

```
import java.applet.*;
import java.awt.*;
import java.util.*;

// testNav Class
public class testTime extends Applet {
    Button B1;
    long downTime;

    public testTime() {
        setLayout(new FlowLayout());
        B1 = new Button("Click Me!");
        show(); add("Center", B1);
    }

    public boolean mouseEnter(Event evt, int x, int y) {
        downTime = evt.when;
        return true;
    }

    public boolean mouseExit(Event evt, int x, int y) {
        downTime = 0;
        return true;
    }

    public boolean mouseMove(Event evt, int x, int y) {
        if ((evt.when - downTime) > 2000) {
            B1.setLabel("Too Long!");
        } else {
            B1.setLabel("Click Me!");
```

```
      }
      return true;
   }

   public void init(){
      testTime TT = new testTime();
   }

} // End testNav
```

Keyboard Events

Handling keyboard events is similar to handling mouse events. The big difference is that when you process a mouse event, you have only one mouse button to work. On the other hand, the user can press one of many possible keys, so processing keyboard events requires an extra step. The two methods you can use, **keyDown**() and **keyUp**(), are very similar to the **mouseDown**() and **mouseUp**() event methods. The only difference is that the keyboard events *do not* generate a location where the event has occurred. Instead, they generate an integer value representing the key that was pressed.

KEY**D**OWN[] AND KEY**U**P[]

Here are the declaration statements for the **keyDown**() and **keyUp**() event methods:

```
public boolean keyDown(Event, int) {}
public boolean keyUp(Event, int) {}
```

The integer argument stores the numeric value of each key on the keyboard— the ASCII equivalent of a key. Java offers us a simple technique for converting this ASCII value to a character representation; we simply cast the integer to a **char** and there we have it. Here is a simple example:

```
public boolean keyDown(Event evt, int key) {
   System.out.println("Value = " + key + ", character = " +
 (char)key);
}
```

This little code snippet simply waits for a key to be pressed then prints the numeric value of the key and the character representation of that value.

If you look back at the variables defined in the **Event** class (Table 11.1), you'll notice all of the key representations. These values represent the keys that do not belong to the standard ASCII character set, including keys like Home, Page Up, and the function keys. Here's a simple code example that waits for you to press the **F1** key to get help and the Ctrl+x combination to quit the program:

```java
import java.awt.*;

class testKeys extends Frame {

    testKeys() {
        super("Test Keys");
        resize(300,200);
        show();
    }

    public boolean keyDown(Event evt, int key) {
        if (evt.controlDown()) {
            if (key == 24) {
                System.exit(0);
                return true;
            }
        }
        if (key == Event.F1) {
            setTitle("No help here!");
            return true;
        }
        return false;
    }

    public boolean keyUp(Event evt, int key) {
        if (key == Event.F1) {
            setTitle("Test Keys");
            return true;
        }
        return false;
    }

    public static void main(String args[]) {
        testKeys TK = new testKeys();
    }
}
```

Hierarchy Of Events

Now that you've seen how to create event handlers for specific events, let's look at how you can create event handlers that capture everything in one central location. Why would you want to do that? Assume that you have an applet that uses a set of buttons that perform related operations. You can create separate event handlers for each control individually, or you can create an event handler that captures all the events at one location and then uses the information in the **Event** object to determine what happened to a certain control.

If you recall from Chapter 11, we created an applet with four buttons. Each button had a caption that represented a URL for a Web site. When a button is pressed, the event handler of the applet, not the buttons themselves, processes the event. This "centralized" approach makes the events easier to process; however, sometimes it can get a little crowded, especially if you have many components that must respond differently to certain events. In these cases it is up to you to decide where to handle the events.

If you do not handle an event at the component level, make sure that a system is in place to hand that event off to the container the particular control resides in. Let's create a little program that has two buttons in a frame. In the first example we will use a standard button and catch its events with the frame. In the second example we will create our own button by subclassing the **Button** class and adding our own event handler to that button. Here is the first example:

```java
import java.awt.*;

class testEvents extends Frame {

  testEvents() {
        super("Test Keys");
        setLayout(new FlowLayout());
        add(new Button("Hello!"));
        add(new Button("Goodbye!"));
        resize(300,200);
        show();
  }
```

```
      public boolean handleEvent(Event evt) {
          setTitle((String)evt.arg);
          return true;
      }

  public static void main(String args[]) {
          testEvents TK = new testEvents();
  }
}
```

The second example we create our own event handler:

```
import java.awt.*;

class testEvents extends Frame {
 myButton B1;
 myButton B2;

 testEvents() {
      super("Test Keys");
      setLayout(new FlowLayout());
      B1 = new myButton("Hello!", this);
      B2 = new myButton("Goodbye!", this);
      add(B1);
      add(B2);
      resize(300,200);
      show();
 }

 public static void main(String args[]) {
      testEvents TK = new testEvents();
 }
}

class myButton extends Button {

 myButton(String s, Frame f2) {
      super(s);
 }

 public boolean handleEvent(Event evt) {
      Frame f;
      f = (Frame)getParent();
      f.setTitle((String)evt.arg);
      return true;
 }
}
```

Processing System Events

Not only can you decide where to place your event handlers, Java also gives you options for capturing events. Instead of creating separate event handlers for each type of event, you can also create a single centralized event handler that accepts all events and then figures out what they are and which components are responsible for generating them.

For processing system-related events, Java provides **handleEvent()** and **action()**. The **action()** method captures all of the standard mouse and keyboard events. The **handleEvent()** method handles all of those and more. It can also catch all the system messages that might be sent to your program.

If you have several different methods in your code that all catch the same event, you need to know what order the methods will be fired in. For example, assume you have a class that has a **mouseDown()** method, an **action()** method, and a **handleEvent()** method. If the user clicks the mouse button, which method will get called? The first method to get called will be the **handleEvent()** method—the mother of all event handlers. If it does not handle the event, the event will be passed on to the **action()** method. Finally, if the **action()** method does nothing with the event, the event is passed on to the **mouseDown()** method.

With this knowledge in hand, you can better direct the flow of operations in your code. You can even handle events in multiple locations. The key here is to do something with the event, then pass it on as if it were never processed. In the case of the event methods, you would usually return a value of true at the end of a method where you handled an event. If you change the return value to false, you will see that the event continues down the chain. Here is a sample applet that illustrates this technique:

```
import java.applet.*;
import java.awt.*;

public class testEvents4 extends Applet {
    Label L1 = new Label();
    Label L2 = new Label();
    Label L3 = new Label();
```

```
public testEvents4() {
    setLayout(new GridLayout(2, 3));
    add(new Label("handleEvent()"));
    add(new Label("action()"));
    add(new Label("mouseMove()"));
    add(L1);
    add(L2);
    show(); add(L3);
}

public boolean handleEvent(Event evt) {
    if (evt.id == Event.MOUSE_MOVE) {
        L1.setText("" + evt.when);
        this.action(evt, evt.target);
        return super.handleEvent(evt);
    } else {
        return false;
    }
}

public boolean action(Event evt, Object arg) {
    L2.setText("" + evt.when);
    return true;
}
public boolean mouseMove(Event evt, int x, int y) {
    L3.setText("" + evt.when);
    return true;    }

public void init(){
    testEvents TN = new testEvents();
}
} // End Application
```

Try switching some of the return statements and see what happens. Figure 13.1 shows the applet in action. The applet consists of six **Label** controls. They are arranged in a grid. The top three labels list the three methods we are handling. The three lower labels show the time at which the last event of the respective type took place.

ACTION() METHOD

The **action()** method is useful for responding to a multitude of user actions. It will capture any events that are caused directly by the user. For example,

Netscape - [file:///D|/java/lib/test.html]

File   Edit   View   Go   Bookmarks   Options   Directory   Window   Help

Location: file:///D|/java/lib/test.html

handleEvent()   action()   mouseMove()

82722349 2170   82722349 2170   82722349 2170

Applet testEvents4 running

Figure 13.1   The sample events applet.

it will catch mouse clicks, but it will not catch system calls. Here is the declaration for the **action**() method:

```
public boolean action(Event, Object) {}
```

HANDLEEVENT() METHOD

The **handleEvent**() method is probably the most versatile of the event handling methods. It can catch all the standard user interface events as well as system events. The ability to catch system events is crucial to larger, more complex programs. It is also essential to applications. Without the ability to catch system events, applications would never know when the user has pressed any of the title bar buttons or selected any of the title bar options.

Here is the declaration for the **handleEvent**() method:

```
public boolean handleEvent(Event) {}
```

You probably have seen this method in use in several of our example programs. When the user of an application clicks on the close icon for your application, it sends a message indicating that the close icon has been pressed. This message comes in the form of **WINDOW_DESTROY**. We need to catch this event and then tell the application to quit. The following is a code snippet that will do just that:

```
public boolean handleEvent(Event evt) {
   if (evt.id == Event.WINDOW_DESTROY) {
      System.exit(0);
      return true;
   } else {
      super. HandleEvent(evt);
      return false;
   }
}
```

This simply checks the event **id** variable to see if it equals the static variable **WINDOW_DESTROY** defined in the **Event** class. If we receive this event message, we tell the application to close by calling the **exit**() method of the **System** class.

Problems with processing events.

Java does not handle all events very well yet. In particular, the current Java interpreters often make mistakes or do not respond correctly to all events. The most common errors involve the mouse event methods. Sometimes the parent objects do not receive any stimulation when they should. For example, if you place a button in the middle of an applet, you should be able to catch all the mouse events that happen to the button with an event handler belonging to the applet. This SHOULD work, but in practice it is a little flaky.

Dances With Databases

Peter Aitken

**Here's the lowdown on using
Visual J++ to access databases.**

We all know that the Web is hot, and perhaps the hottest topic on the Web is database development. Everyone and their grandmother, it seems, wants to be able to use the Web to access remote databases. If you think about it for a moment, we think you'll see why. Almost any commercial or informational use of computers could use databases in some way, and with more and more people wanting to provide services over the Web, the need for Web database connectivity is obvious.

The folks who developed Java have been perfectly aware of this need for some time. As powerful as "plain" Java is, the addition of serious database capabilities would have a major positive impact on the usefulness and widespread adoption of the language. One of the libraries, or *Application Programming Interfaces* (APIs), being developed is the Java DataBase Connectivity API, or JDBC. Its primary purpose is to tie connectivity to databases intimately with the Java language.

Before you get too excited, we have to tell you the bad news. First, the JDBC API is itself still under development. Second, Visual J++ does not support JDBC in any form at present, at least not the pre-release version that we are using to write this book. JDBC support is undoubtedly coming in a subsequent release of Visual J++, but we can't tell you when. Still, if you are going to be a Java programmer, you need to know something about

JDBC programming and now is as good a time as any to start. We won't be able to provide any programming examples, of course, but we can discuss the reasoning behind the JDBC as well as the design of the JDBC and its associated API. We'll also provide basic reference information on the contents of the JDBC API.

The design of the JDBC is tied closely to the technologies used in the operation of the Internet. The other dominant design basis for the JDBC is the database standard known as *Structured Query Language*, or SQL. Hence, the JDBC is a fusion of these three discrete computer areas: Java, Internet technology, and SQL. With the growing implementation of these Internet technologies in "closed" networks, called *intranets*, the time was right for the development of Java-based enterprise APIs. In this book, intranet and Internet are both used to describe the software technology behind the network, such as the World Wide Web.

What Is The JDBC?

What exactly is JDBC? It refers to several things, depending on context:

◆ It's a specification for using data sources in Java applets and applications.

◆ It's an API for using low-level JDBC drivers.

◆ It's an API for creating these low-level drivers, which do the actual connecting/transactions with data sources.

◆ JDBC is based on the X/Open SQL Call Level Interface (CLI) that defines how client/server interactions are implemented for database systems.

Confused yet? It's really quite simple: The JDBC defines every aspect of making data-aware Java applications and applets. The low-level JDBC drivers perform database-specific translation to the high-level JDBC interface. This interface is used by the developer so he doesn't need to worry about the database-specific syntax when connecting to and querying different databases. The JDBC is a package, much like the other Java packages such as java.awt. It's not currently a part of the standard Java Developer's Kit (JDK) distribution, but it is slated to be included as a standard part of the general Java API as the java.sql package. Soon after its official incorporation into the JDK and Java API, it will also become a standard package in Java-enabled Web browsers, though there is no definite time frame for this inclusion. The exciting aspect of the JDBC is that the drivers necessary for connection to respective databases do not require any pre-installation on the clients—a JDBC driver can be downloaded along with an applet!

The JDBC project was started in January of 1996, and the specification was frozen in June of 1996. Javasoft sought the input of industry database vendors so that the JDBC would be as widely accepted as possible when it was ready for release. JDBC has already been widely accepted by the software industry.

The JDBC is heavily based on the ANSI SQL-92 standard, which specifies that a JDBC driver should be SQL-92 entry-level compliant to be considered a 100 percent JDBC-compliant driver. This is not to say that a JDBC driver has to be written for an SQL-92 database; a JDBC driver can be written for a legacy database system and still function perfectly. Even though a driver does not implement every single SQL-92 function, it is still a JDBC driver. This flexibility will be a major selling point for developers who are bound to legacy database systems and who want to extend their client applications.

JDBC Structure

As we mentioned at the beginning of the chapter, the JDBC is two-layered. The reason for the split is to separate the low-level programming from the high-level application interface. The low-level programming is the JDBC driver. The idea is that database vendors and third-party software vendors will supply pre-built drivers for connecting to different databases. JDBC drivers are quite flexible; they can be local data sources or remote database servers. The implementation of the actual connection to the data source/database is left entirely to the JDBC driver.

The structure of the JDBC includes these key concepts:

◆ The goal of the JDBC is a DBMS independent interface, a generic SQL database access framework, and a uniform interface to different data sources.

♦ The programmer writes only *one* database interface. Using JDBC, the program can access any data source without recoding.

Figure 14.1 shows the architecture of the JDBC. The **DriverManager** class is used to open a connection to a database via a JDBC driver, which must register with the **DriverManager** before the connection can be formed. When a connection is attempted, the **DriverManager** chooses from a given list of available drivers to suit the explicit type of database connection. After a connection is formed, the calls to query and fetch results are made directly with the JDBC driver. The JDBC driver must implement the classes to process these functions for the specific database, but the rigid specification of the JDBC ensures that the drivers will perform as expected. Essentially, the developer who has JDBC drivers for a certain database does not need to worry about changing the code for the Java program if a different type of database is used (assuming that the JDBC driver for the other database is available). This is especially useful in the scenario of distributed databases.

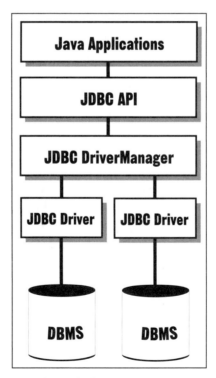

Figure 14.1   The architecture of the JDBC.

The JDBC uses a URL syntax for specifying a database. For example, a connection to an mSQL database is:

```
jdbc:msql://mydatabase.server.com:1112/testdb
```

This statement specifies the transport to use (jdbc), the database type (msql), the server name, the port (1112), and the database to connect to (testdb).

The data types in SQL are mapped into native Java types when possible. When a native type is not present in Java, a class is available for retrieving data of that type. Consider, for example, the **Date** type in the JDBC. A developer can assign a date field in a database to a JDBC **Date** class, after which the developer can use the methods in the **Date** class to display or perform operations against. The JDBC also includes support for binary large objects, or BLOB, data types. You can retreive and store images, sounds, documents, and other binary data in a database with the JDBC.

ODBC's Part In The JDBC

Open Database Connectivity, or ODBC, is an existing and widely used database standard. JDBC and ODBC share a common parent—both are based on the same X/OPEN call level interface for SQL. Though there are JDBC drivers emerging for many databases, you can write database-aware Java programs using existing ODBC drivers. Figure 14.2 shows the place of the JDBC-ODBC Bridge in the overall architecture of the JDBC. However, the JDBC-ODBC Bridge requires pre-installation on the client, or wherever the Java program is actually running, because the Bridge must make native method calls to do the translation from ODBC to JDBC. This pre-installation issue is also true for JDBC drivers that use native methods. Only 100 percent Java JDBC drivers can be downloaded across a network with a Java applet, thus requiring no pre-installation of the driver.

ODBC drivers function in the same manner as "true" JDBC drivers. In fact, the JDBC-ODBC bridge is actually a sophisticated JDBC driver that does low-level translation to and from ODBC. When the JDBC driver for a certain database becomes available, you can easily switch from the ODBC driver to the new JDBC driver with few, if any, changes to the code of the Java program.

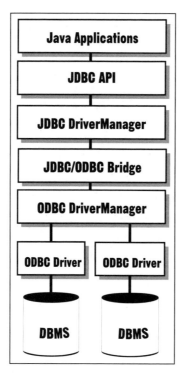

Figure 14.2   ODBC in the JDBC model.

In summary, you can see that the JDBC is not only a specification for using data sources in Java applets and applications, but that it also allows you to create and use low-level drivers to connect and "talk" with data sources. You explored the JDBC architecture and saw how the ODBC fits into the picture. The important concept to remember about the JDBC is that the modular design of the JDBC interface allows you to change between drivers—hence databases—without recoding your Java programs.

Now it's time to get to the reference information. We have provided a summary of the classes, interfaces, and exceptions available in the JDBC API version 1.01, which was the most current version at the time of this writing. Although this chapter's primary purpose is to serve as a reference, you should read through the sections completely so you are aware of all of the constructors, variables, and methods available.

JDBC Classes

We'll begin with the class listings. Each class listing includes a description, and the class' constructors, methods, and variables.

public class Date

This class extends the java.util.Date object, but stores the day, year, and month, whereas the java.util.Date stores time. This is for strict matching with the SQL date type.

CONSTRUCTOR

Constructor	Additional Description
Date(int Year, int Month, int day)	Constructs a java.sql.Date object with the appropriate parameters

METHODS

Method Name	Additional Description
public String toString()	Formats a Date object as YYYY-MM-DD
public static Date valueOf(String str)	Converts a String str to an sql.Date object

VARIABLES

None

public class DriverManager

This class is used to load a JDBC driver and establish it as an available driver. This class is usually not instantiated, but called by the JDBC driver.

CONSTRUCTOR

DriverManager()

METHODS

Method Name	Additional Description
public static void deregister Driver (Driver JDBCdriver) throws SQLException	Drops a driver from the available drivers list
public static synchronized Connection getConnection (String URL) throws SQL Exception	Establishes a connection to the given database URL, with the given parameters
public static synchronized Connection getConnection (String URL, String Login Name, String LoginPassword) throws SQLException	
public static synchronized Connection getConnection (String URL, Properties LoginInfo) throws SQLException	
public static Driver getDriver (String URL) throws SQLException	Finds a driver that understands the JDBC URL from the registered driver list
public static Enumeration getDrivers()	Gets an Enumeration of the available JDBC drivers
public static int getLoginTimeout()	Indicates the maximum time (seconds) that a driver will wait when logging into a database
public static PrintStream getLogStream()	Gets the logging PrintStream used by the DriverManager and JDBC drivers

Method Name	Additional Description
public static void println (String msg)	Sends message to the current JDBC logging stream (fetched from above method)
public static synchronized void registerDriver (Driver JDBCdriver) throws SQLException	Specifies that a new driver class should call registerDriver when loading to "register" with the DriverManager
public static void setLogin Timeout(int sec)	Indicates the time (in seconds) that all drivers will wait when logging into a database
public static void setLogStream (PrintStream log)	Defines the PrintStream that logging messages are sent to via the println method above.

VARIABLES

None

public class DriverPropertyInfo

This class is for developers who want to obtain and set properties for a loaded JDBC driver. It's not necessary to use this class, but the class is useful for debugging JDBC drivers and advanced development.

CONSTRUCTOR

Constructor	Additional Description
public DriverPropertyInfo (String propName, String propValue)	The propName is the name of the property, and propValue is the current value; if it has not been set, it may be null

METHODS

None

VARIABLES

Variable Name	Additional Description
choices	If the property value is part of a set of values, then choices is an array of the possible values
description	The property's description
name	The property's name
required	This is true if this property is required to be set during Driver.connect
value	The current value of the property

public final class Numeric

This special fixed-point, high-precision number class is used to store the SQL data types **NUMERIC** and **DECIMAL**.

CONSTRUCTORS

Constructor	Additional Description
public Numeric (String strNum)	Produces a Numeric object from a string; strNum can be in one of two formats: "1234.32" or "3.1E8"
public Numeric (String strNum, int scale)	Produces a Numeric, and scale is the number of digits right of the decimal
public Numeric (int intNum)	Produces a Numeric object from an int Java type parameter
public Numeric (int intNum, int scale)	Produces a Numeric object from an int, and scale gives the desired number of places right of the decimal

Constructor	Additional Description
public Numeric (long x)	Produces a Numeric object from a long Java type parameter
public Numeric (long x, int scale)	Produces a Numeric object from a long parameter, and scale gives the desired number of places right of the decimal
public Numeric (double x, int scale)	Produces a Numeric object from a double Java type parameter, and scale gives the desired number of places right of the decimal
public Numeric (Numeric num)	Produces a Numeric object from a Numeric
public Numeric (Numeric num, int scale)	Produces a Numeric object from a Numeric, and scale gives the desired number of places right of the decimal

METHODS

Method Name	Additional Description
public Numeric add (Numeric n)	Performs arithmetic addition on the reference Numeric object and the Numeric argument
public static Numeric createFromByteArray (byte byteArray[])	Produces a Numeric object from the byte array parameter
public static Numeric createFromIntegerArray (int intArray[])	Produces a Numeric object from the int array parameter
public static Numeric createFromRadixString (String str, int radix)	Produces a Numeric object from the String and int radix parameters

Method Name	Additional Description
public static Numeric createFromScale (long longNum, int power)	Produces a Numeric object by taking the longNum to the 10^power
public Numeric divide (Numeric q)	Divides the Numeric by the Numeric parameter q and returns the result
public double doubleValue()	Returns the Numeric as a Java type double
public boolean equals (Object objct)	Returns true if the Numeric object equals the objct parameter
public float float Value()	Returns the Numeric as a Java type float
public static int getRoundingValue()	Returns the roundingValue used in rounding operations in the Numeric object
public int getScale()	Returns the number of places to the right of the decimal
public long getScaled()	Returns the Numeric object as a long, but removes the decimal (1234.567 -> 1234567); precision may be lost
public boolean greaterThan (Numeric num)	Returns true if the Numeric object is greater than the Numeric num argument
public boolean greaterThanOrEquals (Numeric num)	Returns true if the Numeric object is greater than or equal to the Numeric num argument
public int hashCode()	Returns an integer hashcode for the Numeric object

Method Name	Additional Description
public Numeric[] integerDivide (Numeric x)	Returns an array with two Numeric objects: the first one is the quotient, the second is the remainder
public int intValue()	Returns the Numeric as a Java type int, digits after the decimal are dropped
public boolean isProbablePrime()	Returns true if the number is prime; it divides the Numeric object by several small primes, and then uses the Rabin probabilistic primality test to test if the number is prime—the failure rate is less than $(1/(4^N))$
public boolean lessThan (Numeric num)	Returns true if the Numeric object is less than the Numeric num argument
public boolean lessThanOrEquals (Numeric num)	Returns true if the Numeric object is less than or equal to the Numeric num argument
public long longValue()	Returns the Numeric as a Java type long
public Numeric modExp(Numeric numExp, Numeric numMod)	The two parameters are used to do a numMod modulus to the numExp exponent calculation; returns the result as a Numeric
public Numeric modInverse (Numeric numMod)	The modular multiplicative inverse is returned using numMod as the modulus
public Numeric multiply (Numeric num)	Returns the product of the Numeric object and the Numeric num parameter

Method Name	Additional Description
public static Numeric pi(int places)	Returns pi to the number of decimal places
public Numeric pow(int exp)	Returns a Numeric object using the current Numeric object taken to the power of the given exponent
public static Numeric random(int bits, Random randSeed)	Returns a Numeric object that is a random number using randSeed as a seed, having size in bits equal to the bits parameter
public Numeric remainder(Numeric num)	Returns the remainder resulting from dividing this Numeric object by the Numeric num parameter
public static void setRoundingValue (int val)	Sets the rounding value used in rounding operations for the Numeric object
public Numeric setScale(int scale)	Returns a Numeric object from the current object with the specified scale parameter
public Numeric shiftLeft(int number OfBits)	Returns the Numeric object with the specified numberOfBits shifted left
public Numeric shiftRight (int numberOfBits)	Returns the Numeric object with the specified numberOfBits shifted right
public int significantBits()	Returns the number of significant bits in the Numeric object
public Numeric sqrt()	Returns the square root of this Numeric object
public Numeric subtract(Numeric num)	Returns the difference between the Numeric object and the Numeric num parameter

Method Name	Additional Description
public String toString()	Returns a String type that is the String representation of the Numeric object
public String toString(int radix)	Returns a String type that is the String representation of the Numeric object, in the representation of the Numeric object, in the specified radix

VARIABLES

Variable Name	Additional Description
public final static Numeric ZERO	A Numeric equivalent to the value of 0
public final static Numeric ONE	A Numeric equivalent to the value of 1

public class Time

This is another SQL-JDBC data coversion class. This class extends java.util.Date, and basically implements the time-storing functions that are not present in the **java.sql.Date** class shown earlier.

CONSTRUCTOR

Constructor	Additional Description
public Time (int hour, int minute, int second)	Makes a Time object with the specified hour, minute, and second

METHODS

Method Name	Additional Description
public String toString()	Returns a String with the Time formatted this way: HH:MM:SS

Method Name	Additional Description
public static Time valueOf(String numStr)	Returns a Numeric object from the String numStr parameter that is in the format: HH:MM:SS

public class TimeStamp

This class is used to map the SQL data type **TIMESTAMP**. It extends **java.util.Date**, and has nanosecond precision for time-stamping purposes.

CONSTRUCTOR

Constructor	Additional Description
public Timestamp (int year, int month, int date, int hour, int minute, int second, int nano)	Builds a Timestamp object using the int parameters: year, month, date, hour, minute, second, and nano

METHODS

Method Name	Additional Description
public boolean equals(Timestamp tstamp)	Compares the Timestamp object with the Timestamp parameter tstamp; returns true if they match
public int getNanos()	Returns the Timestamp object's nanoseconds
public void setNanos(int n)	Sets the Timestamp object's nanosecond value
public String toString()	Returns a formatted String object with the value of the Timestamp object in the format: YYYY-MM-DD HH:MM:SS.F
public static Timestamp valueOf (String strts)	Returns a Timestamp object converted from the strts parameter that is in the previous format

public class Types

This class contains the SQL data types as constants. It is used by other classes as the standard constant for the data types.

CONSTRUCTOR

Constructor	Additional Description
public Types()	Builds a Types object; not usually necessary as they can be accessed as so: Types.BIGINT

VARIABLES

BIGINT
BINARY
BIT
CHAR
DATE
DECIMAL
DOUBLE
FLOAT
INTEGER
LONGVARBINARY
LONGVARCHAR
NULL
NUMERIC
OTHER (for a database=specific data type, not a standard SQL-92 data type)
REAL
SMALLINT
TIME
TIMESTAMP
TINYINT
VARBINARY
VARCHAR

Interfaces

Next are the interface listings. As with the class listings, each interface listing includes a description and the interface's methods and variables.

public interface CallableStatement

This is the primary interface to access stored procedures on a database. If OUT parameters are specified, after a query is executed via this class, its results are fetched from this class and not the **ResultSet** class. This class extends the **PreparedStatement** class; thus it inherits many of its methods.

Methods

The first 15 methods (the **get** methods) are identical in functionality to those in the **ResultSet** class, but are necessary if OUT parameters are used. See the **ResultSet** class for a description of the methods.

Method Name

public abstract boolean
getBoolean(int parameterIndex)
throws SQLException

public abstract byte getByte
(int parameterIndex) throws
SQLException

public abstract byte[]
getBytes(int parameterIndex)
throws SQLException

public abstract Date getDate
(int parameterIndex) throws
SQLException

public abstract double
getDouble(int
parameterIndex) throws
SQLException

Method Name

public abstract float
getFloat(int parameterIndex)
throws SQLException

public abstract int getInt
(int parameterIndex)
throws SQLException

public abstract long
getLong(int parameterIndex)
throws SQLException

public abstract Numeric
getNumeric(int parameterIndex,
int scale) throws SQLException

public abstract Object
getObject(int parameterIndex)
throws SQLException

public abstract short
getShort(int parameterIndex)
throws SQLException

public abstract String
getString(int parameterIndex)
throws SQLException

public abstract Time
getTime(int parameterIndex)
throws SQLException

public abstract Timestamp
getTimestamp(int parameterIndex)
throws SQLException

Method Name	Additional Description
public abstract void registerOutParameter(int paramIndex, int sqlDataType) throws SQLException	Each parameter of the stored procedure must be registered before the query is run; paramIndex is the stored procedures parameter location in the output sequence, and sqlDataType is the data type of the parameter at the specified location (sqlDataType should be setfrom the Type class using one of its variables, for example, Types.BIGINT)
public abstract void registerOutParameter(int parameterIndex, int sqlDataType, int scale) throws SQLException	Specifies the number of places to the right of the decimal desired when getting Numeric data objects
public abstract boolean wasNull() throws SQLException	Returns true if the stored procedure parameter was value NULL

public interface Connection

This is the high-level class used to interact with a database. The object is established from the **DriverManager.getConnection** method, which returns this object (**Connection**). This class obtains information via the instantiated JDBC driver about the specific database connection, and this class' primary use is to perform queries via the **createStatement**, **prepareCall**, and **prepareStatement** methods, which return **Statement**, **PreparedCall**, and **PreparedStatements** objects, respectively.

METHODS

Method Name	Additional Description
public abstract void clear Warnings() throws SQLException	Clears the warnings for the connection

Method Name	Additional Description
public abstract void close() throws SQLException	Closes the connection to the database
public abstract void commit() throws SQLException	Functions as the JDBC equivalent of the standard database commit command; it applies all commands and changes made since the last commit or rollback, including releasing database locks; results from queries are closed when commit in invoked
public abstract Statement createStatement() throws SQLException	Returns a Statement object, which can then be used to perform actual queries
public abstract boolean getAutoClose() throws SQLException	Returns true if automatic closing of the connection is enabled; automatic closing results in the closing of the connection when commit or rollback is performed
public abstract boolean getAutoCommit() throws SQLException	Returns true if automatic commiting of the connection is on; automatic commit is on by default, and means that the connection is committed on individual transactions; the actual commit occurs when the last row of a result set is fetched, or when the ResultSet is closed
public abstract String getCatalog() throws SQLException	Returns the current catalog name for the connection

Method Name	Additional Description
public abstract DatabaseMetaData getMetaData() throws SQLException	Returns a DatabaseMetaData object for the current connection
public abstract int getTransactionIsolation() throws SQLException	Returns the transaction isolation mode of the connection
public abstract SQLWarning getWarnings() throws SQLException	Returns the SQLWarning object with the warnings for the connection
public abstract boolean isClosed() throws SQLException	Returns true if the connection has been closed
public abstract boolean isReadOnly() throws SQLException	Returns true if the connection is a read only connection
public abstract String nativeSQL(String sqlQuery) throws SQLException	Returns the native SQL that the JDBC driver would send to the database for the specified sqlQuery parameter
public abstract CallableStatement prepareCall(String sqlQuery) throws SQLException	Returns a CallableStatement object used to perform stored procedures; note that the SQL query must be passed in as the sqlQuery parameter
public abstract PreparedStatement prepare-Statement(String sqlQuery) throws SQLException	Returns a PreparedStatement object used to perform the specified sqlQuery; this query can be executed repeatedly, if desired, by using the PreparedStatement.execute method

Method Name	Additional Description
public abstract void rollback() throws SQLException	Drops changes made since the last commit or rollback, and closes respective results; database locks are also released
public abstract void setAutoClose(boolean auto) throws SQLException	Sets the connection to auto close mode if the auto parameter is true
public abstract void setAutoCommit(boolean auto) throws SQLException	Sets the connection to auto commit mode if the auto parameter is true
public abstract void setCatalog(String catalog) throws SQLException	The catalog may be changed by specifying the catalog
public abstract void setRead-Only(boolean readOnly) throws SQLException	Sets the connection to read only mode
public abstract void setTransactionIsolation (int level) throws SQLException	Sets translation isolation to the specified level

VARIABLES

The following constants are used in the **setTransactionIsolation** method as the level parameter:

TRANSACTION_NONE

TRANSACTION_READ_COMMITTED

TRANSACTION_READ_UNCOMMITTED

TRANSACTION_REPEATABLE_READ

TRANSACTION_SERIALIZABLE

public interface DatabaseMetaData

This class contains useful information about the open connection to the database. The **Connection.getMetaData** method returns a **Database MetaData** object that is specific to the open connection.

METHODS

Method Name	Additional Description
public abstract boolean allProceduresAre-Callable() throws SQLException	Returns true if all the procedures available to the user are callable
public abstract boolean allTablesAreSelectable() throws SQLException	Returns true if all of the tables are accessible to the user on the open connection
public abstract boolean dataDefinitionCauses-TransactionCommit() throws SQLException	Returns true if data definition causes the transaction to commit
public abstract boolean dataDefinitionIgnored-InTransactions() throws SQLException	Returns true if data defintion is ignored in the transaction
public abstract boolean doesMaxRowSize-IncludeBlobs() throws SQLException	Returns true if the getMaxSize method does not account for the size of LONGVARCHAR and LONGVARBINARY SQL data types

Method Name	Additional Description
public abstract Result getBestRowIdentifier (String catalog, String schema, String table, int scope, boolean nullok) throws SQLException	Returns ResultSet object for the specified Set parameters that gets the specified table's key or the attributes that can be used to uniquely identify a row, which may be composite. The scope parameter is one of the constants: bestRowTemporary, bestRowTransaction, or bestRowSession. The nullok parameter allows columns that may be null. The ResultSet is composed of the following columns: scope (of the same types as above scope parameter), column name, SQL data type, name of the data type dependent on the database, precision, buffer length, significant places if a Numeric type, and pseudo column (one of the constants bestRowUnknown, bestRowNot Pseudo, or bestRowPseudo)
public abstract ResultSet getCatalogs() throws SQLException	Returns a ResultSet object that contains a column for the catalog names that are in the database
public abstract String getCatalogSeparator() throws SQL	Returns the separator between the catalog and the table name
public abstract String getCatalogTerm() throws SQLException	Returns the database-specific term for "catalog"
public abstract ResultSet getColumnPrivileges (String catalog, String schemaString table, String column NamePattern) throws SQLException	Returns a ResultSet object that contains information about the specified table's matching columnNamePattern. The returned ResultSet object contains the following columns: catalog name that the table is in, the schema the table is in, the table name, the column name, owner of the table, grantee,

Method Name	Additional Description
	type of access (SELECT, UPDATE, etc.) and if the grantee can grant access to others, "YES," "NO," or null (if unknown)
public abstract ResultSet getColumns(String catalog, String schema-Pattern, String table-NamePattern, String columnNamePattern) throws SQLException	Returns a ResultSet object that contains information about the matching columns for the matching tables and schemas. The ResultSet contains the following columns: catalog name, schema name, table name, column name, SQL data type, name of the type specific to the database, the maximum number of characters or precision depending on the data type, buffer length (not used), the number of digits (if applicable), radix (if applicable), nullability (one of constant columnNoNulls, columnNullable, column-NullableUnknown), comments for the column, default value (if it exists, else null), empty column, empty column, maximum number of bytes in the column of type CHAR (if applicable), index number of column, the last column set to "YES" if it can contain NULLS, "NO" if it can't, else it's empty if the status is unknown
public abstract ResultSet getCrossReference (String primaryCatalog, String primarySchema, String primaryTable, String foreignCatalog, String foreignSchema, String foreignTable) throws SQLException	Returns a ResultSet object that describes the way a table imports foreign keys. The ResultSet object returned by this method contains these columns: primary key's table catalog, primary key's table schema, primary key's table, primary key's column name, foreign key's table catalog, foreign key's table schema, foreign key's table, foreign key's column name, sequence number within foreign key, action to foreign key when primary key is updated (one

Method Name	Additional Description
	of the constants importedKeyCascade, importedKeyRestrict, importedKeySetNull), action to foreign key when primary key is deleted (one of the constants importedKeyCascade, importedKeyRestrict, importedKeySetNull), foreign key identifier, and primary key indentifier
public abstract String getDatabaseProduct-Name() throws SQLException	Returns the database product name
public abstract String getDatabaseProduct-Version() throws SQLException	Returns the database product number
public abstract int getDefaultTransaction Isolation() throws SQLException	Returns the default transaction isolation level as defined by the applicable constants in the Connection class
public abstract int getDriverMajor-Version()	Gets the driver's major version
public abstract int getDriverMinorVersion()	Gets the driver's minor version
public abstract String getDriverName() throws SQLException	Returns the name of the JDBC driver
public abstract String getDriverVersion() throws SQLException	Returns the version of the JDBC driver

Method Name	Additional Description
public abstract ResultSet getExportedKeys(String catalog, String schema, String table) throws SQLException	Returns a ResultSet object that describes the foreign key attributes that reference the specified table's primary key. The ResultSet object returns the following columns: primary key's table catalog, primary key's table schema, primary key's table, primary key's column name, foreign key's table catalog, foreign key's table schema, foreign key's table, foreign key's column name, sequence number within foreign key, action to foreign key when primary key is updated (one of the constants importedKeyCascade, importedKeyRestrict, importedKeySetNull), action to foreign key when primary key is deleted (one of the constants importedKeyCascade, imported KeyRestrict, importedKeySetNull), foreign key identifier, and primary key indentifier
public abstract String getExtraName-Characters() throws SQLException	Returns characters that can be used in unquoted identifier names besides the standard A through Z, 0 through 9, and _
public abstract String getIdentifierQuote-String() throws SQLException	Returns the String used to quote SQL identifiers
public abstract ResultSet getImportedKeys(String String schema, String table) throws SQLException	Returns a ResultSet object that describes the primary key attributes that are referenced by the specified table's foreign key attributes. The ResultSet object contains the following columns: primary key's table catalog, primary key's table schema, primary key's table, primary key's column name, foreign key's table catalog, foreign key's table schema, foreign key's table,

Method Name	Additional Description
	foreign key's column name, sequence number within foreign key, action to foreign key when primary key is updated (one of the constants importedKeyCascade, importedKeyRestrict, importedKeySetNull), action to foreign key when primary key is deleted (one of the constants importedKeyCascade, importedKey-Restrict, importedKeySetNull), foreign key identifier, and primary key indentifier
public abstract ResultSet getIndexInfo (String catalog, String schema, String table, boolean unique, boolean approximate) throws SQLException	Returns a ResultSet object that describes the specified table's indices and statistics. The ResultSet object contains the following columns: catalog name, schema name, table name, false boolean (if tableIndexStatic is the type), index catalog (or null if type is tableIndexStatic), index type, sequence number, column name, column sort sequence, number of unique values in the table or number of rows (if tableIndexStatic), number of pages used for the index (or the number of pages used for the table if tableIndexStatic), and filter condition (if it exists)
public abstract int getMaxBinaryLiteral-Length() throws SQLException	Returns the number of hex characters allowed in an inline binary literal
public abstract int getMaxCatalogName-Length() throws SQLException	The maximum length for a catalog name

Method Name	Additional Description
public abstract int getMaxCharLiteral-Length() throws SQLException	Returns the maximum length for a character literal
public abstract int getMaxColumnName-Length() throws SQLException	Indicates the maximum length for a column name
public abstract int getMaxColumnsIn-GroupBy() throws SQLException	Indicates the maximum number of columns in a GROUP BY clause
public abstract int getMaxColumns InIndex() throws SQLException	Indicates the maximum number of columns in an index
public abstract int getMaxColumnsIn OrderBy() throws SQLException	Indicates the maximum number of columns allowed in an ORDER BY clause
public abstract int getMaxColumnsIn-Select() throws SQLException	Indicates the maximum number of columns in a SELECT statement
public abstract int getMaxColumnsIn-Table() throws SQLException	Indicates the maximum number of columns allowed in a table

Method Name	Additional Description
public abstract int getMaxConnections() throws SQLException	Indicates the maximum number of simultaneous connections allowed to the database
public abstract int getMaxCursorName-Length() throws SQLException	Returns the maximum allowed length of a cursor name
public abstract int getMaxIndexLength() throws SQLException	Returns the maximum length of an index in bytes
public abstract int getMaxProcedure-NameLength() throws SQLException	Returns the maximum allowed length of a procedure name
public abstract int getMaxRowSize() throws SQLException	Indicates the maximum row size
public abstract int getMaxSchemaName-Length() throws SQLException	Returns the maximum allowed length of a schema name
public abstract int getMaxStatement-Length() throws SQLException	Returns the maximum allowed length of a SQL statement
public abstract int getMaxStatements() throws SQLException	Returns the maximum number of statements allowed at one time

Method Name	Additional Description
public abstract int getMaxTableName-Length() throws SQLException	Returns the maximum allowed length of a table name
public abstract int getMaxTablesInSelect() throws SQLException	Indicates the maximum number of tables allowed in a SELECT statement
public abstract int getMaxUserName-Length() throws SQLException	Returns the maximum allowed length of a user name
public abstract String getNumericFunctions() throws SQLException	Returns a comma-separated list of the math functions available
public abstract Result-Set getPrimaryKeys (String catalog, String schema, String table) throws SQLException	Returns a ResultSet object that contains the primary key's description for the specified table. The ResultSet object contains the following columns: catalog name, schema name, table name, column name, sequence number, primary key name, and, possibly, NULL)
public abstract Result-Set getProcedure-Columns(String catalog, String schema-Pattern, String procedureNamePattern, String columnName-Pattern) throws SQLException	Returns a ResultSet object that describes the catalog's stored procedures and result columns matching the specified procedureNamePatten and columnNamePattern. The ResultSet object contains the following columns: catalog name, schema name, procedure name, column or parameter name, column type, data type, data name, precision, length in bytes, scale, radix, nullability, and comments

Method Name	Additional Description
public abstract Result-Set getProcedures(String catalogString String procedureNamePattern) throws SQLException	Returns a ResultSet object that describes the catalog's procedures. The ResultSet object contains the following columns: catalog name, schema name, procedure name, empty column, empty column, empty column, comments about the procedure, and kind of procedure
public abstract String getProcedureTerm() throws SQLException	Returns the database-specific term for procedure
public abstract ResultSet getSchemas() throws SQLException	Returns a ResultSet object that describes the schemas in a database. The ResultSet object contains one column that contains the schema names
public abstract String getSchemaTerm() throws SQLException	Returns the database-specific term for schema
public abstract String getSearchStringEscape() throws SQLException	Returns the escape characters for pattern searching
public abstract String getSQLKeywords() throws SQLException	Returns a comma-separated list of keywords that the database recognizes, but the keywords are not SQL 92 keywords
public abstract String getStringFunctions() throws SQLException	Returns a comma-separated list of string functions in the database
public abstract String getSystemFunctions() throws SQLException	Returns a comma-separated list of system functions in the database

Method Name	Additional Description
public abstract ResultSet getTablePrivileges (String catalog, String schemaPattern, String tableNamePattern) throws SQLException	Returns a ResultSet object that describes the privileges for the matching schemaPattern and tableNamePattern. The ResultSet object contains the following columns: catalog name, schema name, table name, grantor, grantee, type of access, and "YES" if a grantee can grant other access
public abstract Result Set getTables(String catalog, String schema-Pattern, String table-NamePattern, String types[]) throws SQLException	Returns a ResultSet object that describes tables matching the schemaPattern and tableNamePattern. The ResultSet object contains the following columns: catalog name, schema name, table name, table type, and comments
public abstract Result-Set getTableTypes() throws SQLException	Returns a ResultSet object that describes the table types available in the database. The ResultSet object contains the column that is a list of the table types
public abstract String getTimeDate-Functions() throws SQLException	Returns the date and time functions for the database
public abstract Result Set getTypeInfo() throws SQLException	Returns a ResultSet object that describes the SQL data types supported by the database. The ResultSet object contains the columns: type name, SQL data type constants in the Types class, maximum precision, prefix used to quote a literal, suffix used to quote a literal, parameters used to create the type, nullability, case sensitivity, searchability, signed or unsigned (boolean), is it a currency, auto incrementable or not, local version of data

Method Name	Additional Description
	type, minimum scale, maximum scale, empty column, empty column, and radix
public abstract String getURL() throws SQLException	The URL for the database
public abstract String getUserName() throws SQLException	Returns the user name as known by the database
public abstract Result-Set getVersionColumns (String catalog, String String table) throws SQLException	Returns a ResultSet object that describes the specified table's columns that are updated when any column is updated in the table. The ResultSet object contains the following columns: empty column, column name, SQL datatype, type name, precision, column value length in bytes, scale, and pseudoColumn or not
public abstract boolean isCatalogAtStart() throws SQLException	Returns true if the catalog name appears at the start of a qualified table name
public abstract boolean isReadOnly() throws SQLException	Returns true if the database is in read only mode
public abstract boolean nullPlusNonNullIs-Null() throws SQLException	Returns true if a concatentation between a NULL and non-NULL is NULL
public abstract boolean nullsAreSortedAtEnd() throws SQLException	

Method Name

public abstract boolean
nullsAreSortedAtStart()
throws SQLException

public abstract boolean
nullsAreSortedHigh()
throws SQLException

public abstract boolean
nullsAreSortedLow()
throws SQLException

public abstract boolean
storesLowerCaseIdentifiers()
throws SQLException

public abstract boolean
storesLowerCaseQuotedIdentifiers()
throws SQLException

public abstract boolean
storesMixedCaseIdentifiers()
throws SQLException

public abstract boolean
storesMixedCaseQuotedIdentifiers()
throws SQLException

public abstract boolean
storesUpperCaseIdentifiers()
throws SQLException

public abstract boolean
storesUpperCaseQuotedIdentifiers()
throws SQLException

public abstract boolean
supportsAlterTableWithDropColumn()
throws SQLException

Method Name

public abstract boolean
supportsANSI92EntryLevelSQL()
throws SQLException

public abstract boolean
supportsANSI92FullSQL()
throws SQLException

public abstract boolean
supportsANSI92IntermediateSQL()
throws SQLException

public abstract boolean
supportsCatalogsInDataManipulation()
throws SQLException

public abstract boolean
supportsCatalogsInIndexDefinitions()
throws SQLException

public abstract boolean
supportsCatalogsInPrivilegeDefinitions()
throws SQLException

public abstract boolean
supportsCatalogsInProcedureCalls()
throws SQLException

public abstract boolean
supportsCatalogsInTableDefinitions()
throws SQLException

public abstract boolean
supportsColumnAliasing()
throws SQLException

Method Name

public abstract boolean
supportsConvert()
throws SQLException

public abstract boolean
supportsConvert(int fromType,
int toType) throws SQLException

public abstract boolean
supportsCoreSQLGrammar()
throws SQLException

public abstract boolean
supportsCorrelatedSubqueries()
throws SQLException

public abstract boolean
supportsDataDefinitionAndData-
ManipulationTransactions()
throws SQLException

public abstract boolean
supportsDataManipulationTransactions-
Only() throws SQLException

public abstract boolean
supportsDifferentTableCorrelationNames()
throws SQLException

public abstract boolean
supportsExpressionsInOrderBy()
throws SQLException

public abstract boolean
supportsExtendedSQLGrammar()
throws SQLException

Method Name

public abstract boolean
supportsFullOuterJoins()
throws SQLException

public abstract boolean
supportsGroupBy()
throws SQLException

public abstract boolean
supportsGroupByBeyondSelect()
throws SQLException

public abstract boolean
supportsGroupByUnrelated()
throws SQLException

public abstract boolean
supportsIntegrityEnhancementFacility()
throws SQLException

public abstract boolean
supportsLikeEscapeClause()
throws SQLException

public abstract boolean
supportsLimitedOuterJoins()
throws SQLException

public abstract boolean
supportsMinimumSQLGrammar()
throws SQLException

public abstract boolean
supportsMixedCaseIdentifiers()
throws SQLException

Method Name

public abstract boolean
supportsMixedCaseQuotedIdentifiers()
throws SQLException

public abstract boolean
supportsMultipleResultSets()
throws SQLException

public abstract boolean
supportsMultipleTransactions()
throws SQLException

public abstract boolean
supportsNonNullableColumns()
throws SQLException

public abstract boolean
supportsOpenCursorsAcrossCommit()
throws SQLException

public abstract boolean
supportsOpenCursorsAcrossRollback()
throws SQLException

public abstract boolean
supportsOpenStatementsAcrossCommit()
throws SQLException

public abstract boolean
supportsOpenStatementsAcrossRollback()
throws SQLException

public abstract boolean
supportsOrderByUnrelated()
throws SQLException

public abstract boolean
supportsOuterJoins()
throws SQLException

Method Name

public abstract boolean
supportsPositionedDelete()
throws SQLException

public abstract boolean
supportsPositionedUpdate()
throws SQLException

public abstract boolean
supportsSchemasInDataManipulation()
throws SQLException

public abstract boolean
supportsSchemasInProcedureCalls()
throws SQLException

public abstract boolean
supportsSchemasInTableDefinitions()
throws SQLException

public abstract boolean
supportsSelectForUpdate()
throws SQLException

public abstract boolean
supportsStoredProcedures()
throws SQLException

public abstract boolean
supportsSubqueriesInComparisons()
throws SQLException

public abstract boolean
supportsSubqueriesInExists()
throws SQLException

Method Name

public abstract boolean
supportsSubqueriesInIns()
throws SQLException

public abstract boolean
supportsSubqueriesInQuantifieds()
throws SQLException

public abstract boolean
supportsTableCorrelationNames()
throws SQLException

public abstract boolean
supportsTransactionIsolationLevel
(int level) throws SQLException

public abstract boolean
supportsTransactions()
throws SQLException

public abstract boolean
supportsUnion()
throws SQLException

public abstract boolean
supportsUnionAll()
throws SQLException

public abstract boolean
usesLocalFilePerTable()
throws SQLException

public abstract boolean
usesLocalFiles() throws SQLException

Variables

public final static int bestRowNotPseudo
public final static int bestRowPseudo
public final static int versionColumnUnknown
public final static int versionColumnNotPseudo
public final static int versionColumnPseudo
public final static int importedKeyCascade
public final static int importedKeyRestrict
public final static int importedKeySetNull
public final static int typeNoNulls
public final static int typeNullable
public final static int typeNullableUnknown
public final static int typePredNone
public final static int typePredChar
public final static int typePredBasic
public final static int typeSearchable
public final static short tableIndexStatistic
public final static short tableIndexClustered
public final static short tableIndexHashed
public final static short tableIndexOther

public interface Driver

The JDBC driver implements this interface. The JDBC driver must create an instance of itself and register itself with the **DriverManager**.

Methods

Method Name	Additional Description
public abstract boolean acceptsURL(String URL) throws SQLException	If the driver can connect to the specified database in the URL, returns true

Method Name	Additional Description
public abstract Connection connect (String URL, Properties props) throws SQLException	Connects to the database specified in the URL with the specified Properties props
public abstract int getMajorVersion()	Returns the JDBC driver's major version number
public abstract int getMinorVersion()	Returns the JDBC driver's minor version number
public abstract DriverPropertyInfo[] getPropertyInfo(String URL, Properties props) throws SQLException	Returns an array of DriverPropertyInfo that contains possible properties based on the supplied URL and props
public abstract boolean jdbcCompliant()	Returns true if the JDBC driver can pass the JDBC compliance suite

VARIABLES

None

public interface PreparedStatement

This object extends **Statement** and is used to perform queries that will be repeated. This class exists primarily to optimize queries that will be executed repeatedly.

METHODS

Note: The **set** methods set the parameter at the **paramIndex** location in the prepared query to the specified **paramType** object.

Method Name	Additional Description
public abstract void clearParameters() throws SQLException	Resets all of the PreparedStatment's query parameters
public abstract boolean execute() throws SQLException	Runs the prepared query against the database; this method is used primarily if multiple ResultSets are expected
public abstract ResultSet executeQuery() throws SQLException	Executes the prepared query
public abstract int executeUpdate() throws SQLException	Executes the prepared query; this method is used for queries that do not produce a ResultSet (such as Update); returns the number or rows affected, or 0 if nothing is returned by the SQL command
public abstract void setAsciiStream(int paramIndex, InputStream paramType, int length) throws SQLException	
public abstract void setBinaryStream(int paramIndex, InputStream paramType, int length) throws SQLException	
public abstract void setByte (int paramIndex, byte paramType[]) throws SQLException	

Method Name

public abstract void
setBoolean(int paramIndex,
boolean paramType) throws
SQLException

public abstract void
setBytes(int paramIndex,
byte paramType[])
throws SQLException

public abstract void
setDate(int paramIndex,
Date paramType) throws
SQLException

public abstract void
setDouble(int double
paramType) throws
SQLException

public abstract void
setFloat(int paramIndex,
float paramType) throws
SQLException

public abstract void
setInt(int paramIndex,
int paramType) throws
SQLException

public abstract void
setLong(int paramIndex,
long paramType) throws
SQLException

Method Name

public abstract void
setNull(int paramIndex,
int sqlType) throws
SQLException

public abstract void
setNumeric(int
paramIndex, Numeric
paramType) throws
SQLException

public abstract
void setObject(int
paramIndex, Object
paramType) throws
SQLException

public abstract void
setObject(int paramIndex,
Object paramType,
int targetSqlType)
throws SQLException

public abstract void
setObject(int paramIndex,
Object paramType,
int targetSqlType,
int scale) throws
SQLException

public abstract
void setShort(int
paramIndex, short
paramType) throws
SQLException

Method Name

public abstract void
setString(int paramIndex,
String paramType)
throws SQLException

public abstract void
setTime(int
paramIndex,
Time paramType)
throws SQLException

public abstract void
setTimestamp(int
Timestamp
paramType)
throws SQLException

public abstract void
setUnicodeStream(int
paramIndexInputStream
paramType, int length)
throws SQLException

public interface ResultSet

The results of a query are stored in this object, which is returned when the respective query execute method is run for the **Statement**, **Prepared-Statement**, and **CallableStatement** methods. The **get** methods in this class fetch the result for the specified column, but the proper data type must be matched for the column. The **getMetaData** method in this class can facilitate this process of checking the data type in each column of the result set.

METHODS

Method Name	Additional Description
public abstract void clearWarnings() throws SQLException	Clears the warnings for the ResultSet
public abstract void close() throws SQLException	Closes the ResultSet
public abstract int findColumn- (String columnName) throws SQLException	Gets the column number for the specified columnName in the ResultSet
public abstract ResultSetMetaData getMetaData() throws SQLException	Returns a ResultSetMetaData object that contains information about the query's resulting table
public abstract InputStream getAsciiStream- (int columnIndex) throws SQLException	Fetches the result from the current row in the specified column (the column number- columnIndex) in the resulting table
public abstract InputStream getAsciiStream- (String columnName) throws SQLException	Fetches the result from the current row in the specified column (the column name- columnName) in the resulting table
public abstract InputStream getBinaryStream- (int columnIndex) throws SQLException	Fetches the result from the current row in the specified column (the column number- columnIndex) in the resulting table

Method Name	Additional Description
public abstract InputStream getBinaryStream-(String columnName) throws SQLException	Fetches the result from the current row in the specified column (the column name-columnName) in the resulting table
public abstract boolean getBoolean(int columnIndex) throws SQLException	Fetches the result from the current row in the specified column (the column number-columnIndex) in the resulting table
public abstract boolean getBoolean(String columnName) throws SQLException	Fetches the result from the current row in the specified column (the column name-columnName) in the resulting table
public abstract byte getByte(int columnIndex) throws SQLException	Fetches the result from the current row in the specified column (the column number-columnIndex) in the resulting table
public abstract byte getByte(String columnName) throws SQLException	Fetches the result from the current row in the specified column (the column name-columnName) in the resulting table
public abstract byte[] getBytes(int columnIndex) throws SQLException	Fetches the result from the current row in the specified column (the column number-columnIndex) in the resulting table
public abstract byte[] getBytes(String columnName) throws SQLException	Fetches the result from the current row in the specified column (the column name-columnName) in the resulting table

Method Name	Additional Description
public abstract String getCursorName() throws SQLException	This returns a String with this ResultSet's cursor name
public abstract Date getDate(int columnIndex) throws SQLException	Fetches the result from the current row in the specified column (the column number-columnIndex) in the resulting table
public abstract Date getDate(String columnName) throws SQLException	Fetches the result from the current row in the specified column (the column name-columnName) in the resulting table
public abstract double getDouble-(int columnIndex) throws SQLException	Fetches the result from the current row in the specified column (the column number-columnIndex) in the resulting table
public abstract double getDouble-(String columnName) throws SQLException	Fetches the result from the current row in the specified column (the column name-columnName) in the resulting table
public abstract float getFloat(int columnIndex) throws SQLException	Fetches the result from the current row in the specified column (the column number-columnIndex) in the resulting table
public abstract float getFloat(String columnName) throws SQLException	Fetches the result from the current row in the specified column (the column name-columnName) in the resulting table
public abstract int getInt(int columnIndex) throws SQLException	Fetches the result from the current row in the specified column (the column number - columnIndex) in the resulting table

Method Name	Additional Description
public abstract int getInt(String columnName) throws SQLException	Fetches the result from the current row in the specified column (the column name-columnName) in the resulting table
public abstract long getLong(int columnIndex) throws SQLException	Fetches the result from the current row in the specified column (the column number-columnIndex) in the resulting table
public abstract long getLong(String columnName) throws SQLException	Fetches the result from the current row in the specified column (the column name-columnName) in the resulting table
public abstract Numeric getNumeric (int columnIndex, int scale) throws SQLException	Fetches the result from the current row in the specified column (the column number-columnIndex) in the resulting table
public abstract Numeric getNumeric-(String columnName, int scale) throws SQLException	Fetches the result from the current row in the specified column (the column name-columnName) in the resulting table
public abstract Object getObject(int columnIndex) throws SQLException	Fetches the result from the current row in the specified column (the column number-columnIndex) in the resulting table
public abstract Object getObject(String columnName) throws SQLException	Fetches the result from the current row in the specified column (the column name-columnName) in the resulting table

Method Name	Additional Description
public abstract short getShort(int columnIndex) throws SQLException	Fetches the result from the current row in the specified column (the column number-columnIndex) in the resulting table
public abstract short getShort(String columnName) throws SQLException	Fetches the result from the current row in the specified column (the column name-columnName) in the resulting table
public abstract String getString(int columnIndex) throws SQLException	Fetches the result from the current row in the specified column (the column number-columnIndex) in the resulting table
public abstract String getString(String columnName) throws SQLException	Fetches the result from the current row in the specified column (the column name-columnName) in the resulting table
public abstract Time getTime(int columnIndex) throws SQLException	Fetches the result from the current row in the specified column (the column number-columnIndex) in the resulting table
public abstract Time getTime(String columnName) throws SQLException	Fetches the result from the current row in the specified column (the column name-columnName) in the resulting table
public abstract Timestamp getTimestamp(int columnIndex) throws SQLException	Fetches the result from the current row in the specified column (the column number-columnIndex) in the resulting table

Method Name	Additional Description
public abstract Timestamp get Timestamp(String columnName) throws SQLException	Fetches the result from the current row in the specified column (the column name-columnName) in the resulting table
public abstract InputStream getUnicodeStream-(int columnIndex) throws SQLException	Fetches the result from the current row in the specified column (the column number-columnIndex) in the resulting table
public abstract InputStream getUnicodeStream-(String columnName) throws SQLException	Fetches the result from the current row in the specified column (the column name-columnName) in the resulting table
public abstract SQLWarning getWarnings() throws SQLException	Returns the warnings for the ResultSet
public abstract boolean next() throws SQLException	Retrieves the next row of the resulting table
public abstract boolean wasNull() throws SQLException	Returns true if the last column read by one of the get methods was NULL

VARIABLES

None

public interface ResultSetMetaData

These methods allow access to information about a query's results, not the results themselves. This object is created by the **ResultSet.getMetaData** method.

METHODS

Method Name	Additional Description
public abstract String getCatalogName- (int column) throws SQLException	Returns the name of the catalog hit by the query
public abstract int getColumnCount() throws SQLException	Returns the number of columns in the resulting table
public abstract int getColumnDisplaySize- (int column) throws SQLException	Returns the specified column's maximum size
public abstract String getColumnLabel(int column) throws SQLException	Gets a label, if it exists, for the specified column in the Resultset
public abstract String getColumnName(int column) throws SQLException	Gets a name for the specified column number in the resulting table
public abstract int getColumnType(int column) throws SQLException	Returns a constant in the Type class that is the JDBC type of the specified column in the ResultSet

Method Name	Additional Description
public abstract String getColumnTypeName-(int column) throws SQLException	Gets the name of the type of the specified column in the ResultSet
public abstract int getPrecision(int column) throws SQLException	Returns the precision of the data in the specified column, if applicable
public abstract int getScale(int column) throws SQLException	Returns the scale of the data in the specified column, if applicable
public abstract String getSchemaName(int column) throws SQLException	Returns the name of the schema that was accessed in the query to produce the ResultSet for the specified column
public abstract String getTableName(int column) throws SQLException	Returns the name of the table from which the specified column in the ResultSet came from
public abstract boolean isAuto-Increment(int column) throws SQLException	Returns true if the specified column is automatically numbered
public abstract boolean isCaseSensitive (int column) throws SQLException	Returns true if the specified column's contents are case sensitive, if applicable
public abstract boolean isCurrency(int column) throws SQLException	Returns true if the contents of the specified column in the ResultSet are a currency

Method Name	Additional Description
public abstract boolean isDefinitelyWritable(int column) throws SQLException	Returns true if a write operation in the specified column can be done for certain
public abstract int isNullable(int column) throws SQLException	Returns true if the specified column accepts NULL entries
public abstract boolean isReadOnly(int column) throws SQLException	Returns true if the specified column is read only
public abstract boolean isSearchable(int column) throws SQLException	Returns true if the WHERE clause can be a part of the SQL query performed on the specified column
public abstract boolean isSigned(int column) throws SQLException	Returns true if the data contained in the specified column in the ResultSet is signed, if applicable
public abstract boolean isWritable(int column) throws SQLException	Returns true if a write on the specified column is possible

VARIABLES

Variable Name	Additional Description
public final static int columnNoNulls	NULL values not allowed
public final static int columnNullable	NULL values allowed
public final static int columnNullableUnknown	NULL values may or may not be allowed, uncertain

public interface Statement

This class is used to execute a SQL query against the database via the **Connection** object. The **Connection.createStatement** returns a **Statement** object. Methods in the **Statement** class produce **ResultSet** objects used to fetch the result of the query executed in this class.

METHODS

Method Name	Additional Description
public abstract void cancel() throws SQLException	If a query is running in another thread, a foreign thread can cancel it by calling this method on the local Statement object's instantiation
public abstract void clearWarnings() throws SQLException	Clears the warnings for the Statement
public abstract void close() throws SQLException	Closes the Statement and frees its associated resources, including any ResultSets
public abstract boolean execute- (String sql) throws SQLException	Executes the parameter sql, which is an SQL query; this method accounts for multiple ResultSets
public abstract ResultSet execute- Query(String sql) throws SQLException	Executes a query that returns a ResultSet object (produces some results), using the sql parameter as the SQL query
public abstract int executeUpdate- (String sql) throws SQLException	Executes a query that does not produce a resulting table; the method returns the number of rows affected or 0 if no result is produced

Method Name	Additional Description
public abstract int getMaxFieldSize() throws SQLException	Returns the maximum amount of data returned for a resulting column; applies only to the following SQL datatypes: BINARY, VARBINARY, LONGVARBINARY, CHAR, VARCHAR, and LONGVARCHAR
public abstract int getMaxRows() throws SQLException	Returns the maximum number of rows a ResultSet can contain
public abstract boolean getMoreResults() throws SQLException	Returns true if the next ResultSet of the query is present, and moves the ResultSet into the current result space
public abstract int getQueryTimeout() throws SQLException	Returns the number of seconds that the JDBC driver will wait for a query to execute
public abstract ResultSet getResult-Set() throws SQLException	Returns a ResultSet object that is the current result of the query. Only one of these is returned if only one ResultSet is the result of the query; if more ResultSets are present the getMoreResults method is used to move to the next ResultSet
public abstract int getUpdateCount() throws SQLException	Returns the update count; if the result is a ResultSet, 1 is returned
public abstract SQLWarning getWarnings() throws SQLException	Returns the warnings encountered for the query of this Statement object
public abstract void setCursorName-(String name) throws SQLException	Sets the name of a cursor for future reference and uses it in update statements

Method Name	Additional Description
public abstract void setEscapeProcessing- (boolean enable) throws SQLException	Sets escape substitution processing
public abstract void setMaxFieldSize(int max) throws SQLException	Sets the maximum amount of data that can be returned for a column of type BINARY, VARBINARY, LONGVARBINARY, CHAR, VARCHAR, and LONGVARCHAR
public abstract void setMaxRows(int max) throws SQLException	Sets the maximum number of rows that can be retrieved in a ResultSet
public abstract void setQueryTimeout(int seconds) throws SQLException	Sets the time a driver will wait for a query to execute

Variables

None

Exceptions

Finally, we get to exceptions. As with the other sections, the exception listings include a description, and the class' constructors and methods.

public class DataTruncation

This class extends **SQLWarning**. An exception is produced when data transfer is prematurely terminated on a write, and a warning is generated when data transfer is prematurely terminated on a read operation. You can use the methods contained here to provide debugging information as the JDBC driver should throw this exception when a data transfer problem is encountered.

CONSTRUCTOR

Constructor	Additional Description
public DataTruncation-(int index, boolean paramter, boolean read, int dataSize, int transferSize)	Builds a Throwable DataTruncation object with the specified properties

METHODS

Method Name	Additional Description
public int getDataSize()	Returns the number of bytes that should have been transferred
public int getIndex()	Returns the index of the column or parameter that was interrupted
public boolean getParameter()	Returns true if the truncated value was a parameter or false if it was a column
public boolean getRead()	Returns true if truncation occurred on a read; false means truncation occurred on a write
public int getTransferSize()	Returns the number of bytes actually transferred

public class SQLException

This class extends **java.lang.Exception**. It is the responsibility of the JDBC driver to throw this class when a problem occurs during an operation.

CONSTRUCTORS

These constructors are used to create an **SQLException** with the specified information. Creating an exception is not normally necessary unless the developer is working on creating a driver or higher-level JDBC interface.

public SQLException()

public SQLException(String problem)

public SQLException(String problem, String SQLState)

public SQLException(String problem, String SQLState, int vendorCode)

METHODS

Method Name	Additional Description
public int getErrorCode()	Returns the error code that was part of the thrown exception
public SQLException getNextException()	Returns the next exception as an SQLException object
public String getSQLState()	Returns the SQL state that was part of the thrown exception
public synchronized void setNextException-(SQLException excp)	Sets the next exception as excp for the SQLException object

public class SQLWarning

This class extends **SQLException**. It is the responsibility of the JDBC driver to throw this class when a problem occurs during an operation.

CONSTRUCTORS

These constructors build an **SQLWarning** object with the specified information. An **SQLWarning** is not normally needed to be created unless the developer is working on creating a driver or higher-level JDBC interface.

public SQLWarning()

public SQLWarning(String problem)

public SQLWarning(String problem, String SQLstate)

public SQLWarning(String problem, String SQLstate, int vendorCode)

METHODS

Method Name	Additional Description
public SQLWarning getNextWarning()	Returns an SQLWarning object that contains the next warning
public void setNextWarning-(SQLWarning warn)	Sets the next SQLWarning warning warn for the SQLWarning object

Networking With Java 15

David H. Friedel, Jr.

Java supports a number of classes and methods so that you can make connections to the Internet and perform a variety of operations from processing Web content to transferring files.

*S*ince you are reading this book, it's likely that you are connected to the Internet in one way or another. And after writing a few Java applets, you're probably aware that networking plays a key role in the development of Java. So, whether you are just stepping into the world of networking or you already realize what a pain networking can be, this chapter should help you use Java to connect your applications to other resources via networks.

We'll begin by examining the basics of how networking works across the Internet. As you'll see, the two key networking components for the Internet are protocols and ports. We'll then show you how to use special classes defined in the java.net package to set up network sockets and support client/server network communications. We'll also show you how to use the URL class to access content from the Web. In the last part of the chapter, we'll look at techniques for communicating between applets.

Understanding The Basics Of Networking

You may not be aware of it, but you already know the basics of computer networking, especially if you use a telephone. A telephone provides a means for two or more people at different locations to talk back and forth. In order for voices (data) to be sent back and forth, a *protocol* is used that defines how each party will interact with each other. In the case of a telephone, the protocol involves speaking into a transmitter and listening to a receiver.

When it comes to computer networks that connect with the Internet, the set of key protocols that are used include:

◆ TCP/IP

◆ SMTP

◆ FTP

◆ HTTP

◆ NNTP

◆ Finger

◆ WhoIs

Let's take a few moments and discuss the basics of each of these protocols.

TCP/IP

The full name of this protocol is *Transmission Control Protocol/Internet Protocol*. It was proposed as a standard in 1973 but was not adopted as a standard until 1982. TCP/IP serves as a hardware-independent protocol for allowing different types of networking systems to connect and send data back and forth. Actually, TCP/IP consists of a collection of different protocols.

The Unix operating system was the first major OS to incorporate this protocol for network communications. With the proliferation of the Internet, this protocol has become widely used for both Internet connections and for networking computers in local area networks. To take advantage of Java's networking capabilities, you'll need to have a TCP/IP connection to the Internet. Fortunately, newer PC operating systems, such as Windows NT, are incorporating TCP/IP into the system.

SMTP

SMTP stands for *Simple Mail Transfer Protocol*. It is the protocol that is used by email programs such as Eudora to send and receive email. The communications work of handling email is actually controlled by three protocols: SMTP, POP3, and MIME. The primary protocol used to process email is SMTP.

FTP

FTP stands for *File Transfer Protocol*—the protocol that allows files to be transferred from one computer to another across the Internet. This protocol is the most widely used, since most Internet users spend a majority of their time transferring files. Programs that automate the process of sending and receiving files for you use this protocol behind the scenes to make sure that all data is transferred correctly.

HTTP

HTTP stands for *Hyper Text Transfer Protocol*—the protocol that drives the World Wide Web. Since you've probably written countless HTML documents, you already know that information is processed on the Web in the form of hypertext links. HTTP ensures that Web content is transferred correctly from a server to a client computer so that information can be displayed in the correct format. Web browsers like Netscape live and die by the HTTP protocol. You've probably used this protocol numerous times since Web addresses are usually specified by first including the HTTP protocol (for example, http://www.coriolis.com).

NNTP

NNTP stands for *Network News Transfer Protocol*. If you have ever been involved with an Internet newsgroup, you've probably used this protocol hundreds of times, without ever knowing it existed. NNTP works behind the scenes to deliver messages from newsgroups that you belong to.

Finger

Imagine having a finger so large that you could reach out and touch anyone who is connected to the Internet to see if they are currently available. This might sound a little ridiculous, but this is the goal of the Finger protocol.

With this protocol, you can "finger" an Internet user to obtain information that the user has declared as public. Some of this information might include the user's full name, mailing address, phone number, and so on.

WhoIs

If you live in a big city and you want to locate someone, you can go to a phone book and look the person up. On the Internet, you can use the WhoIs protocol to do your detective work for you. As long as a person, organization, or company is registered with the Internet address assignment agency (InterNIC), this protocol will give you the information you need.

The Client/Server Model

Using our simple phone analogy, let's investigate the concepts of client/ server technology—the driving force that makes networks like the Internet come to life. At one time or another, we've all stood by the phone in anticipation waiting for a call to come in. The caller has the option to pick up the phone at any time and make the call. When they do, we can pick up the phone after a few rings to complete the connection. Since we are the party who is waiting for the call, we operate as the *server.* The person making the call, on the other hand, operates as the *client,* since by making the call, he or she is simply "requesting information" from us—the server.

Computers connected in a network pass information back and forth in the form of *messages.* The computer, acting as the client, sends messages to the server. The server processes the messages and returns information in the form of messages back to the client.

Ports Of Interest

In addition to performing complex calculations quickly, today's computers are great at performing multiple tasks at the same time. (Or at least they create the illusion that they can, as we learned in Chapter 8 when we explored threads.) Computers connected to the Internet as servers can provide many services at once. They do this by using *ports* that link up different channels set up at a single address. A computer may set up a port with a number between 0 and 65535, known as a 16-bit number. Each request that comes in from a client requires a port specification as shown in Figure 15.1. If the server has a service running for that port, it is addressed with a certain message defined by the protocol. Currently, ports have been established for the default protocols. For example, port 80 is reserved for HTTP, port 21 is reserved for FTP, port 119 is reserved for News, and so on. The set of key protocols and their associated ports are listed in Table 15.1.

Establishing new ports and protocols.

You can create your own ports and protocols for the Internet—in fact new ones are being established for the Internet all the time. Just remember that the basic principal behind a network is to be able to communicate; thus, standards are needed. To make sure that everyone follows standard practices for setting up communication links on the Internet, a system of REQUEST FOR COMMENTS (RFCs) have been established. RFCs are documents that are submitted for the purpose of defining specifications or the guidelines for the Internet. For example, the FTP protocol was submitted and reviewed by many Internet developers and users until it was officially adapted as RCF0959. This particular document presents all of the specifications for the protocol. If you were to create a protocol, you could submit it for review and it to would go through the process of being reviewed. Think of it as a bill on Capitol Hill on its windy path to becoming a law. There are many chances for it to be vetoed along the way.

Table 15.1   Key Internet protocols and their associated ports.

Protocol	Port
HTTP	80
FTP	21
NNTP	119
WhoIs	43
SMTP	25
Finger	79

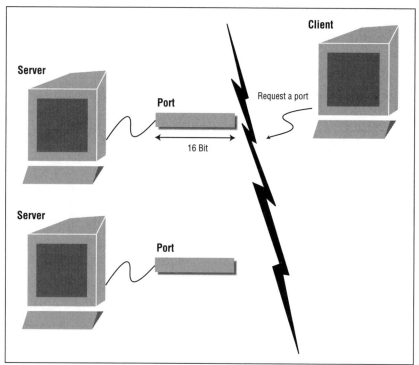

Figure 15.1   Processing a request from a client.

Introducing The
java.net Package

As we've explored topics like creating GUI interfaces, controlling threads, and writing exceptions, we've seen that Java's developers put a lot of care into creating packages and classes to handle important activities. Fortunately, when it comes to networking, the Java developers came through again. The java.net package provides several classes for handling key Internet protocols. With these classes, you can perform a number of Internet related operations, including transferring files, setting up and controlling mail servers, creating search agents, processing Web content, and much more.

The structure of the java.net package is shown in Figure 15.2. Table 15.2 provides a summary description of each key class. To understand how these key classes operate, you'll need to be familiar with the client/server model of networking and how sockets are used to facilitate network communications. Because of their complexity and depth, we won't cover every class in detail; but we will cover the essentials so that you can use some of these classes to develop network-capable Java applets and applications.

Networking Applications

Although you may only be creating Java applets right now, opportunities will emerge for creating more powerful distributed programs, especially as Java compilers get better at generating more tightly compiled code. The incredible flexibility and power that Java's portability provides across multiple platforms allows you to create programs for wide distribution. As you gain more experience developing with Java, you'll find yourself building applications that perform networking related tasks that were never possible in the past using traditional languages like C and C++. The key is learning how to exploit the client/server model of developing networked applications.

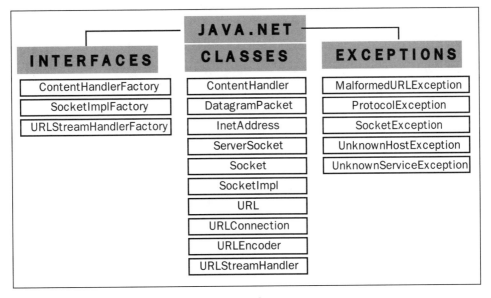

Figure 15.2   The structure of the java.net package.

Table 15.2   The main classes in the java.net package.

Class	Description
ContentHandler	This is an abstract class that processes data in a specific format from a stream and creates an appropriate object.
InetAddress	Used to process an Internet address.
ServerSocket	Used to set up a connection-oriented server socket.
Socket	Used to set up a socket for a client.
SocketImpl	Used to create a specific implementation of a socket.
URL	Used to set up a URL.
URLConnection	Used to set up a connection to a URL.
URLStreamHandler	Used to manage data read from or written to a URL.

Working With Internet Addressing

Before we jump in and start using some of the java.net classes to set up client/server communications, you'll need to know the basics of TCP/IP Internet addressing. Actual Internet addresses are represented using a series of four numbers separated by dots. Here's an example:

```
189.12.49.123
```

Each number must be in the range from 0 to 255.

Since you should already have your own Internet address, you can easily determine what it is by using the **InetAddress** class defined in the java.net package. This class provides five key methods as listed in Table 15.3.

To see how the **InetAddress** class can be used, let's write a simple Java program that checks your local computer and displays your Internet address:

```
import java.net.*;  // Must be included to use the InetAddress class

public class checkMyIP {
  public static void main(String args[]) {
```

```
        InetAddress localA = null;
        try {
            // Returns the name of the local address
            localA = InetAddress.getLocalHost();
        }
        catch {
        }
        system.out.println("The local address is " + localA);
    }
}
```

First notice that the **import** statement is used to include the classes from the java.net package. The variable **localA** is declared as type **InetAddress**. A call to the method **getLocalHost**() returns the address of the local host computer. Notice that no parameters are provided.

The Role Of The Client

A client application interacts with other clients to perform certain functions through *sockets*. In order for a client to communicate to other clients, a server must be established for connection. The server is discussed later in the chapter, but for now all you need to know is that a client requires a server to make a connection from which all communication originates.

Table 15.3   The key methods in the InetAddress class.

Method	Description
getHost()	Returns the name of the host being stored by the InetAddress class. An example would be coriolis.com.
getAddress()	Returns the numerical address of the host being stored by the InetAddress class.
getLocalHost()	Returns the name of the local host.
getByName()	Returns the name of the host specified by a supplied argument to this method.
getAllByName()	Returns a list of addresses for the host name provided as an argument to this method.

Creating A Socket

A socket provides a means for information to flow to and from a computer, much like the way a wall socket provides a channel for electricity to flow through. To initiate a socket, the client application must create an instance of the **Socket** class. This is a class that Java provides to facilitate Internet communications. It uses Internet protocol (IP) addresses and port numbers. The IP address indicates with which computer you want to establish communication. Here is an example of how a socket object is created using the **Socket** class:

```
Import java.net.*;
...
Socket mrClient = null;
```

First, notice that the package java.net must be imported so that you can access the **Socket** class. Here the socket object, **mrClient**, is declared and set to null. To initialize **mrClient**, you use a statement like the following:

```
mrClient = new Socket(165.247.88.17, 10);
```

This code creates an instance of the **Socket** class with an IP address of 165.247.88.17 and a port value of 10.

Using Sockets

After creating the gateway for data to enter your program, you need to create a repository for the data to come and go. Streams provide a method of reading and writing data to a socket. For our example and most uses, we'll need two separate streams. The first stream is an input stream and calls a method to receive the information from the socket. The second stream is used to send data out from the socket:

```
InputStream rawDataIn = mrClient.getInputStream();
OutputStream rawDataOut = mrClient.getOutputStream();
```

The first statement instantiates the object **rawDataIn** as type **InputStream**. Any data that flows to the client, **mrClient**, will be stored in **rawDataIn**. The other stream is the **OutputStream**. As you might have guessed, this stream is responsible for passing the data from the client. If you recall from Chapter 12, the Input/OutputStream is difficult to parse all data through because not all of the data processed is just simple bytes. To use some of the more complex data types available in Java, we need to pass our stream through the **DataInput** and **DataOutput** interfaces. This allows for more control over the data that is to be received and sent. To pass both the incoming and outgoing data through the **DataInput** and **DataOutput** interfaces, you'll need to use code like the following:

```
DataInputStream DataIn = new DataInputStream(rawDataIn);
DataOutputStream DataOut = new DataOutputStream(rawDataOut);
```

An InputStream/OutputStream is used because of the extensive ability to manipulate more complex streams than simple bytes. For example, you can test the stream to see if it is at the end of a line by using a **readLine()** method. This method explicitly checks for *returns, newlines,* and *return-newline* combinations in a string of characters read from the stream.

Creating A Sample Client Application

Now that you've been introduced to the basics of how client applications communicate using sockets and IP addresses, let's write a sample Java program that creates a socket object and reads in data:

```
import java.io.*;
import java.net.*;  // Must be included to use Socket class
import java.awt.*;

public class mrClient extends Frame {
   mrClient() { }
   mrClient(String s) {
      // Create the text display for the application
      super("Client Application");
      TextArea clientScreen = new TextArea("mrClient's Screen:\n",
         10, 40);
      add("Center", clientScreen);
   pack();
   show();

   Socket mrClient = null;
   // Setup the input and output streams
   InputStream rawDataIn = null;
   OutputStream rawDataOut = null;
```

```
        try {
          mrClient = new Socket(s, 10 );    // Create the socket object

          rawDataIn = mrClient.getInputStream();
          rawDataOut = mrClient.getOutputStream();
          // Create a data input stream
          DataInputStream DataIn = new DataInputStream(rawDataIn);
          // Create a data output stream
          DataOutputStream DataOut = new DataOutputStream(rawDataOut);
          int Value = DataIn.readInt();   // Read in data from the socket
          clientScreen.appendText( "mrClient receives -  " + Value +
          // "\n");

          switch(Value) {    // Determine which value has been obtained
          // from the socket
           case 1:
             clientScreen.appendText("Your Number 1");
             DataOut.writeInt( 1 );
             break;
           case 2:
             clientScreen.appendText("Your Number 2");
             DataOut.writeInt( 2 );
             break;
           case 3:
             clientScreen.appendText("Your Shakey");
             DataOut.writeInt( 3 );
             break;
          case 4:
             clientScreen.appendText("Your a loser");
             DataOut.writeInt( 4 );
             break;
          case 5:
             clientScreen.appendText("This is my lucky number!");
             DataOut.writeInt( 5 );
             break;
          default:
             clientScreen.appendText("What was your Number?");
             DataOut.writeInt( 6 );
          }
          mrClient.close();    // Close the socket
     }

 // Handle exceptions that have occurred
 catch( UnknownHostException e ) {
      clientScreen.appendText("Can't find Server");
     }
    catch( IOException e ) {
      clientScreen.appendText("an IO Error has occurred");
```

```
    }
}

public static void main( String args[] ) {
   new mrClient(args[0]);
}

   // Handle events that have occurred
   public boolean handleEvent(Event evt)
   {
      switch(evt.id)
      {
         System.out.println(evt.target.toString());
         case Event.WINDOW_DESTROY:
         {
            System.out.println("Exiting...");
            System.exit(0);
            return true;
         }
      }
   return true;
   }

}
```

When you run this code, remember to pass the address of the computer to connect to. Otherwise, you will throw an **ArrayOutOfBoundsException**. In this case, you should pass the address of your local computer as the command line argument. A sample output produced by the program is shown in Figure 15.3.

Figure 15.3   Output produced by the Client Application.

Most of the interesting code is found in the **mrClient**() constructor. After setting up an introductory message, the constructor declares objects that will be used for creating a socket and the input and output streams:

```
Socket mrClient = null;
InputStream rawDataIn = null;    // Set up the input and output
  streams
OutputStream rawDataOut = null;
```

Next, notice the **try** statement that comes before the line of code that creates the socket object, **mrClient**:

```
try {
   mrClient = new Socket(s, 10);    // Create the socket object
...
```

Because all sockets, as well as streams, are capable of throwing **IOExceptions**, it is good practice to check for an IOException when creating a socket and using the socket to perform critical operations such as sending and receiving data. (For more information on exceptions, review Chapter 9.)

The next set of statements perform the actual reading and writing to the socket. In the line shown next, **DataIn** is the reference to the **DataInput** which is linked to the **InputStream** of the socket:

```
int Value = DataIn.readInt();
```

In this case, the integer **Value** receives the value of the **DataIn** at that instance and clears the buffer. Once the data has been read from the socket, we use a **switch** statement to check the input and display an appropriate message. After the input data has been processed, the **close**() method is called to close the socket.

Networking Concerns

When communicating across a network, certain factors should be taken into consideration. In a perfect world, all users would have a fast connection with no lag. Unfortunately that "perfect" world doesn't exist, so you must take the bandwidth of your connections into consideration. To optimize your applications, the use of return codes allows for quick transmission of integers or small clauses that have more complicated procedures attached to them on either side. In our example, the receiving and returning of integers actually fall into a switch statement that performs a more complicated task. The following line is responsible for sending the integer "5" to DataOutputStream interface:

```
DataOut.writeInt( 5 );
```

From here, the data is passed through the interface and converted to bytes for the OutputStream to be able to handle the data.

Bring On The Server

Now that we have the client under our belt, we need to learn how to connect to another application. This is accomplished by having the client connect to a server. Essentially, a server is a computer that provides a service for others to utilize. The server is set to listen to a particular port. Once a client requests information on that port, the server springs into action.

For setting up and controlling servers, Java provides a counterpart to the **Socket** class called the **ServerSocket** class. Objects created from this class do not connect to an address like socket objects do. Instead, a server socket object creates a port for another socket to plug in to. To declare a variable of the **ServerSocket** class, you use a statement like the following:

```
ServerSocket mrsServer = null;
```

Then, you can create an instance of the **ServerSocket** class by supplying the appropriate parameter to the class' constructor:

```
mrsServer = new ServerSocket( 10 );
```

This line creates an instance of a **ServerSocket** class named **mrsServer**. The object, **mrsServer**, is initialized with a port setting of 10. Essentially, the server is now set up to listen for incoming sockets at port 10. In addition to specifying the port, you can set a time limit. Here's an example:

```
mrsServer = new ServerSocket(10, 5);
```

Once you have created an object of type **ServerSocket**, you must put the server in motion by using the **accept()** method. This method effectively places a hold on the program until a socket comes along to connect to the server. So, it would be wise to place this method call in a thread if you want to perform other functions while you are waiting for a socket to connect to the server. Once a socket shows up, the **accept()** method returns a socket. Then, the server operates just like the client, by allowing sockets to communicate back and forth.

Creating A Sample Server Application

Let's combine everything we know about clients and servers and create a program that uses both the **ServerSocket** and **Socket** classes. This program will create a server socket object and then wait for a client object to connect up. Once the client connects, the server will try to read data from the client. Here's the complete program:

```
import java.io.*;
import java.net.*;
import java.awt.*;

public class mrsServer extends Frame {
   TextArea serverScreen;

   mrsServer() {
    super("Server Application");
    serverScreen = new TextArea("mrsServer's Screen:\n", 10, 40);
    add("Center", serverScreen);
    pack();
    show();

    ServerSocket mrsServer = null;    // Initialize the server socket
    Socket socketReturn = null;       // Initialize the client socket
    InputStream rawDataIn = null;
    OutputStream rawDataOut = null;

   try {
      mrsServer = new ServerSocket( 10 ); // Create the server
                                          // object
      socketReturn = mrsServer.accept(); // Wait for the client
                                         // socket to come in
      serverScreen.appendText( "Connected to the mrsServer \n" );
```

```
        rawDataIn = socketReturn.getInputStream();
        rawDataOut = socketReturn.getOutputStream();
        DataInputStream DataIn = new DataInputStream(rawDataIn);
        DataOutputStream DataOut = new DataOutputStream(rawDataOut);
        DataOut.write( 5 );
        int Value = DataIn.read();

        switch(Value)
        {
        case 1:
          serverScreen.appendText("You sent me Number 1");
          break;
        case 2:
          serverScreen.appendText("You sent me Number 2");
          break;
        case 3:
          serverScreen.appendText("You sent me Number 3");
          break;
        case 4:
          serverScreen.appendText("You sent me Number 4");
          break;
        case 5:
          serverScreen.appendText("You sent me Number 5");
          break;
        default:
          serverScreen.appendText("What was your Number?");
        }

        }
      catch( UnknownHostException e ) {
        clientScreen.appendText("Can't find Server");
      }
      catch( IOException e ) {
        clientScreen.appendText("an IO Error has occurred");
      }
}

public static void main( String args[] ) {
    new mrsServer();
}

 // Handle events that have occurred
 public boolean handleEvent(Event evt)
 {
   switch(evt.id)
   {
     System.out.println(evt.target.toString());
     case Event.WINDOW_DESTROY:
     {
```

```
        System.out.println("Exiting...");
        System.exit(0);
        return true;
    }
  }
  return true;
  }
}
```

This program is essentially an extension of the client example we created earlier. A sample output is shown in Figure 15.4. This time around we added server capabilities by using the **ServerSocket** class. The key code is found in the **mrsServer()** constructor. As you start to read this code, you might want to compare it with the code found in the **mrClient()** constructor from the previous example.

The first two important lines in **mrsServer()** declare the variable **mrsServer** of type **ServerSocket** class and **socketReturn** of type **Socket**:

```
ServerSocket mrsServer = null;    // Initialize the server socket
  (server)
Socket socketReturn = null;       // Initialize the client socket
```

In addition to the **ServerSocket**, we must declare a socket that is returned when we connect to another socket. In the following lines of code, we create an instance of the **ServerSocket** class and initialize the port to 10. Then, the **accept()** method is called to instruct the program to wait for the incoming socket. The returning socket will be assigned to **socketReturn**:

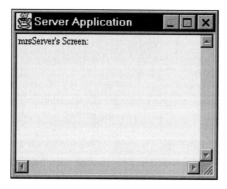

Figure 15.4   **Output produced by the Server Application.**

```
try {
    mrsServer = new ServerSocket( 10 ); // Create the server object
    socketReturn = mrsServer.accept(); // Wait for the client socket
                                       // to come in
```

In the event of a connection, the server will write a "5" to the socket stream and not to the server socket stream. After this occurs, the server will attempt to read data from the client, and the data will be processed by the server by displaying an appropriate message.

Web Content Only Please

If communicating across the Internet to access Web content is your only concern, Java has a few special classes for you—**URL** and **URLConnection**. You can use these classes for creating objects to read, manipulate, and write Web content. Here is the syntax you use to declare a Uniform Resource Locator (**URL**) variable:

```
URL aURL = null;
```

In this case, **aURL** is the name of the variable being declared. To create and initialize an object you would use a statement like this:

```
aURL = new URL(http, www.coriolis.com, 80, index.html);
```

This line passes the **URL** class four parameters including the Internet protocol, Web address, Internet port, and the name of an HTML file to access. Although we are using four arguments with this constructor call, other variations are available including:

```
URL(String protocol, String host, String file);
URL(URL context, String spec);
URL(String spec);
```

Since the **URL()** constructor is called to create an object based upon a value, you should use **try...catch** statements to check for errors that might occur. This will allow you to check for a **MalformedURLException** that could be thrown whenever a URL is not specified properly.

Once a URL object has been created, you can easily use it to access Web content. Let's look at an example that grabs a file and prints it to the screen:

```java
import java.io.*;
import java.net.*;

public class GrabAFile {
    BufferedInputStream holdingRoom1;
    String holdingRoom2;

    GrabAFile() {
    }

    GrabAFile( String userURL ) {
        URL aURL;
        InputStream rawDataIn;
        DataInputStream refinedDataIn;
        int aCharDataIn;

        try {
            aURL = new URL(userURL);
            rawDataIn = aURL.openStream();
            holdingRoom1 = new BufferedInputStream( rawDataIn );
            refinedDataIn = new DataInputStream( holdingRoom1 );

            while((aCharDataIn = refinedDataIn.read() ) >= 0 ) {
                    System.out.print((char)aCharDataIn);
            }

            System.out.print( refinedDataIn );
        }
        catch( MalformedURLException e ) {}
        catch( IOException e ) {}
        catch( Exception e ) {}
    }

    public static void main(String args[]) {
        new GrabAFile(args[0]);
    }
}
```

First, this code declares and initializes a URL object as explained earlier. Then, we open a stream for the input. To do this we declare an object as type **InputStream** and assign it a variable. Then, we make reference to the method **openStream**() using the name of the object of type URL we wish to connect to the input stream.

Using The URLConnection Class

Another class worth mentioning when reading and writing data to a URL is the **URLConnection** class. This class is an abstract class and must be subclassed to implement the methods that are contained within it. It offers an abundance of useful methods for extracting data from files and setting up properties for writing to a URL.

To utilize any of the methods available in the **URLConnection** class, you first declare a variable of type **URLConnection** as shown here:

```
URLConnection anotherURL;
```

Next, you need to open the connection to an instance of an existing URL. To accomplish this task, you would use a statement like this:

```
anotherURL = aURL.openConnection();
```

The variable, **anotherURL**, is declared as type **URLConnection** as shown in the previous statement. The variable **aURL** in the call, **aURL.openConnection()**, is an object instantiated as type **URL**. The method **openConnection()** creates an object of type **URLConnection** and establishes a connection between the remote object declared in the URL. Let's look at an example where we extract the content type of the file being accessed:

```java
import java.net.*;

public class GrabInfo {

    GrabInfo() {
    }

    GrabInfo( String userURL ) {
        URL aURL;
        URLConnection anotherURL;

        try {
            aURL = new URL(userURL);
            anotherURL = aURL.openConnection();
            anotherURL.connect();
            System.out.print(anotherURL.getContentType() + "\n\n");
        } catch( MalformedURLException e ) {
        } catch( Exception e ) {
```

```
        }
    }

    public static void main(String args[]) {
        new GrabInfo(args[0]);
    }
}
```

Here we call the method **getContentType()** defined in the **URLConnection** class and print out what was returned from the object. This method can be extremely useful for determining file types. If you need a more thorough check of a file type, try the method **guessContentTypeFromStream()** and apply it to the previous example by passing the stream to it.

Networking Between Applets

Situations may arise where you want applets on the same Web page to be able to communicate with each other. For example, if you want a certain event to occur in an applet when another applet reaches a point in an animation, you could have the animation applet send a message to the other applet at the appropriate time. The only limitation for this type of communication is that both applets must be present on a page to communicate back and forth. Currently, there is no way to have one applet send information to another applet on another page. Hopefully, this feature will be added in the near future.

Passing Information To A Fellow Applet

Let's write some Java code that allows one applet to communicate with another. After you compile and run the code, you should see the responses shown in Figures 15.5 through 15.7. One of the applets is named Gentleman and the other is named Lady.

This example can quickly be modified to perform even more complex tasks with little or no effort. But first, let's discuss exactly what is taking place. The first applet, the Lady, looks like any other applet except for the **handleEvent()** method:

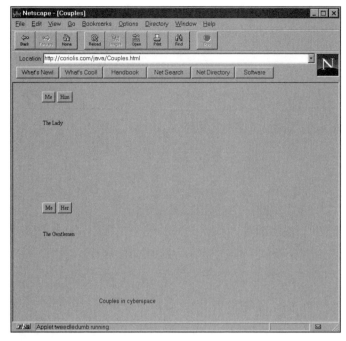

Figure 15.5 A shot of the opening screen showing the two applets.

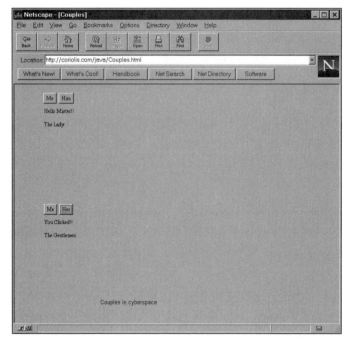

Figure 15.6 A shot of the Gentleman applet's Me button pressed and the Her button pressed.

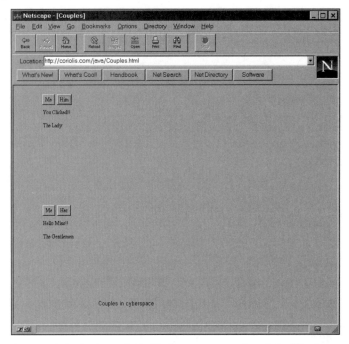

Figure 15.7   A shot of the Lady applet's Me button pressed and the Him button pressed.

```java
public boolean handleEvent(Event evt)
{
  if (evt.target instanceof Button) {
    if("Him".equals(evt.arg))
    {
      Gentleman tweedledee=
        (Gentleman)getAppletContext().getApplet("tweedledee");
      if ( tweedledee != null) {
        return  tweedledee.handleEvent(evt);
      } else {
        return false;
      }
    }
    else if("Me".equals(evt.arg))
    {
      str ="You Clicked!!";
      repaint();
      return true;
    }
    else if("Her".equals(evt.arg))
    {
      str ="Hello Mister!!";
      repaint();
      return true;
```

```
    }
        return super.handleEvent(evt);
}
return super.handleEvent(evt);
}
```

The actual communication code is found in the second **if** statement. The first line actually retrieves the applet named tweedledee. This applet is named within the declaration of an applet in the HTML file named Couples:

```
<applet code="Gentleman" name=tweedledee width=187 height=232></
  applet>
```

Using the methods **getApplet()** from the **AppletContext** class and the **getAppletContext()** from the **Applet** class, we create an interface in which to call the methods of the **Gentleman** class and apply it to the applet itself. This allows us to control the applet by calling it with the name of the variable and the name in the **<applet>** tag assigned to it. In this case, **tweedledee** controls the applet from within the **Lady**.

Now we need to make sure when calling handling events that we make reference to the particular event:

```
// From the Lady
return tweedledee.handleEvent(evt);

// From the Gentleman
else if("Him".equals(evt.arg))
    {
        str ="Hello Miss!!";
        repaint();
        return true;
    }
```

In the event that a user clicks the "Him" button from the "Lady" applet, the Gentleman must address the event that will be passed to it. Otherwise, the **evt** object will slip by without being acted upon. The same goes for the Lady addressing the events that will occur in the Gentleman. Everything here is just reversed for the other applet to communicate in the reverse direction.

Which came first ... the chicken or the egg?

When compiling the two source files for our applets listed at the end of this chapter, it is important to remember that both source files must be typed in and saved before compiling one or the other. This is because both reference each other's class file. When no class file is present, as in the event of requiring a class in both directions, the Java compiler reads the source file and compiles it from the definitions within. This would be comparable to a deadlock when relating this situation to threads.

The complete code for the Lady applet is:

```
import java.awt.*;
import java.applet.*;

public class Lady extends Applet
{
     String str = "";

   public void init()
   {
     Button a = new Button("Me");
     Button b = new Button("Him");
       add("East", a);
       add("West", b);

   }

public boolean handleEvent(Event evt)
{
  if (evt.target instanceof Button) {
     if("Him".equals(evt.arg))
       {
Gentleman tweedledee=
  (Gentleman)getAppletContext().getApplet("tweedledee");
       if ( tweedledee != null) {
         return tweedledee.handleEvent(evt);
       } else {
         return false;
       }
     }
     else if("Me".equals(evt.arg))
     {
        str ="You Clicked!!";
```

```
            repaint();
            return true;
        }
        else if("Her".equals(evt.arg))
        {
            str ="Hello Mister!!";
            repaint();
            return true;
        }
        return super.handleEvent(evt);
}
return super.handleEvent(evt);
}
        public void paint(Graphics g) {
            g.drawString(str, 60,50);
            g.drawString("The Lady", 60, 80);
        }
}
```

And here is the complete code for the Gentleman applet:

```
import java.awt.*;
import java.applet.*;

public class Gentleman extends Applet
{
        String str = "";

    public void init()
    {
      Button a = new Button("Me");
      Button b = new Button("Her");
        add("East", a);
        add("West", b);

    }

public boolean handleEvent(Event evt)
{
  if (evt.target instanceof Button) {
     if("Her".equals(evt.arg))
     {
        Lady tweedledumb= (Lady)
          getAppletContext().getApplet("tweedledumb");
        if ( tweedledumb != null) {
          return tweedledumb.handleEvent(evt);
        } else {
          return false;
```

```
        }
      }
      else if("Me".equals(evt.arg))
      {
          str ="You Clicked!!";
          repaint();
          return true;
      }
      else if("Him".equals(evt.arg))
      {
          str ="Hello Miss!!";
          repaint();
          return true;
      }
        return super.handleEvent(evt);
}
return super.handleEvent(evt);
}
   public void paint(Graphics g) {
       g.drawString(str, 60,50);
       g.drawString("The Gentleman", 60, 80);
   }
}
```

THE COUPLES.HTML FILE

```
<HTML>
<HEAD>
<TITLE>Couples</TITLE>
</HEAD>
<BODY>
<applet code="Lady" name=tweedledumb width=187 height=232></applet>
<br>
<br>
<applet code="Gentlemen" name=tweedledee width=187 height=232></
 applet>
Couples in cyberspace
</BODY>
</HTML>
```

Debugging

16

Peter Aitken

If you're lucky, you'll never need to debug your Java programs. However, it seems that no one is ever that lucky! Fortunately, Visual J++ has a capable set of debugging tools that makes this job relatively easy.

What Is Debugging?

A *bug* is a problem with a program that keeps it from running properly. Bugs are distinct from build errors which prevent a program from compiling. A buggy program will compile and execute, but the bug will cause the program to produce incorrect results—or, in more serious cases, to "crash."

Let's look at some examples. If a mortgage calculator program produces incorrect figures for monthly payments, that is a bug. If a graphics program displays picture elements in incorrect colors, that is a bug, too. Also, if an applet causes your browser to crash and the operating system to freeze, this is most definitely a bug. In practice, this latter type of bug is quite uncommon with Java programs because of the language's built-in security features—but one can never be sure!

The process of debugging has two major parts. First, you can control program execution by processing program statements one at a time, executing up to a particular program location, then pausing to control execution of methods, and so on. Secondly, you can examine and manipulate the values of program variables. These two methods are almost always used together. For example, if a program is producing incorrect results in its mathematical calculations, you would execute the program up to the section of code that you suspect is at fault. At that point, you would pause execution at a *breakpoint* and examine the contents of relevant program variables. Next, you might execute the program one line at a time, keeping track of the variable values and watching for the error to occur. Once you have located the line of Java code that is at fault, it is usually a simple matter to examine the code and fix the mistake.

What is a breakpoint?

During debugging, you can set a breakpoint on any line of code in the program. Execution pauses whenever it reaches a breakpoint.

Starting The Debugging Process

The first step in a debugging session is usually to set one or more breakpoints where you want execution to pause. The only time that you do not need to set breakpoints is when you are going to single-step through the code, which can be thought of as placing an automatic breakpoint on every line. If you need to pause execution at only a single location, simply place the cursor on that line of source code. To set multiple breakpoints, follow these steps:

1. Place the editing cursor on the line of code where you want the breakpoint.

2. Select Breakpoints from the Edit menu, or press Ctrl+B. The breakpoint dialog box is displayed, as shown in Figure 16.1.

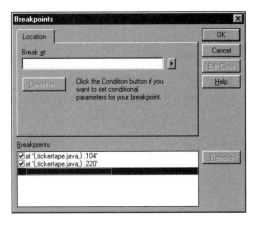

Figure 16.1   The Breakpoint dialog box.

3. Click the arrow at the right end of the Break at box, then click the line number that is displayed (this is the number of the current line).

4. Click OK. The dialog box closes, and the breakpoint is indicated by a red dot displayed next to the line of code in the left margin.

Existing breakpoints are listed at the bottom of this dialog box, identified by file name and line number. To remove a breakpoint, highlight it in the list, and then click the Remove button. To temporarily disable a breakpoint, click the check box next to the breakpoint's entry to remove the check. A disabled breakpoint is marked by an open circle in the source code listing.

Once you have set the desired breakpoints, you are ready to start debugging. To initiate debugging in Visual J++, select Debug from the Build menu. A submenu will appear with the following three choices:

◆ Go: Starts the program and executes code until a breakpoint or the end of the program is reached.

◆ Step Into: Single-steps through instructions in the program and enters each method call that is encountered. This command is the equivalent of having a breakpoint set on every line.

◆ Run to Cursor: Executes the program as far as the code line that contains the insertion point.

Depending on the project options, your program will start executing either within your browser or in its own window. You can resize and arrange the Visual J++ and application windows to make them both visible on your screen, or you can use the standard Windows techniques (e.g., Alt+Tab) to switch from one to the other. In any case, the program will execute up to the first breakpoint and pause. The source code window will be displayed, with a yellow arrow in the left margin indicating the line where execution is paused. Note that execution pauses before the breakpoint line—not after it.

While debugging is in progress, the Build menu is replaced by the Debug menu, and the Debug toolbar is displayed. Many, but not all, commands are duplicated on the menu and toolbar. Remember, like all Visual J++ toolbars, the Debug toolbar can be moved to the most convenient screen location.

Looking At Variables

One of the most important things you'll need to do while a program is paused is to examine the contents of variables. Visual J++ provides the Variables window that automatically displays the values of the variables that programmers most often need to view during debugging. You can also set up a *watch* to keep an eye on any variable or expression you desire.

Using The Variables Window

The Variables window is normally displayed at the lower left of the screen during debugging. If it is not, click the Variables button on the Debug toolbar. The Variables window has three tabs:

◆ The Auto tab displays information about variables used in the current statement and the previous statement.

◆ The Locals tab displays information about variables local to the current function.

◆ The "this" tab displays information about the object pointed to by **this**.

On each tab, the variable names are listed in one column and the value (when appropriate) in the other column. Because many Java variables contain objects rather than simple numerical or text values, some items listed in the Variables window will not have a value per se and will display {…} instead. An example of the Variables window display is shown in Figure 16.2. You can see, for example, that the variable **fMetrics** (an object) does not have a value displayed for it, while **fontHeight** (a simple type Integer variable) does.

Some items listed in the Variables window will have a plus sign next to them. This means that more information is available about this item, which you can display by clicking on the plus symbol. In Figure 16.2, you can see that **fMetrics** has a plus sign next to it. Figure 16.3 shows the display after opening **fMetrics** by clicking its plus sign.

We see now that **fMetrics** is derived from the **java.Lang.Object** class—which is not very helpful, since every object in Java is eventually based on this class. We also see that **fMetrics** contains something called font, which has its own plus sign next to it. Click that and you'll see the display in Figure 16.4 (we have enlarged the Variables window so it can show everything at once).

Now, we can see that font itself is derived from **java.Lang.Object** (again, no surprise) and contains some instance variables such as **PLAIN**, **ITALIC**, and **BOLD**, as well as some other objects, such as **family** and **name**. You could click the plus sign next to these items to see details at the next level, but we'll stop here. We're sure you get the idea. Click the minus sign next to an expanded Variables window item to collapse it and hide its details again.

Figure 16.2 The Variables window display.

Figure 16.3   Displaying detailed information about fMetrics.

The Variables window not only lets you view the value of variables—you can change them as well (as appropriate). Click on an entry in the Value column to edit it; when you resume program execution, the variable will contain the new value that you entered. This can be a powerful debugging technique when you suspect that the value of a particular variable is responsible for the bug.

If you right-click anywhere in the Variables window, its Context Menu will be displayed. The following menu commands are available:

◆ Toolbar: Toggles display of the Variables window toolbar on and off.

◆ Docking View: Toggles window display between docked and floating.

◆ Hexadecimal Display: Toggles numerical value display between hexadecimal and decimal.

◆ Hide: Hides the Variables window.

Figure 16.4   Viewing the details of the font object.

◆ Properties: Displays the properties of the currently selected item. This is useful because it gives you the type as well as the value of variables.

The Variables window toolbar contains only one item, the Context list. You can pull down this list and select the scope to which the Variables window applies. The scopes that are available depend on the details of the project being debugged, and the default scope is almost always the most useful.

Using Watches

Visual J++'s Watch window is similar to the Variables window in that it permits you to view and modify the values of program variables. It differs in allowing you to specify the variables to work with, rather than displaying an automatically defined set of variables as the Variables window does. In addition to individual variables, the Watch window can be used to view the value of Java expressions, which can be extremely useful. Sometimes during debugging, you are more interested in the value to which an expression evaluates than in the values of its individual variables. The Watch window is normally displayed in the lower-right corner of the screen during debugging. You can toggle its display on and off by clicking the Watch button on the debug toolbar.

The Watch window has four tabs that you can use to group related variables together. For example, you can group the variables related to a particular dialog box on one tab, and the variables related to another part of the program on another tab, then view the appropriate tab as needed. Two ways are available to add a variable or expression to the Watch box:

◆ Click an empty box in the Name column, and type the variable name or expression.

◆ Select the variable name or expression in a code editing window, and drag it to the Watch window.

The debugger continually evaluates Watch entries and displays the results in the Value column. If, for some reason, the value is unavailable—for example, you misspelled a variable name—the Value column will display an error message to that effect. If the item in the Watch window is not a simple variable, it is displayed in the same manner as in the Variables window: You see {...} in the Value column, and a plus sign is displayed next to the item name. Click the plus sign to view more details about the item.

Quick Watches

You can use the QuickWatch window to quickly see the value of a variable or expression which you may not want to add to the Watch window. To display QuickWatch, select QuickWatch from the Debug menu, or press Shift+F9. This window is shown in Figure 16.5. Type the variable name or expression into the Expression box, and click the Recalculate button. If you decide to add the expression to the Watch window, click the Add Watch button.

Instant Watch.

For a quick look at a variable value without adding it to the Watch window, highlight the variable in the source code, and point at it with the mouse. A small window will be displayed next to the mouse cursor with the variable name and value.

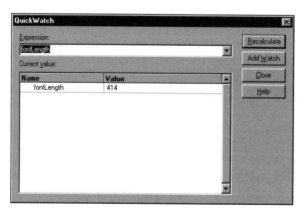

Figure 16.5 Using the QuickWatch window to check a variable's value.

You can edit a Watch window entry by clicking it and using the usual editing methods. When editing is complete, press Enter, and the Value column will update to display the value of the edited entry. You can select a Watch window item and drag it to a code window—for example, to replace your original Java expression with a modified one. To remove an item from the Watch window, select it, and press Del.

Controlling Program Execution

Along with keeping track of variables, control of program execution is a crucial part of debugging.

Advanced Breakpoints

We have already seen how to set simple breakpoints to pause program execution at specific lines of code. These are called *unconditional* breakpoints because execution always pauses when it reaches the line of code containing the breakpoint. You can also set *conditional* breakpoints that pause program execution only if a specific condition is met. For example, you could specify a breakpoint that will pause the program only if a certain variable is equal to 0.

To set a conditional breakpoint, move the cursor to the desired line of code and select Edit Breakpoint, or press Ctrl+B, to display the Breakpoints dialog box. Enter the line number in the Break at box, as you learned how to do earlier in the chapter. Next, click the Condition button to display the Breakpoint Condition dialog box, which is shown in Figure 16.6.

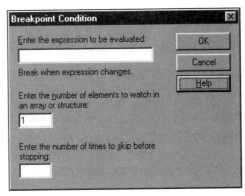

Figure 16.6 **Specifying conditional breakpoints in the Breakpoint Condition dialog box.**

In the first text box, enter the expression or condition to be evaluated. You have two options:

♦ If you enter a boolean expression, one that will evaluate as **true** or **false**, the breakpoint will be active only when the expression evaluates as **true**. For example, if you enter **total<0**, the breakpoint will pause execution only when the value of the variable **total** is less than 0.

♦ If you enter a non-boolean expression such as **a+b**, the breakpoint will be active only when the value of the expression changes.

The next entry in the dialog box is relevant only if you have entered an array name as the variable to watch for changes. It lets you specify how many elements of the array should be monitored for changes. If you enter **data[0]** as the expression and 10 as the number of elements, the breakpoint will be active if any element **data[0]** through **data[9]** has changed.

The third entry in this dialog box is applicable only if you have entered a boolean conditional expression, or no conditional expression at all. It tells the debugger to pause at this breakpoint every *n*th time it is encountered. For example, if you enter 4 here, then execution will pause at the specified line every fifth time execution comes to it, and the specified condition (if any) is met.

Multiple breakpoints?

You can set more than one conditional breakpoint on a single line of text, then use the Watch window to determine which of the conditions caused execution to pause.

Program Flow Commands

Once you have started the debugging process, several commands are available to control program execution. You'll find these commands on the Debug menu and also on the Debug toolbar.

♦ Go: Executes from the current statement (where execution is paused) to the next breakpoint or to the end of the program.

- Restart: Terminates debugging, reloads the program, and pauses at the first line. The Restart command is equivalent to issuing Stop Debugging followed by Step Into.

- Stop Debugging: Terminates debugging and returns you to program editing mode.

- Step Into: Steps to the next program statement, entering any method calls that are encountered.

- Step Over: Steps to the next program statement, but executes through any method calls and stops at the next statement following return from the method call.

- Step Out: When execution is paused within a method, executes the remainder of the method and pauses when execution exits the method call. Use this command when you are single-stepping through a method and have determined that the bug is not located within the current method.

- Run to Cursor: Executes from the current location to the cursor location. This command is available only if the cursor is located past the current location.

Debugging And Exceptions

You learned about Java exceptions in Chapter 9. To recap briefly, exceptions are a method that you utilize to detect and deal with certain types of program errors. Despite the powerful Visual J++ debugging capabilities that we have covered in this chapter, the proper use of exceptions is still the most important method you'll use for dealing with bugs. Still, exceptions cannot do everything. Times will arise when you'll need to debug a program that uses exceptions, and the Visual J++ debugger gives you a great deal of control over how the debugger interacts with exceptions.

What can the debugger do? When an exception occurs, the debugger is always notified—regardless of whether the exception is handled in your code or not. For each type of exception, you can specify that the debugger always stops, or that the debugger stops only if the exception is not handled.

Stop If Not Handled causes the debugger to write a message to the Output window when an exception occurs. The program is not halted and a notification dialog box is not displayed *unless* the exception handler fails to handle the exception. Once this happens, it is too late to fix the problem or examine the source code to see where the exception took place, since the program is already past the point where the exception occurred.

Stop Always causes the debugger to stop the program and display a notification dialog immediately when an exception occurs, before any handler code is invoked. At that point, you can look at the source window to see where the exception occured and use the Watch and Variables windows and QuickWatch to see current variable values. In some cases, you may be able to fix the exception by modifying variable values. When you continue the program after the exception, you are asked whether you want to pass the exception back to the program's exception handlers. If you fixed the problem, choose the No button. Otherwise, choose the Yes button to invoke the exception handler. If the exception handler cannot fix the problem, the debugger halts the program and notifies you again, just as if you had selected Stop If Not Handled.

To set exception options, select Exceptions from the Debug menu (this is possible only while a program is in the process of being debugged). Visual J++ will display the dialog box as shown in Figure 16.7.

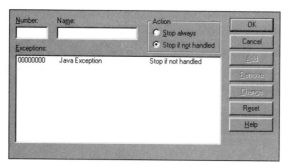

Figure 16.7   The Exceptions dialog box.

In this dialog box, enter the exception number and name in the boxes provided, select the Action you want the debugger to take for this exception, then click Add. Where do you get the exception numbers? To be honest, this is still a bit of a mystery at this time. The beta version of Visual J++ that we are using does not provide this information, and we can only assume it will be part of the online Help in the final release. Click Help in the Exceptions dialog box, and you'll probably find this information.

Working With Images

Peter Aitken

It's hard to imagine a Web page without some images. The Visual J++ Graphics Editor provides basic image editing capabilities.

It's All In The Image

Images are an important part of many Web pages. Getting the most out of Java and the Web demands that you be able to create and modify images. As you may know, many different file formats are used to store images. At present, however, Java and the Web can utilize only two formats: Joint Photographic Expert Group (JPEG) files, which typically have the .JPG or .JPEG extension, and Graphical Interchange Format files with the .GIF extension. Visual J++ has a graphics editor that allows you to create JPG and GIF files from scratch, as well as converting other graphics formats to GIF or JPG.

While the Visual J++ Graphics Editor is a competent program, it cannot hold a candle to dedicated graphics programs when it comes to special effects and other sophisticated graphics manipulations. When the Graphics Editor becomes limiting, you should consider moving up to a professional image editor, such as Adobe Photoshop or Corel Paint. If you find the price tags of these commercial products a bit too much to handle, we strongly suggest that you try the shareware version of Paintshop Pro, available at http://www.jasc.com/. It's a very powerful program, and the shareware fee is quite reasonable.

Starting The Graphics Editor

To create a new image with the Graphics Editor, first select Insert Resource followed by Bitmap from the dialog box. The editor will open with a blank image area, ready for you to start creating your image. If you want to open an existing image for editing or conversion, select Open from the File menu. In the Open dialog box, open the Files of Type box and select Image Files, then select the image file to open. The Graphics Editor will either display a blank image or the image you selected for editing.

Icons, anyone?

To create a standard icon, select Icon from the Insert Resource dialog box. The Graphics Editor will open a predefined 32 by 32 pixel image area (standard icon size).

Image Conversion

To convert an image to JPG or GIF format, you must first open it in the editor as described above. If it requires editing, this is the time to do it. Then:

1. Select File Save As.

2. Tab or click to activate the File Name box.

3. Edit the file name, if desired, but this is not necessary.

4. Add the desired extension (.GIF or .JPG) to the file name.

5. Select OK.

Perhaps the most serious limitation of the Graphics Editor is the fact that it supports a severely limited number of image formats. If your images exist as TIF, CGM, or PCX format files (to name just a few), you are out of luck.

Image Editing

Like all computer images, the images you work with in the Graphics Editor are pixel-based. The image is comprised of a grid of dots, or pixels. Each pixel can be white, black, or just about any color you like. Creating and editing an image, therefore, consists of working with pixels. Sometimes you'll be working at the level of individual pixels, while at other times you'll be working with larger graphics elements, such as lines, circles, and text. It's all pixel-based, however. The Graphics Editor is not similar to some other graphics programs you may have seen in which each element you add—text or a shape, for example—remains an independent object that can be removed or manipulated independently. Once you add something to an image in the Graphics Editor, it becomes part of the basic image and cannot be removed except by changing its pixels back to the way they were originally. If you act quickly, you can "remove" an object (or undo any other change) by selecting the Undo command from the Edit menu.

Split-Screen View

The Graphics Editor has the capability of displaying your image in a split-screen view. The image is shown actual size on one side and enlarged on the other. An example is shown in Figure 17.1. You can perform your editing actions on either the normal or the enlarged view; the other view will instantly show the changes. Each view can be scrolled independently.

The Graphics Editor will normally start in split-screen view for images below a certain size. For larger images, the default displays only the normal-size view. You can control the view as follows:

◆ To change the relative size of the two panes, point at the vertical bar separating the normal and enlarged panes, and drag it to a new position.

◆ To close one pane, point at the vertical bar separating the normal and enlarged panes, and drag it to the left or right edge of the editor's work area.

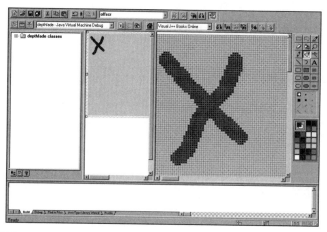

Figure 17.1   Using the split-screen view.

◆ To "open" split-screen view when only one pane is visible, point at the vertical bar which will be docked at either the left or right edge of the editor's work area. You can tell when you've found it because the mouse pointer will change to a pair of parallel vertical lines with left- and right-pointing arrowheads. Then you can drag the bar to the desired split position.

Full-screen graphics.

To edit graphics using the full screen, select Full Screen from the View menu. All of Visual J++'s screen elements, except for the image and the graphics tools, will be hidden, permitting the maximum possible view of the image. A very small window containing a single button will also be displayed. Click that button to return to normal view.

Changing Image Size

If you select the normal view image by clicking on it, you'll see an outline with small handles displayed around the image borders. You can change the image size and proportions by pointing at one of the black handles and dragging the outline to the new size. As you drag, the image size (in pixels) is displayed in the status bar.

If you make the image larger, the new areas will be blank (white). If you make the image smaller, the parts of the image that are cut off will be lost and cannot be recovered by again making the image larger. However, it is possible to reverse the effects of image size changes with the Undo command if you act immediately.

Drawing Tools

The Graphics Editor provides a set of drawing tools for various tasks, such as lines, curves, and text. Each tool is represented by a button on the Graphics Toolbar displayed on the right side of the work area. Like other Microsoft toolbar buttons, these buttons display tool tips, identifying their function if you rest the mouse pointer over them for a few seconds. The Graphics Toolbar is identified in Figure 17.2.

To use a tool, click its button on the Graphics Toolbar, and then use the mouse to draw. Most tools work by dragging the mouse. For example, to draw a straight line:

1. Click the Line button.

2. Point at the image location where you want the line to begin.

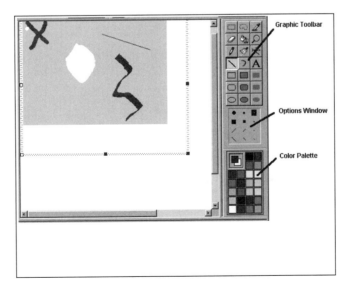

Figure 17.2   Elements of the Graphics Editor screen.

3. Press and hold the left mouse button.

4. Drag to the line's end location, and release the button.

The Tool Options window is displayed immediately below the Graphics Toolbar. This window displays the available options (if any) for the currently selected drawing tool. For example, if you select the Brush tool, the Options window displays several different brush sizes and shapes. Click the desired option to select it.

If you drag on the image with the right mouse button, you will draw with the background color instead of the foreground color. The best way to get acquainted with the various drawing tools is simply to try them out. Some are very obvious, such as the Line and Rectangle tools. Others, such as the Airbrush, may take a little experimentation before you begin to feel comfortable. Go ahead and practice—the paper is free!

Selecting Colors

At any moment, an image has one foreground color and one background color. You can change these colors; the current settings are displayed by the overlapping color squares in the Color Palette, as identified in Figure 17.2. The current foreground color is used to draw items when the left mouse button is used. The current background color is used to draw items when the right mouse button is used, as well as filling the interior of items and coloring parts of the image that are erased. Note that changing the background color does not change existing image background, which starts out at the default setting—white.

To change the foreground or background color, point at the desired color in the Color Palette; the mouse pointer will change to an eyedropper. Click with the left or right button to designate the color as the new foreground or background color, respectively.

You may find that the default color palette is not sufficient for your needs. While you are limited to a palette of 24 colors visible at once, you can define custom colors for any or all of those 24 palette positions. Note that the image can have more than 24 colors—it's just the palette that has the limitation.

To create a custom color:

1. Make the color you want to change into the foreground color.

2. Select Adjust Colors from the Image menu. Visual J++ displays the Custom Color Selector dialog box, as shown in Figure 17.3.

3. Use the controls in the dialog box to create the desired color. You can click the color you want in the color window or enter specific numerical settings.

4. Select OK.

If you change a palette color, parts of the image that had been drawn with the old color do not change to the new color. The change affects only subsequently drawn items.

Erasing, Cutting, And Copying

To erase parts of an image, select the Erase tool and then select the desired eraser width in the Options window. Then, drag over the parts of the image you want erased. Erasing an area has the effect of setting it to the current background color.

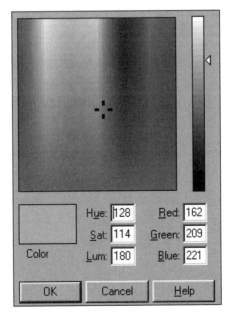

Figure 17.3 The Custom Color Selector dialog box.

You can cut or copy part of an image and then paste it in another location. First, choose the Select tool or the Select Region tool. The former is used to cut or copy rectangular areas, while the latter lets you specify an irregularly shaped region. Then:

1. Drag in the image to select the region to be cut or copied. If you make a mistake, simply release the mouse button and drag again.

2. Select either Cut or Copy from the Edit menu.

3. Select Paste from the Edit menu. The selection is placed in the upper-left corner of the image surrounded by handles.

4. Point at the selection and drag it to the desired location.

5. Click anywhere outside the selection to make the Paste operation final.

Other Image Manipulations

The Image menu, which is displayed only while you are working in the Graphics Editor, provides some other useful commands for image manipulation. They are described in the Table 17.1.

Table 17.1   Image menu commands.

Command	Function
Invert Colors	Changes each color in the image to its complement. In a black-and-white image, the result looks like a negative. With colors, the effects depend on the specific image colors.
Flip Vertical	Inverts the image.
Flip Horizontal	Flips the image left-to-right.
Rotate 90 Degrees	Rotates the image one-quarter turn clockwise. Issue this command two or three times for 180 or 270 degree rotations.
Load Palette	Loads a previously saved color palette.
Save Palette	Saves a palette with custom colors to disk for later retrieval.

Index